Caribbean Story

Caribbean Story

BOOK ONE: FOUNDATIONS

William Claypole
John Robottom

Longman Caribbean

Longman Caribbean Limited
Trinidad and Jamaica

Longman Group Limited
London and New York

Associated companies, branches and representatives throughout the
world

First published 1980

Claypole, William
  Caribbean story.
  Book 1: Foundations
  1. Caribbean area – History
  I. Title II. Robottom, John
  972.9   F2175   79–40567

  ISBN 0–582–76534–X

Printed in Hong Kong by
Sing Cheong Printing Co Ltd

Contents

List of maps

Acknowledgements

The authors are grateful to the many people who advised on the manuscript. In particular they would like to thank Dr Bridget Brereton, Anne Hickling-Hudson and Professor Keith Laurence.

The publishers are grateful to the following for permission to reproduce photographs in the text:

American History Picture Library for figs 1.4, 3.3, 12.3, 16.3, 17.1, 18.1 and 25.3; British Museum for figs 1.3, 2.1, 2.2, 2.5 and 3.2; The Church Missionary Society for fig. 23.3; Mary Evans Picture Library for figs 4.1, 4.2, 4.3, 4.4, 4.5, 5.2, 5.3, 6.2, 6.3, 7.3, 7.4, 8.3, 8.4, 8.5, 12.2, 15.1, 19.2, 21.1, 22.1, 23.1, 23.2, 23.5, 24.1 and 24.2; Werner Forman Archive for fig. 12.1; Agence Hoa-Qui for fig. 11.2; Irongate Studios Ltd for fig. 1.5; The Mansell Collection for figs 1.2, 2.4, 5.4, 8.1, 13.1, 20.1, 20.2, 24.3, 25.1 and 25.2; D. Lloyd Matheson for fig 14.1; Museum of Mankind for fig. 11.5; National Maritime Museum for figs 7.2, 15.2 and 15.3; Radio Times Hulton Picture Library for figs 3.1, 6.1, 6.4, 10.1, 10.2 and 18.3; RIDA Photo Library for fig. 11.1 (B. Wood); Royal Commonwealth Society Library for figs 8.2, 13.4, 13.5, 14.3, 14.4, 17.2, 19.1, 21.2 and 25.4; United Society for the Propagation of the Gospel for fig. 9.2; West India Committee for figs 2.3, 5.1, 7.1, 9.1, 13.2, 13.3, 14.2, 16.1, 18.2, 21.3 and 23.4; Adrian Deeve-Jones for fig. 1.1.

The tables on p.94 are adapted from Richard B. Sheridan, *Sugar and Slavery: An Economic History of the British West Indies 1623–1775*, Caribbean University Press, 1974.

The publishers regret that they are unable to trace the copyright holders of figs 11.3 and 11.4, and apologise for any infringement of copyright caused.

The cover photograph was kindly supplied by the British Museum.

Fig 1.1 *The remains of a Mayan step-pyramid with its temple at the summit (Chichén Itzá, Yucatan, Mexico).*

1   *The first Americans*

Hunters

The story of the peoples of the American islands and continents begins in pre-historic times, long before any written records. It is thought that hunters first entered America over 50,000 years ago following animals across the land or ice bridge which then joined Alaska to Asia. Before the bridge disappeared many other groups of hunters followed, pushing those who had come before them further south. 12,000 years ago they were crossing the isthmus of Panama into South America. 5,000 years later their descendants were building the first fires on the frozen tip of the continent at Tierra del Fuego, the land of fire.

These hunters of pre-historic times were the forefathers of the people living in the Americas at the time of the European explorer, Columbus. He called them 'Indians', for he believed he had discovered India in Asia. But, of course, he had discovered a new continent whose people had developed in completely different ways from those of India and the East Indies; so, today, they are given the name of Amerindians.

The first Amerindians followed herds of caribou, buffalo and seals as they moved from one feeding ground to the next. It was impossible to do this and have a permanent camp or many bulky possessions. Numbers had to be kept small, as too many people in one area would lead to the death of too many animals and then to starvation. So they lived in small groups. Larger numbers were not possible until a settled way of life based on farming was developed.

Farming for subsistence

Agriculture had its small beginnings about 7,000 B.C. when people living in the Mexican highlands found a wild grass which grew tiny ears of edible grain. For centuries the wild grass was carefully cultivated until it produced the first kernels of Indian maize. One discovery led to another. By 5,000 B.C. the Mexican

Amerindians were eating a varied diet of maize squash, beans and chili. At the same time, the people of the Caribbean shores were learning to cultivate yams, cacao and tobacco. The Amerindians of the rainforests of South America discovered how to remove the poisonous liquid from bitter cassava by grating and straining the pulp through a weighted wicker basket. Some wild animals were domesticated, too. All Amerindians kept and ate small dogs, but the Mexicans also had flocks of turkeys and ducks. Amerindians in Peru kept llamas, alpacas and vicunas, which they used as beasts of burden and for meat and wool.

Where the climate was too harsh for farming Amerindians were forced to remain hunters and gatherers; Eskimos in the Arctic had no choice but to hunt seal and fish. Where game was still plentiful there was no need to change; the plains' Amerindians had their needs supplied by enormous herds of buffalo. Other groups combined hunting and gathering with farming. Among them were the Huron and Iroquois people in North America and the Arawaks and Caribs in the West Indies. They grew only enough in one season to meet their needs and, when supplies ran out, they turned to fishing, hunting and gathering wild fruits. We speak of men who grew food only for their own survival as subsistence farmers.

Surplus farming

The people who became totally dependent on agriculture were the Maya in Central America, the Aztecs in Mexico and the Incas in Peru. The farmers in these societies produced a surplus so that there was not only food to eat and store but some to trade for other goods and pay taxes to rulers. The food surplus made it possible for the numbers of Aztecs, Incas and Mayas to increase and for their societies to become very complex, and divided into people of different groups and occupations. Kings and nobles rose to power and

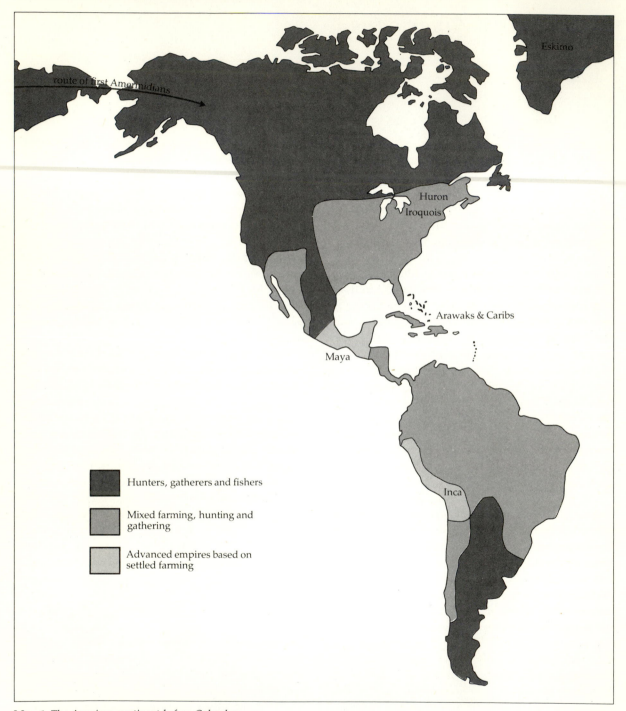

Map 1 *The American continent before Columbus.*

organised the yearly round of work according to calendars worked out by priests, whose task was to take charge of religious ceremonies. Next in rank were the warriors who conquered neighbouring peoples and created large empires. Towns grew up where craftsmen cut building blocks, wove cloth and made fine jewelry and ornaments. At the bottom of the society were the common people and slaves, who

Fig 1.2 *Machu Picchu, a fortified city in the Andes which was used by local governors of the Inca Empire. The highest building to the left is a sun temple. The city could be approached only from one side.*

Map 2 *The main sites of the Maya. The sites in the centre and south were used between 300–900 A.D. They were then replaced by those in the Yucatan.*

grew the food and toiled to build magnificent stone cities, fine bridges, aqueducts and roads. The Aztecs ruled an empire of over seven million people from their beautiful stone city, Tenochtitlan, built on a series of islands in the centre of Lake Texcoco. The Incas in Peru organised an empire paid for by taxing conquered people along three thousand kilometres of the western coast of South America. Both the Incas and Aztecs had learned much from the older society of the Maya who lived in Central America.

The Maya

At the height of their civilisation the Mayas occupied a region of 324,000 square kilometres, which included the modern Mexican states of Yucatan, Campeche and Tobasco, as well as all of Belize, Guatemala and the western edge of Honduras. Unlike the Incas, the Mayas never tried to build a centralised empire ruled from one capital. Instead they lived in many independent city-states. In each there was a hereditary 'priest-king' who ruled the countryside around its central temple-city with the aid of priests and nobles.

Remains of the temple cities show that they were a collection of temples and monuments. The most usual arrangement was a courtyard with pyramids on three sides and public meeting rooms on the fourth. Steps up the sides of each pyramid led to a temple on its flat top. The larger cities had several of these sets of build-

Fig 1.3 *A pottery figure of a god with a feathered headdress. Made in the first century A.D., it was found in Mexico.*

ings and the spaces in-between were filled with stone blocks or pillars, put up to mark the passing of every twenty years. All the buildings were decorated with elaborate carvings and wall paintings.

Fig 1.4 *Maya noblemen playing their ball game at Chichén Itzá. The game was like a violent form of basketball in which the players tried to pass a solid rubber ball through a stone ring. Notice the sloping heads of the players.*

The temple-cities are proof of the power and importance of Maya priests. This power came from their skill in working out calendars, so necessary to growing crops. As time went on the measurement of time became completely mingled with worship of the gods. Each day was under the protection of one god and each night of another. The will of these gods could be worked out by observing sunrise and sunset and the position of the sun, moon and planets. Some of the temples were built to serve as observatories for the priests. There were also other gods who watched over corn, wind, water, war, human sacrifice and violent death; goddesses controlled floods, childbirth and weaving. There was a god for every number and symbol in the Maya alphabet. When displeased, *Chac*, the raingod, refused to send rain; the corn did not grow and the Maya faced famine. Only the priests might then save the people.

Every twenty days peasants brought gifts to be offered to the gods in the temples. Once a year they came with a percentage of their crops; this was the tax they paid to the priest-king, the warriors and the priests. On these occasions the courtyards before the temples were used for music, dancing and religious ceremonies. The peasants never entered the temples; only the priests were allowed to do this. In fact the whole success of Maya civilisation depended on the

corn grown by peasants. The Maya grew enough to support a large number of priests and nobles, who could be easily recognised by their long narrow skulls, created by fixing boards to the heads of young babies. The work of the peasant farmers did not stop at corn growing; they were also forced to spend time working on the pyramids and temples. The many remains show that these were continually being added to with more and more elaborate stone work and decoration.

The second Maya

This way of life went on for hundreds of years from the second century A.D. to the seventh or eighth. Then, in one city after another, the temples were abandoned. Buildings were left unfinished and cornfields went unplanted. Fierce-looking stone gods fell from their bases. No-one has fully explained why. Some archaeologists think it was caused by a shortage of corn due to soil exhaustion; others believe that a series of deadly diseases swept through the city states. In some places there may have been wars between states or a peasant revolt against the priests and nobles. Whatever happened, the Maya civilisation re-appeared in the tenth century but only in northern Yucatan.

This second Maya civilisation was never as fine as the first. Wars were common and made peaceful farming difficult. The temples and monuments were less grand and sculpture and painting less beautiful. Yet the Maya only collapsed altogether in the face of Europeans. The first Spanish arrived in 1511. Soon the new conquerors were destroying one city after another. The Mayas retreated to their last stronghold at the city of Tayasal deep in the jungle. This finally fell to the Spaniards in 1597. The stone of its temples was used to build Christian churches, and the Maya books were burnt.

Other circum-Caribbean people

No other people of the circum-Caribbean area ever had the same skills in farming, building and science as the Maya. In the Colombian highlands the Chibchas were skilled workers with gold but they built no great cities. Other Amerindian people, who spoke a

Chibcha language, were the Chocho and Cuna in Panama, and the Mosquito-coast Indians in Belize. None of these reached large numbers and they built no temples or other lasting monuments. Their agriculture was purely for subsistence, to meet their own needs, with cassava as the main crop. The rest of their food was gathered from the forests and seas. Tools were simply made from stones and shell. They had no system of writing or mathematics, although they were skilled at making dugout canoes, hammocks and clay pottery. Their homes were made from flimsy sticks and thatch and grouped together in small tribal villages. Two other peoples living at these simple levels were the Arawaks and Caribs. Some of them made permanent homes on the South American mainland and were the ancestors of people such as the Warraws and Wapisians who live in present day Guyana and Venezuela. Other Arawaks and Caribs left the mainland and made the Caribbean their home.

Fig 1.5 *A Chibcha gold ornament. The upper part shows a human head with a royal headdress.*

Map 3 *Peoples of the circum-Caribbean.*

2 Arawaks and Caribs

Sources of history

There were perhaps 200,000 people living in the Caribbean at the time when Columbus' ships brought the first Europeans in 1492. That was the year in which the *written* history of the Caribbean begins, for we can read about the Caribs and Arawaks in the journals of Columbus and some of the men who came with him. Their accounts are useful to historians, especially when they describe the Amerindians' dress and ornaments, their crops and the foods they ate. Nowadays it is thought that these early writings are much less reliable when they talk about the customs and beliefs of the Amerindians or about the way they organised their societies. The writers looked on the Caribbean people through European eyes; they also needed to describe the Arawaks and Caribs as more primitive than they really were to justify the harsh treatment they were given by Spanish settlers.

Much more accurate information can come from the work of archaeologists who have given years of patient work to build up a picture of Amerindian life. Archaeologists working in the Caribbean are less fortunate than those who have studied the Maya and can look at the ruins of cities and stone carvings or even books and calendars made by priests. In the islands they have to begin with long abandoned sites of villages, usually now covered with earth and vegetation. Careful removal of the soil will lead the archaeologist to the kitchen middens, which were heaps of rubbish piled up outside villages. By sifting through the middens, it is possible to find pieces of pottery, stone axe-heads or celts, weights for fishnets and ornaments.

Archaeologists then record the distribution of all the remains which have a similar design. This will tell them how far the people who made objects in that way were spread over the Caribbean islands. If they can date the objects they will know the order in which different groups of Arawaks or Caribs came to an area. Some tools are of more advanced design than others

Fig 2.1 *A stone axe-head, 26cm long, found in the Dominican Republic. It bears a simple carving of a human face.*

and these, of course, are usually reckoned to be the most recent. Sometimes the differences in date can tell a story. If archaeologists find earlier, more primitive, tools in one midden, and nearby come across remains which include later, and more efficient, spears and swords, they may be able to reconstruct the history of a settlement whose people were conquered by invaders. On some islands it is possible to see that the earlier people were forced to move inland, or into the mountains, to avoid being destroyed altogether by new arrivals who settled near the coast. Trade and raiding routes can be understood by noting whether sites are on the leeward or windward sides of islands and whether the currents would take canoes.

Some Arawak people buried their dead in caves, along with items used in life. Archaeologists lucky enough to find a burial cave may see the remains of canoe paddles, or a *duho*, the chief's ceremonial stool, or *zemis*, the figures which represented Arawak gods. If a cave was dry enough, examples of Amerindian weaving and basket making may have survived for many hundred years to give us a better understanding of the Caribbean's first inhabitants.

Three Caribbean peoples

Archaeologists can tell us that some of the earliest settlers in the Caribbean came to the islands a thousand years or more before Columbus. Remains of these people, the Ciboneys (or Sibonays), have been found in the Bahamas and a few parts of Jamaica, but they were driven from the best sites by the Arawaks whose first home was probably in the forests between the Orinoco and Amazon rivers. No one knows for sure why they left to live in the Antilles a few hundred years before Columbus. It may have been because the islands gave an easier life than the mainland. There was less dense jungle, a fresher climate and no dangerous animals. Perhaps, too, the Arawaks saw the islands as places of safety from the warlike Caribs who were pushing north into Arawak territory from an area across the borders of modern Brazil and Bolivia.

The Arawaks spread across the Antilles reaching Jamaica about 1,000 A.D., but they had not escaped from the Caribs forever. By the time Columbus arrived the Caribs had followed the Arawaks into the Caribbean, destroyed their settlements on the Lesser Antilles, and Carib war canoes were bringing raiders to Puerto Rico and Haiti. The only places in the eastern Caribbean not permanently occupied by Caribs were Barbados and Trinidad. Barbados lies to windward of the other islands in the Lesser Antilles, which may have made it difficult for the Caribs to return there after a trading or raiding expedition. Yet, shell, bone and stone remains in Barbados tell us that many Caribs did visit the island. On Trinidad they occupied the north-west but had not managed to destroy the Arawaks, who had been given aid against the Caribs by relatives from the mainland and by warriors from a similar people, the Nepoyes.

In the main areas of Arawak settlement there were three major groups. The Lucayanos reached as far west as the Bahamas. The Tainos had made their homes on Cuba, Jamaica and Haiti. The third group was the Borequinos who occupied Puerto Rico.

Farming and food

Both Arawaks and Caribs were subsistence farmers, growing food mainly for their own needs and very little for trade. They carried out 'slash and burn agriculture', cutting branches from trees and setting fire to them. Crops were then planted in the ashes among the blackened tree stumps. After about five to ten years the soil was exhausted and the village people moved on to fresh land. Some Arawaks used slightly more advanced methods. In Cuba and Hispaniola, irrigation ditches were dug and fields were fertilised with a mixture of ash and urine. Arawaks in Hispaniola also blocked inland rivers to make artificial fish ponds.

These simple farming methods produced a variety of crops. Maize was widely grown in the Greater Antilles. Cassava was produced in all the islands, along with sweet potatoes and hot pepper. Cotton and tobacco were also grown. Yet Arawaks and Caribs did not need to rely on field crops for all their food. The islands and the surrounding seas were rich in foods which needed little effort or skill to gather: snails, shellfish, barnacles, grubs, gull and turtle eggs. Huge piles of shells have been found among the remains of camp sites. There were no large wild animals to hunt but the Amerindians trapped many small animals including snakes, bats, lizards, iguanas, conies and rabbits and agoutis. Birds were snared or trapped in

Fig 2.2 *Two stone pestles used for grinding food. The right hand one comes from the Dominican Republic and the left hand one may have come from Jamaica.*

finely woven nets strung between trees. As well as parrots, doves and wild ducks there were other birds which are now extinct or very rare. The only domestic animal known to Arawaks and Caribs was a small dog which was fattened on corn meal and then eaten as a great delicacy.

Large numbers of fish were eaten. Fishermen used nets, hooks, spears and the remora. The remora is a fish with suction cups on the back of its head which it uses to cling to larger fish. A cotton line was tied tightly to the remora's tail and was gently let out until it attached itself to a fish or turtle. The remora and its captive were then carefully pulled back to the canoe. The Caribs relied more on sea food than the Arawaks. As well as hooks and nets they used long arrows and a type of poisoned bark which stunned the fish when it was thrown into the water. Manatee and pedro seal, now extinct, were also hunted.

The simplest Arawak and Carib dish was 'pepper-pot'. A large clay pot was set close to the fire and filled with any bits and pieces from the fields and the day's hunting. The mixture was heavily seasoned with red pepper and left to stew. A good pepper-pot lasted for weeks, its flavour changing each day as some new lizard, fish or bat was added. Bread and cakes were prepared from maize and cassava. The green maize was pounded with stone pestles into a watery pulp which was wrapped in green leaves and baked over the fire. Cassava flour was mixed with a little water and cooked into nearly rock-hard cakes on a hot clay griddle.

There were very few wild fruits to add to the diet.

Coconuts, bananas and citrus fruits were all brought to the Caribbean by Europeans. But the Amerindians did eat guava and occasionally avocados and pineapples. Both Arawaks and Caribs feared to eat certain foods. The Arawaks would not touch mammy apples which they believed were food for the souls of the dead; Caribs refused to eat turtles and manatee for fear of becoming slow and stupid like the animal.

Crafts

The Caribs and Arawaks did not master the Maya skills of writing, mathematics, building and astronomy. Pottery was made from the local red, brown and grey clays. The potter's wheel was unknown. Pots were not glazed but were decorated with markings different for each village. They were often made in fanciful shapes of frogs, birds, or heads with wide eyes and large ears to serve as handles. The Caribs were better potters than the Arawaks and gave their pots a rim at the top to add strength and make pouring easier. They also made pots from several layers of clays and then cut patterns through the layers to give their designs different colours. The most elaborate pots were used as funeral urns for holding ancestors' bones or placing food in the grave.

Tools were made from wood, stone, bone and shell. To make baskets, fish traps and lobster pots, wood was soaked and split into supple strips. The Arawaks were excellent basket weavers. A basket for carrying water was made by double-weaving wood and leaves.

Seamanship

Dugout canoes were made with great skill without the aid of any metal tools. A wide silk-cotton tree was first ringed and burnt off at the base. Branches were trimmed and the trunk was hollowed by chipping the upper side and slowly burning out the interior. The canoe was shaped by wetting the hollowed trunk and inserting wooden wedges of different lengths to widen it in the middle and slightly taper it at each end. It was then buried in damp sand to cure before being dried in the sun. Some Arawak canoes were large enough to carry seventy or eighty people or a tonne of trading goods. The Caribs built several different kinds of boats and rafts. Their war canoes,

Fig 2.3 *A drawing of a Carib hammock taken from a book written by Oviedo, a Spaniard who wrote one of the first European accounts of the Americas.*

piraguas, were narrow and high-prowed; that is the front of the boat was the highest part. They were easily manoeuvred, travelled swiftly and could cover great distances. On very long voyages several piraguas were lashed together under a platform on which a shelter was built.

The canoes made it possible for the Arawaks to carry out trade between the islands in cloth, tools, weapons, furniture, tobacco, certain fruits and gold. Puerto Rico and Haiti exported gold to Cuba, Jamaica and the Bahamas. The small island, Petit Goave, was famous for its fine duhos, a ceremonial stool used by Arawak chieftains. Some groups in Puerto Rico grew pineapples and exported them to other islands. The first European explorers used Arawak traders as guides and pilots. Some archaeologists think that Maya carvings found in Cuba show that the Arawaks also traded with the mainland; but it is likely that they were brought by Maya slaves carried there by the Spanish in the sixteenth century. The Caribs were not a trading people. Instead they used their expert seamanship to make lightning raids on the Arawaks and steal food, clothing and slaves.

Weapons

Flint, obsidian (a volcanic rock) and other hard stones were shaped and smoothed with great patience to make tools and weapons. Fishing arrows and spears were tipped with shell and bone. Fishhooks were cut from turtle shell with sisal string, moistened and dipped in sand to make a simple saw. The Arawaks' war weapons were much simpler than the Caribs. Columbus noticed that the Lucayanos on the Bahamas were armed with only wooden javelins. However, on Hispaniola the Tainos had darts with reed shafts and wooden points hardened with fire which were thrown with spear-throwers. The Tainos often used a stout wooden 'sword club', the *macana*, which the Spaniards soon came to fear, as a well-aimed blow could crush even a skull protected by thick armour plating. The Arawaks in the Bahamas, Cuba and Jamaica seldom used bows and arrows, but those in Puerto Rico and Hispaniola used them to defend themselves from Carib attacks.

Carib weapons were altogether more deadly. They used fire- and poison-tipped arrows. The poison was almost always fatal to someone hit by such an arrow. An early English explorer warned his readers that the 'person shot endures the most insufferable torment in the world, and suffers a most ugly and lamentable death, sometimes dying stark mad'. The Caribs also had a variety of clubs and spears. One club, the *butu*, had sharpened flints fixed in its head.

Dress

Arawaks and Caribs went about mostly as Columbus described them: 'a people in their original simplicity . . . stark naked as they were born, men and women'. Yet although they wore hardly any clothing they spent a lot of time adorning their bodies. Newly born babies had their skulls bound between two boards so that they grew up with high elongated heads. This may have been to thicken the skull so that it could stand up to heavy blows. Tales are told of Spaniards who broke their swords on Arawak heads. Clay and fat mixed with bright coloured dyes were smeared in patterns all over the body: 'some of them . . . with black, others white and others red, most of them on their bodies, and some on their faces, and eyes, or only the nose'. Besides being colourful, the clay and grease kept off insects and rain. Small amulets, or charms, were carried in sacks round the neck, and others made from clay, shell and cotton were woven into the hair.

Caribs were more decorative than Arawaks. They applied down, flower petals and gold dust to their body paint before it dried. They also wore chains of

Fig 2.4 *Carib carvings on a rock in Grenada.*

stone and coral around their arms, wrists and legs. They pierced their nose, lips and ears to hold ornaments made from fish spines and plates of turtle shell. Caribs greatly respected crescents of gold and copper which were worn round the neck of chiefs and warriors as a badge of rank. Neither the Caribs nor Arawaks saw gold as anything more than a form of decoration, and were quite ready to trade it to the Europeans. They were bewildered at the great excitement Columbus showed when he saw a woman with 'a little plate of gold hanging at her nose' and immediately ordered her to be brought on board his ship. It was the first American gold seen by any European.

Village society

Little time was spent on housing, as a shelter to keep off the rain was all that the Arawaks and Caribs needed. There was no point in building permanent houses because the villagers moved to fresh gardening plots every few years. Arawak houses were round with steep thatched roofs. The larger ones had a covered porch before the door. The village chieftain's house was rectangular and held several rooms. Arawak villages also had a separate dwelling for the tribal gods. Carib villages were similar, but their houses were made of woven thatch reaching almost to the ground, looking like large beehives. The woven thatch made a strong flexible house which could stand up to hurricanes. The villages were open and not protected by stockades or other defences.

Each Arawak village was the home of related people who obeyed a hereditary headman or chieftain. Often several of these family villages in a district were grouped into a clan headed by a clan chieftain, sometimes called a *cacique*. In Puerto Rico and Hispaniola several such clans were united under a paramount chieftain; there were seven chieftains in Hispaniola. These alliances probably came about as a way of defending the Arawaks against Carib raids. Where the risk was less as in the Bahamas, Cuba and Jamaica, the Arawaks seldom organised anything larger than a family village or clan.

The family idea was reflected in daily village life. Property belonged to everyone in common. Men, women and children shared the chores of planting, hunting, fishing and cooking. Meals were eaten together, first by the men and then by women and children. Like any family, the village group shared what was available. Columbus wrote: 'I could not clearly understand whether this people possess any private property, for I observed that one man had the charge of distributing various things to the rest but especially meat provisions and the like'. Arawak law supported the importance of working together for the good of the tribe. The greatest crime was theft since the whole tribe shared in the loss. A convicted thief suffered a horrible death, impaled on a sharpened stick. A murderer was treated more mercifully, by being banished or executed quickly by strangling.

Leadership

Caciques were treated with great respect and looked on as the father of all the people. Part of the cacique's importance came from his position as religious leader, but he was also an all-powerful ruler. He decided who should hunt, fish or work in the fields and was the final judge in all disputes. He did not demand regular tax payments from the people but received the best food brought in by hunters, fishers and farmers. When a cacique became sick or injured so that he could no longer carry out his duties, he was strangled and replaced by his eldest son. If there was no son, his sister's eldest male child became cacique. As a final mark of respect the cacique was buried with his most valuable articles and a few favourite wives.

In a large village or clan the cacique was helped by a number of nobles or *nitayanos*. Nitayanos were usually the oldest males who were expected to know the borders of their people's land and remember agreements reached with other groups. When the cacique was considering a new treaty with neighbouring groups he would discuss it with the nitayanos in a council meeting. Some nitayanos were also priests and sorcerers; they cared for the clan's gods, supervised religious rites and trained medicine men. Their songs and dances were a way of teaching the younger people about the history and laws of their people.

The Caribs had a more complicated organisation to give them the best leadership in their warlike society. As with the Arawaks they had hereditary chiefs, nobles and priests, but military leaders were elected. The village commander was the *obutu*. Anyone who wished to stand for election as obutu had to have killed several Arawak warriors or at least one cacique with his own hands. The obutu was assisted by a lieutenant or *ubutu maliarici*. Each clan also elected a *naharlene* or commander of the canoes as well as a captain, or *tiubutuli canaoa*, of each crew.

A Carib group's strength was reckoned on the number of male warriors and it was common for it to keep a number of Arawak slave women to produce male children who could be raised as fighters. Before a child could become a warrior he had to undergo a painful initiation in which he fasted and had his flesh scarred. If the child went through the test without flinching he was allowed to enter the *carbet*, a meeting house where only warriors were allowed.

Religion

Amerindian religion was a colourful mixture of nature worship, ancestor worship and protective magic. The Arawaks believed their land had been created by a male sky-god and a female earth goddess. Both were too far away to affect their daily lives, but there were many nature gods and ancestral spirits who controlled wind, rain, sickness, luck and misfortune. Each of these gods could be represented by a *zemi*. Zemis were made from wood, bone or shell in the shape of a human or animal and cotton zemis held the bones of a respected ancestor. The skulls and bones of ancestors could also be neatly packed in a zemi basket and kept in the household. Arawaks believed that trees, rivers and rocks were the homes of evil spirits. To protect themselves they wore amulets, painted their bodies with sacred designs and took specially prepared medicines.

Each village had its zemi house, set aside from the other buildings. It was a shadowy place where the priests and caciques offered food and clothing to the spirits, worshipped them and asked for their help. Powdered tobacco was burnt before the zemis and sometimes it was taken by the priests to send them into a trance in which the spirits would speak to them.

Fig 2.5 *An Arawak carving of a bird-faced figure found in Jamaica. It is made from an extremely hard wood and stands 88cm tall.*

A Y–shaped pipe was placed deeply in the nostrils and the priest breathed the fumes until he fainted. The Arawak word for powdered tobacco, *coyiaba*, also meant 'prayer'.

Arawaks believed that the soul left the body after death and wandered for a while at night feeding on mammy apples. This unhappy time ended when the soul was miraculously carried to magical islands in the south to join other ancestral souls. Death was something to look forward to and not to be dreaded.

Columbus found this belief very strong and was able to persuade several Arawaks to come on board his ship by making the false promise to sail them south to the magical islands.

The Caribs shared the belief that death led to a life in another form. From this arose the belief that their live bodies could become homes for the souls of dead enemies, so eating the flesh of a brave warrior would give them his strength and courage. Enemies killed in a raid were cut up and favourite portions were eaten on the spot. Yet Caribs preferred to take captives live and test their courage before the rest of the warriors. Prisoners were kept tied in a hammock near the roof of the carbet. After several days of fasting they were brought down and horribly tortured. Brave prisoners were expected to take the pain without flinching and to mock at their torturers. Those who did so with the greatest courage were the most valued. They were killed quickly and eaten with great reverence as the central part of a ceremonial feast. The rest of the body was boiled; the fat was skimmed off and rubbed into the bodies of young male children to give them additional strength. Of course, flesh eating was not an everyday practice, and peaceful people whom the Caribs met did not become victims. Yet among Europeans a myth grew up that anyone sailing to the 'Caribees' was in danger of being eaten, and such tales appeared in European books for 300 years.

Caribs too worshipped ancestor spirits. However, they spent more time in trying to please the evil god Maboya and the many sea spirits they believed in. Death for the Carib meant a journey to either a heaven or a hell. The souls of brave warriors went to the 'fortunate' islands where they were waited on by Arawak slaves; cowardly souls went to a dreary desert where they became the slaves of Arawak masters.

3 The Spanish

Land! Land!

It was 2 a.m. on Friday 12 October 1492 when a seaman, high in the crow's nest of the *Pinta*, saw a dark line of land edged with sand gleaming silver in the moonlight. His cry of *Tierra! Tierra!* – land! land! – carried back to the two following ships, the *Nina* and the *Santa Maria*. All three dropped anchor and the fleet's admiral, Christopher Columbus, slept. In the morning he would be, he believed, the first European to put ashore in the East Indies after a voyage entirely by sea. Only many years later was it known for certain that the fleet was rocking gently off the reefs outside the tiny Watling Island which lay on the other side of the world from the Indies he sought.

On that night five centuries ago, Europeans 'discovered' the Americas. Not for the first time. The Vikings, from modern Norway, and the Irish, had sailed the north Atlantic six hundred years before Columbus, but all records of their journeys had been lost. Columbus' voyage was different. It was the start of regular contact between Europe and America because it took place at a time of great developments in ship-building, navigation and map-making. His fleet had sailed from Spain, in a part of Europe which had been eagerly seeking overseas trade and colonies throughout the fifteenth century.

Spain

Columbus' ships had been provided by Isabella, Queen of Castille, a kingdom on the Iberian Peninsula of Europe. She was married to King Ferdinand, ruler of Aragon. The marriage united the two kingdoms which would in future be known as Spain. Ferdinand and Isabella's daughter was married to the King of Portugal, the third kingdom in the Iberian Peninsula. All three kingdoms were Christian, but there was another people on the Peninsula – the Moors. They were the Muslim descendants of people who had

crossed from North Africa in A.D. 711 and occupied almost all of Iberia. 1492 was a great year in the history of the Peninsula for, on 6 January, Ferdinand and Isabella had ridden in triumph into Granada, the Moors' last stronghold which had just fallen to the Christian armies. It was the end of the *reconquista*, seven hundred years of warfare to reconquer the Iberian Peninsula from the Moors.

Hidalgos

This long struggle played its part in the history of the Americas for it produced men of the type who would become the first European conquerors and colonisers. Out of the reconquista had risen a class of knights, the *hidalgos*, who were famous for their courage and independence, their readiness to fight and their eagerness for adventure. Hidalgos were rewarded with many privileges; they were free from taxes and each could wear his own coat-of-arms. But many were poor, and would become even poorer if the end of the reconquista meant there was no more war to give a chance of joining the class of great landowning noblemen who had gained wealth and power during the wars against the Moors. As districts had been retaken by the Christians, the Moors living there had been placed under the rule of a nobleman. This grant of the right to rule, made by the king, was known as an *encomienda*. The hidalgos who followed Columbus to the Americas came in the hope of being granted an encomienda over the people living here.

The Church

The Christian Church had grown wealthy and powerful and its cathedrals, churches and monasteries owned much of the land in the Peninsula. It had played a leading part in the reconquista which it declared to be a holy struggle against unbelievers.

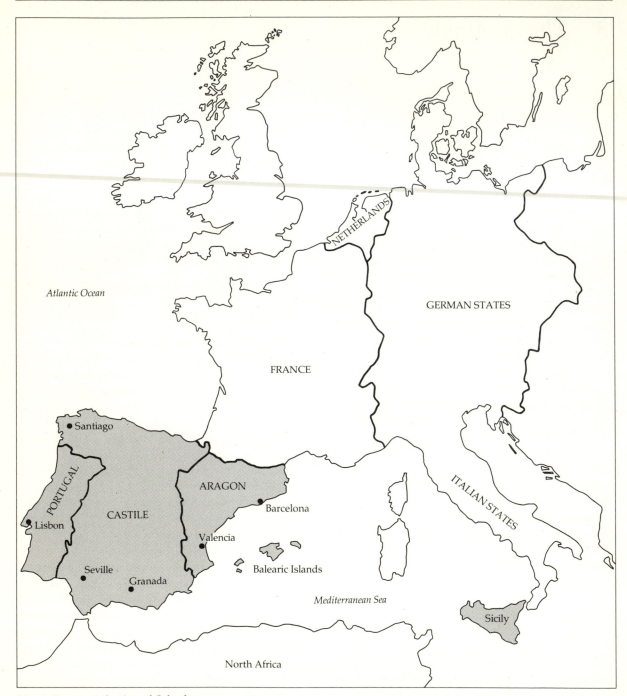

Map 4 *Europe at the time of Columbus.*

Many of the most important advisers of Ferdinand and Isabella were Archbishops, bishops or priests. Both the King and Queen were deeply religious people who believed it was their duty to convert non-believers to Christianity. This often led to great hardship and cruelty; for instance, about 150,000 Jews were expelled from Spain in 1492, and a few years later there was a revolt among the reconquered Moors in Granada who were being forced to accept Christianity.

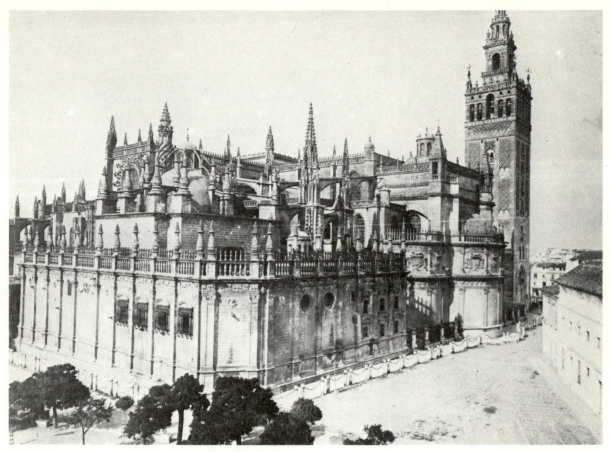

Fig 3.1 *The cathedral of El Alcazar in Seville, Spain.*

Some Church leaders believed that it was possible to make non-believers Christian by more gentle methods, by encouraging them to attend Christian schools for instance. The belief that it was God's work to convert everyone made Churchmen strong supporters of the search for new lands and new peoples.

Hidalgos and Churchmen were two important groups who seized at the chance to carry the reconquista from Spain to the New World. The third group was made up of merchants and traders.

Traders

The Iberians had always been active in trade and commerce. The Peninsula has thin soils which made it necessary to import grain and other foods. On the other hand it was ideal country for raising large flocks of sheep, and great quantities of wool were exported to the weaving factories in northern Europe. In the fifteenth century, however, the biggest profits could be made on goods obtained from Arab merchants in the towns on the southern and eastern shores of the Mediterranean Sea.

The Arab traders controlled trade routes into parts of the world which were then quite unknown to Europeans. From the North African cities of Tunis, Tripoli and Ceuta, Arab caravans made the slow trek across the Sahara Desert to the African cities of Gao and Timbuctu, bringing back gold, ivory and ebony goods. There were three main routes to the Indies. Two of them left from Constantinople by land into Persia, India and China. The third began with a land journey to the Red Sea and then crossed the Indian Ocean by Chinese junk or Arab dhow to India, Indo-China or the spice islands of the East Indies.

Only a few Europeans ever risked their lives by travelling along these Arab trade routes. But many grew wealthy by purchasing goods from Arab merchants and bringing them into Europe. Europeans

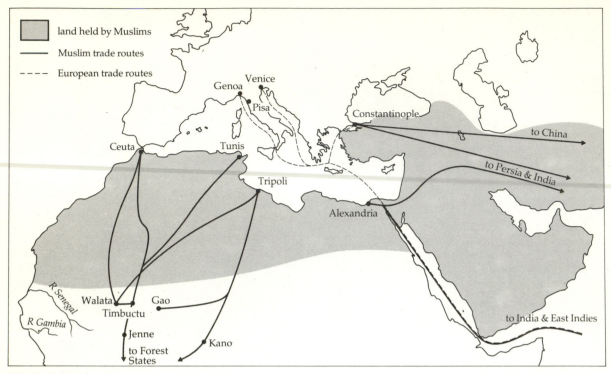

Map 5 *Arab trade routes.*

learned to enjoy food seasoned with pepper, nutmeg, ginger and other spices. For the first time they could drink coffee, sweetened with cane sugar. Fine eastern textiles were used by the wealthy for ladies' dresses, cloaks and costly church vestments. Europeans came to want more and more of the wonderful perfumes, gems, gold, ivory and ebony carvings and leather goods.

All these goods were expensive, especially because of the taxes placed on them by the rulers of the Arab states, who were all Muslim and generally unfriendly to the Christian Europeans.

Because of the high prices European merchants began to consider ways of finding their own sea-route to the Indies. It had been estimated that one ship alone could carry half the amount of all the pepper brought into Europe by land each year. Yet no-one in Europe knew if it was possible to sail to the Far East. Seamen feared to go far west of Gibraltar or south of the northern curve of Africa. They told each other fantastic stories of ship-eating monsters, boiling seas and reaching the edge of the world. Most sailors did not trust those men who told them that the world was round.

The explorations

The people of the three Iberian kingdoms were best placed to begin exploration of a sea route round Africa. The lead was taken by the Portuguese, especially during the time of Prince Henry (1394–1460) who was called 'the Navigator'. In fact he did little navigating himself but made it his business to see that Portuguese sailors knew all the most up to date geographical ideas. Henry lived at a time when there were so many new inventions and theories that Europeans later called it the Renaissance, an age of the rebirth of knowledge. In 1450 a German, Johann Gutenburg invented the first European printing press with movable type. It was now possible to produce many copies of books, and accounts of travellers and explorers could be printed and read by large numbers. Map-making too was mechanised. Instead of expensive hand-drawn maps, known as *Portolani*, cheaper printed maps were produced. These showed coastlines, currents, winds and the position of dangerous shoals and charts. Henry the Navigator collected the newest studies in geography, mathematics, astronomy and map-making into a library at Sagres.

This stands on the south-west tip of Portugal, jutting into the Atlantic Ocean, and Henry made it the head-quarters for his country's seamen.

Henry had improvements made on three new inventions, the astrolabe, the cross-staff and the quadrant. Seamen used them to observe the angle of the Pole star or the sun at noon and work out their ship's latitude. Under Henry's orders, the old mag-netised needle floating on a cork in a bowl of water was replaced by a glass-enclosed box compass which was more accurate. The Prince's shipbuilders pro-duced a new type of ship known as a caravel. This usually had three movable sails which made much lighter work of tacking against the wind. Pulleys, wrenches and pivots were used to aid work on the sails so that fewer sailors were needed for each caravel. This increased the space for cargo and provi-sions and made possible longer voyages without put-ting into land. Finally, Prince Henry's sailors and ships were equipped with the latest European weapons. During the Renaissance, Europeans learned to use gun powder, cannons and small firearms. European sailors soon found that these weapons were superior to those of other peoples and gained confidence in journeying to strange foreign lands.

The map shows the success of Portuguese sailors. In the Atlantic they reached Madeira, the Azores, the Canary and Cape Verde Islands. By the time of Prince Henry's death Portuguese traders in forts along the coast were sending back great wealth in ivory, gold and ebony while sailors were pushing their way further south. In 1488, Bartholomew Diaz, running his ships before the winds of a gale, found he had rounded the tip of Africa and entered the Indian Ocean. Ten years later, Vasco da Gama made the first sea voyage from Europe to India. He returned with a cargo of jewels, spices and silks worth sixty times the cost of the voyage.

The Spanish in the Canary Islands

The Portuguese did not keep the Canary Islands. After their troops had been defeated in a war against Spain a treaty was signed in 1479. By this Treaty of Alcaçovas, Portugal handed over the Canary Islands to Spain while Isabella and Ferdinand agreed to allow Portugal the sole rights to trading routes along the African coast.

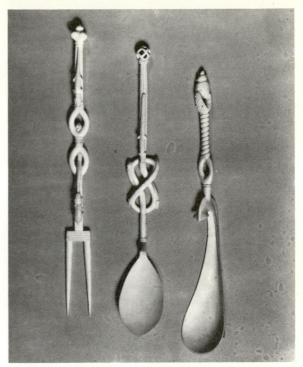

Fig 3.2 *Ivory spoons and fork made in Benin in West Africa in the fifteenth century for sale to Portuguese sailors.*

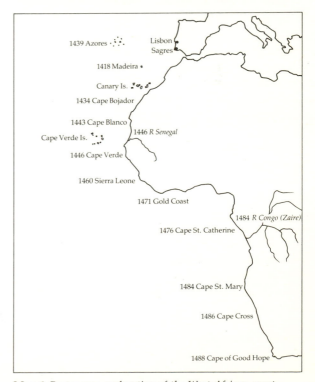

Map 6 *Portuguese exploration of the West African coast.*

The Canary Islanders disliked the Spanish as much as they had the Portuguese. It was several years before Spanish soldiers could bring all the islands under their control. They then treated the conquered people in the same way as the defeated Moors. The soldiers who had taken part in the conquest were granted encomiendas over groups of islanders. Most of them soon found themselves forced to work on plantations producing sugar for export to Spain. When workers were short, the Spanish bought African slaves from Portuguese traders and forced them to work in the canefields.

Some of Isabella's advisers saw another use for the Canary Islands. Now that Spain had given up the right to explore the African coast they hoped to use the islands as a base for westward voyages of exploration. Their hopes were raised by geographers who were convinced that the world was round. The person who in the end persuaded them that this meant that the Indies could be reached by sailing west across the Atlantic was an unknown Italian sailor, Christopher Columbus.

Fig 3.3 *A painting of Vasco da Gama from a palace built for the Portuguese in Goa, India.*

4 Columbus: explorer and coloniser

The idea

Columbus was born with the name Cristoforo Colombo in late 1450 or 1451 in the Italian port of Genoa. For centuries its merchants had traded in the western Mediterranean and Atlantic, and many young Genoese grew up to become sailors. Columbus gained his experience of the sea on voyages to Western Europe, Iceland, Madeira and West Africa. But he was not satisfied with just learning seamanship; he

wanted to be an explorer. He began collecting and studying all the maps and sea charts he could lay his hands on. In 1476 he moved with his brother to Lisbon where they opened a business buying and selling rare maps. At first business was slow, but the brothers prospered once they began printing and selling accounts of the Portuguese sailors' discoveries. Their stock went up when Columbus married Dona Felipa Menez, daughter of the first Portuguese to start a colony in Madeira. Her father's maps and records

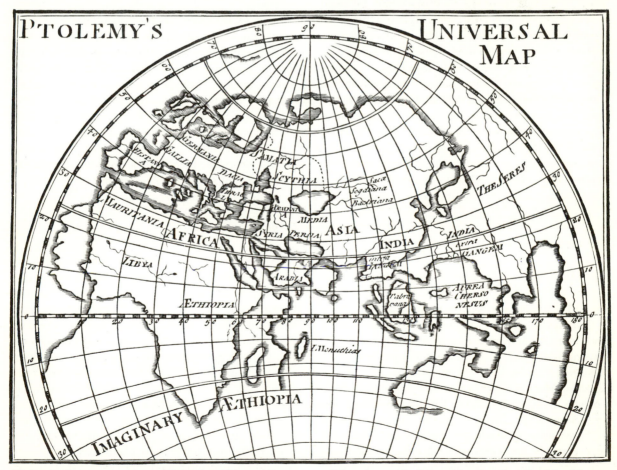

Fig 4.1 *Ptolemy's map of the world showing Africa and Europe on the western edge and India and China (The Seres, or 'land of silk') on the east. He believed that the other side of the globe was only water.*

were part of the marriage settlement Columbus demanded.

Columbus kept the best documents and books for his own personal use and these have been preserved in the Cathedral at Seville. The collection contains books by three authors whose writings helped Columbus to decide that Asia could be reached by sailing west across the Atlantic. Ptolemy, a Greek geographer who lived in the second century, believed that the earth was a perfect sphere. Half of it was land stretching from Western Europe to the eastern edge of Asia. The other half was water, and Columbus thought that if you sailed west across this ocean sea you would reach the Indies. But how wide was the ocean sea? The Arab geographer, Al-Farghani, had calculated that the distance round the earth at the equator was about 29,000 kilometres. Half of this was more than 14,500 kilometres, so clearly Columbus would need a resting place in the middle of the ocean sea where he could refit and take on fresh provisions. He found this while reading about the journeys of Marco Polo, an Italian merchant who travelled the land routes to Asia in the thirteenth century. Marco Polo wrote about the rich island of Cipango (Japan), which he described as lying off the coast of Asia. With more guesswork than good judgement, Columbus worked out that Japan was a mere 3,900 kilometres from the Canary Islands. Columbus had his theory, his calculations and his experience. Now he needed a patron rich enough to finance such a risky voyage and powerful enough to see that he got his fair rewards if he succeeded.

Search for a patron

Columbus first took his plans to the Portuguese, who turned him down because they had already decided to try and reach Asia by sailing round Africa.

Columbus next went to Spain where he was warmly welcomed by merchants who were willing to listen to anyone with plans for a new trade route across the Atlantic to the Far East. The merchants contacted the Duke of Medina Sidonia who had already financed voyages west of the Canary Islands. The Duke was impressed with Columbus and arranged a meeting with the Spanish monarchs. Isabella and Ferdinand were interested, but they were not to be rushed. Their time and money was still taken up with the end of their struggle to drive the Muslims from their last

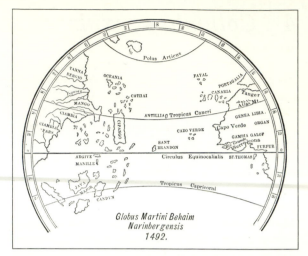

Fig. 4.2 *A map drawn in 1492 showing the world as Columbus expected to find it. Japan (Cipango) is to the west of Europe and Africa, and further west are the Indies.*

stronghold in Spain. In the meantime their royal geographers considered the proposals for five years while Columbus waited. Three times they told him that his plans were 'perilously impractical and ruinously expensive'. Columbus grew weary of the delays and sent his brother, Bartholomew, to look for help from Henry VII of England. King Henry was already considering sending another Genoese, Giovanni Caboto (John Cabot), on a similar voyage. On his way back to Spain, Bartholomew visited King Charles VIII of France, but he showed no interest at all.

Preparation

In 1492 when the long war against the Moors at last ended, Isabella agreed to help Columbus. A trade link with the far east would help to fill the empty Spanish treasury and balance off the Portuguese successes along the African coast. Wealthy Spanish followed their Queen's lead. The treasurer of Castile and some of his friends gave money, as did some Genoese merchants living in Seville and the Pinzon brothers from the port of Palos. All expected to make huge profits on their investment if Columbus was successful. Columbus himself was to get one-tenth of all the profits and be made governor of any lands he discovered. The Queen also promised to make him a nobleman and an admiral of the Spanish navy. She ordered that the port of Palos supply him with three ships. The *Pinta* was named after her owners, the Pinzon brothers, and the *Nina* after her owner, Juan Ninas. The *Santa Maria* which Columbus chose as his flag ship was the most awkward and slowest of the three. On 3 August 1492 the new Spanish admiral set sail from Palos to the Canary Islands where he refitted his ships and took on fresh provisions. On 6 September 1492 the little fleet sailed from the Canary Islands into the uncharted Atlantic Ocean.

Columbus' first voyage

The fears of the seamen grew daily as the trade winds steadily blew their ships further and further west. By mid-September they were on the point of mutiny. Even Columbus began to doubt the wisdom of his plan. According to his earlier reckoning they should have already reached Japan. For a while he quietened his men's fears by showing them a log book in which he had purposely underestimated the true distance they had travelled. A week later the seamen were once again talking about throwing their stubborn admiral into the sea and turning back. Columbus avoided mutiny by telling his men that they were even then sailing between two islands and could at any time turn towards land. Of course the islands didn't exist, but Columbus made his story convincing by marking

Fig 4.3 *Columbus landing at San Salvador (Watling Island). The picture of 'Indians' bringing him trade goods was false and* *probably drawn to impress people in Spain.*

them on his sea chart. By 10 October Columbus himself was discouraged; he promised that the voyage would be abandoned if land was not sighted within forty-eight hours. As the deadline was drawing to a close on Friday 12 October 1492, Rodrigo de Triana, keeping watch high on the rigging of the *Pinta*, sighted land.

Columbus went back to bed convinced that the island was one of the many far eastern spice islands he had read about in Marco Polo's book. His joy was short-lived. A closer look in the morning showed that the island had no exotic spices, jewels, rich clothes or gold. The natives he met had no trade goods at all, except a little inferior cotton. From them he could not learn where he was or what they called their island.

Columbus consoled himself by giving it a new name, San Salvador (Holy Saviour), while pointing out to his disappointed men that the natives were gentle, willing to please and non-believers. At least their souls could be won for the Christian Church and that was sure to please Queen Isabella. Besides, the 'Indians', as Columbus mistakenly called the Arawaks, might be taught to cultivate enough cotton to export for sale in Europe. In the meantime he took several Arawaks on board to guide him to the *real* spice islands.

Hispaniola

The Arawak guides led Columbus along their own

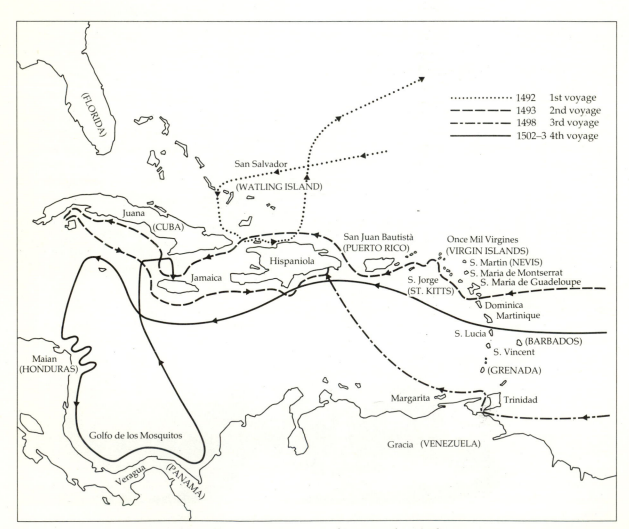

Map 7 *Columbus' four voyages to the Caribbean, showing the names he gave to places in the area.*

trade routes between San Salvador, Cuba and Hispaniola. They continually told him – as they did all European explorers – that there were mountains of gold further inland, or on 'just' the next island. For three months Columbus unsuccessfully looked for the fabled wealth of Asia. He found a little gold in Hispaniola, but the quantities were small and mixed with base metals. The search continued until one day just before Christmas the tired admiral's flag ship, the *Santa Maria*, ran aground on the north shore of Hispaniola, and sank. Thirty-nine seamen who couldn't find a place on the remaining two ships unhappily became the first European settlers in the West Indies. They used timbers from the wrecked *Santa Maria* to build themselves a fort which they called Puerto Navidad.

Columbus abandoned his search for Asia soon after the *Santa Maria* sank. Reluctantly, he ordered the remaining two ships to turn back for Spain. Their strange cargo was not encouraging: a few Arawaks, some cotton samples, an alligator, several parrots, a few hammocks, a small quantity of golden nuggets and trinkets, one wooden canoe and a bundle of tobacco leaves. Columbus wrote that the tobacco was 'highly esteemed among the Indians', but had to admit that he had no idea what it was used for! This, together with the promise of greater success on a return voyage, was all Columbus had to pay back the men who had invested money in his enterprise.

The return to Hispaniola

Columbus returned to Spain in 1493 convinced that he had discovered one of the islands of the Indies. He wrote immediately to Queen Isabella with plans for making Hispaniola the centre of a great trading empire. The first step would be to build towns from which Spaniards could trade with the Indians. The island could also be used as a base for exploring in search of other parts of the Indies.

Isabella gave the task of collecting stores, men and ships to Juan de Fonseca, who was a priest, like most of the officials at her court. Together, he and Columbus gathered seventeen ships and 1,200 men. Among them were builders, masons and carpenters with the materials to start work on the first towns in the 'Indies'. To organise the trade there were merchants and clerks as well as map-makers who would be use-

ful for voyages beyond Hispaniola. To provide food for the colony there were farmers with animals and stocks of seed. An important part of the expedition was a party of priests for the work of converting the Indians to Christianity.

In November 1493 Columbus arrived again on the coast of Hispaniola after a voyage which had taken him round the Lesser Antilles. The fleet sailed first to Navidad, only to find that the fort built a year before had been completely destroyed and the Spaniards killed in the fights with the Amerindians. Columbus decided to replace it with a new trading post named after Queen Isabella, but he chose a poor site, far away from supplies of fresh water. Seeds sprouted but then wilted in the salty soils, and men died from tropical fevers carried by mosquitos in the nearby swamps.

There were soon more disappointments. Columbus sent expeditions into the interior to seek gold, but his men found that the Arawaks lived simple farming lives and had no riches to trade. There was some gold to be panned from rivers but no working mines. These setbacks did not stop Columbus' belief in the wealth of the Indies and he took three ships to explore further west. He sailed to Jamaica but passed quickly on as he was looking for the mainland, not another island. Cuba was then sighted and for a month the ships worked their way along its south coast before returning to Hispaniola. Columbus got the map-makers to swear that they had discovered the mainland of the Indies but, privately, they were sure that Cuba, too, was an island.

Destruction of the Arawaks

While Columbus was away from Hispaniola, the Spaniards had abandoned work on the buildings and farms at Isabella. Instead they forced the Arawaks to provide them with food, at the same time robbing them of trinkets and assaulting their women. Columbus returned to find that the normally peaceful Arawaks had begun a war against the Spanish. He immediately organised expeditions to destroy the Arawak resistance and a one-sided struggle followed. The Arawaks had only primitive bows and arrows, stone clubs and wooden spears. The Spaniards were armed with steel swords, metal-tipped pikes and cross-bows. They used fierce dogs and armour-covered horses which terrified people who had never seen animals larger than a rabbit or coney. Horses gave the Spaniards the advantage of quick attacks and retreats, while the Arawaks suffered dreadful casualties by rushing headlong at the enemy. In a very short time tens of thousands of them were killed.

The fighting marked the end of any pretence that the Spaniards would trade fairly. Instead, Columbus forced the people of the island to pay a tax. Every three months each male over fourteen had to hand over enough gold to fill a hawk's bell and every other Arawak had to supply twenty-five pounds (about twelve kilograms) of spun cotton. Arawaks who failed to pay were forced to give several weeks' free labour. Hundreds of Arawaks who resisted the tax were captured and sent back to Spain for sale as slaves.

In 1496, Christopher Columbus returned to Spain, leaving his brother, Bartholomew, in charge of Hispaniola. The wars against the Arawaks continued and, in a short while, led to Spanish control of the whole island. In 1493 there had been between 200,000 and 300,000 Arawaks on Hispaniola; by the end of 1496 perhaps as many as two-thirds were dead. They were killed not only by Spanish weapons but also by the smallpox brought to the island on Columbus' ships. The Arawaks had no immunity to the disease and it raced through the island, weakening and killing whole tribes. European animals had no natural enemies in Hispaniola and within a few years great herds of cattle, swine and goats were roaming the island destroying the Arawaks' maize and cassava crops.

The first Spanish colony

In three years the Spanish plan for a trading base in Hispaniola had given way to a conquest of the whole island. To complete it, Bartholomew Columbus built a line of forts from the abandoned Isabella to a new Spanish headquarters which he started at Santo Domingo. Hispaniola had become the first Caribbean colony of Spain and Santo Domingo its capital.

Columbus did not return to Spain in triumph as he had done in 1493. Many reports had reached Isabella of the failure to find the wealth of the Indies as well as complaints about the way Columbus governed Hispaniola. At first, the Spanish Queen was unwilling to allow him to return to the Caribbean but, in 1498, she finally agreed to a third voyage.

The third voyage

On his third voyage Columbus plotted a course far to the south. He sighted Trinidad while passing through the Gulf of Paria, but he was interested in the land he could see across the Gulf. The amount of fresh water pouring out of the Orinoco River into the sea told him that the land it drained was too vast to be another island. What Columbus saw was the coast of Venezuela. He did not stop to investigate. The state of Santo Domingo was on his mind, and after taking on fresh water in Trinidad he sailed on west to Hispaniola. The discovery of South America was given only a short entry in his log: 'I believe', he wrote, 'that this is a very large continent which until now has remained unknown'. Columbus reached Hispaniola again, only to find that a revolt had broken out against his brother. He had five of the ringleaders hanged and tried to buy the support of the other Spanish on the island by allowing them to take over parts of the island as private estates. This did not stop a steady stream of complaints to Spain against the Columbus brothers and, in 1499, Isabella sent Francisco de Bobadilla to Hispaniola. He had the title of Chief Justice and Royal Commissioner which gave him special powers to act on the Queen's behalf. Almost his first act was to have the Columbus brothers arrested and sent back to Spain.

The fourth voyage

Isabella forgave Columbus and after a while allowed him to make a fourth voyage to the Caribbean to explore the coastline he had sighted across the Gulf of Paria from Trinidad. She warned him to stay clear of Hispaniola where his presence might lead to further trouble. Columbus did not heed the warning but sailed directly to Santo Domingo to claim his share of the taxes which had been so cruelly taken from the Amerindians. There he found a fleet about to carry the taxes and Francisco de Bobadilla back to Spain. Columbus was not allowed to enter Santo Domingo but had to take on fresh water and supplies at a nearby natural harbour. Only one of the twenty ships in the fleet reached Spain. The other nineteen and five hundred seamen along with Bobadilla were lost in a storm.

Meanwhile, Columbus had left Hispaniola and

Fig 4.4 *Columbus on board one of his ships using an astrolabe to work out the angle between the sea and the sun or a star.*

Fig 4.5 *A drawing of Amerindians trying to prevent Amerigo Vespucci landing.*

sailed west to the coast of Honduras. Between January and May he sailed south-east along the coast before turning his worm-eaten ships north again to Hispaniola. The ships were not fit for the voyage and sank near St. Ann's Bay, Jamaica. Columbus sent Diego Mendez by canoe to Hispaniola to beg for a rescue ship. It was almost a year before he could hire a vessel to collect Columbus and the survivors of his crews. Columbus finally arrived back in Spain in 1504 and died there in 1506, probably still believing that he had discovered part of the Indies.

Mapping the New World

At first geographers were baffled by Columbus' descriptions, which were unlike anything they had heard about Asia. Their doubts increased as more explorers crossed the Atlantic and mapped the mysterious lands. The first man to publish accounts of these journeys was an Italian who visited the Ven-

ezuelan and Guyanese coast, Amerigo Vespucci. Vespucci's book was widely read and his descriptions of the American coastline gave support to the growing belief that Columbus had discovered a separate continent. A German geographer, Martin Waldseemuller, used Vespucci's account to produce the first map of the discoveries calling the new land 'America' in honour of Vespucci. The map showed only a small section of the American coastline between Florida and Venezuela. There was still no proof that it was part of a new continent or continents. Before they could be absolutely certain of that, the Europeans had to find out what was on both ends and on the other side of Waldseemuller's coastline.

By 1518 explorers from Spain had brought back enough information to fill in the South American coastline and the western shores of the Pacific Ocean. No-one knew how wide the Pacific Ocean was or what lay beyond. The mystery was solved in 1522 when Ferdinand Magellan, a Portuguese sailor commissioned by the Spanish King, became the first European to sail round the globe. For the first time Europeans knew for certain that the world was round and that the new discoveries were separated from Asia by an ocean several thousand kilometres wide.

Now it was clear beyond all doubt that Columbus had failed to find the Indies. But he and the voyagers who followed had done more than lay claims to new lands for the King and Queen of Spain. They had charted the winds and currents which decided the sea

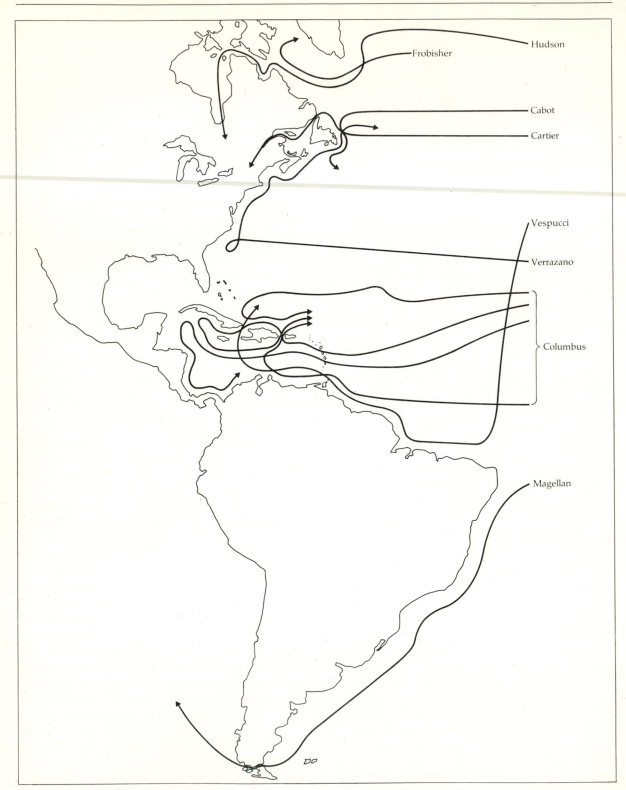

Map 8 *European explorers of the American continent.*

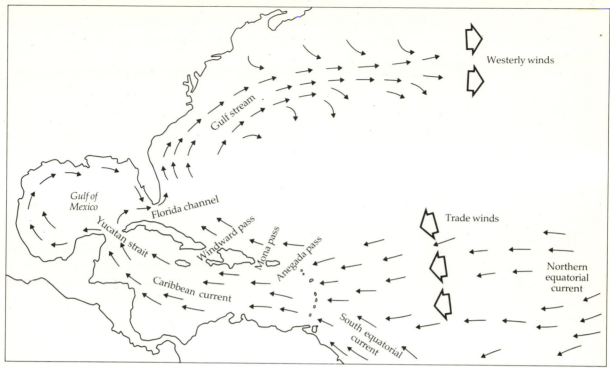

Map 9 *Winds and currents in the Caribbean.*

routes which connected the colonies with Europe. Columbus had discovered the importance of the Trade Winds when he had picked the Canary Islands to start his first voyage. These winds 'take their strength from the masses of air which move towards the equator from the north pole. Near the equator the spinning of the earth forces the air currents to turn towards the Caribbean basin. They become the Trade Winds, which blow almost continuously from east to west at the latitiude of the Canary Islands. After Columbus, ships from Europe sailed towards the Canaries to catch the Trades and they could then choose either to stay in the southern level, which would bring them to Trinidad and the coast of South America, or in the northern section which brought them to the Lesser Antilles. From here they entered the Caribbean through one of the many passes between the small islands. Ships sailing the southern route ran the risk of running into the Doldrums, a windless region. Here they might be stuck for weeks waiting for a breeze to blow them back into the Trades.

Once the Caribbean was reached the Trades were less welcome. It was difficult to sail against them on an

easterly voyage. If a ship sailed leeward of its destination it could take weeks to 'tack' back against the Trades. A voyage from Barbados to Jamaica took about a week; to go in the opposite direction needed five or six weeks!

The Spanish were also the first to chart the Caribbean currents. Like the Trade Winds they flow from east to west. The North Equatorial Current and the South Equatorial Current flow in from the Atlantic and join north of Tobago to become the Caribbean Current. This flows to the Gulf of Mexico where it turns back through the Florida channel as the Gulf Stream. The currents flow only at three or four knots an hour and did not influence sailing as much as the Trades, but they still forced ships in a westerly direction. On his return voyage, Columbus fought against the awkward currents and winds as he left the Caribbean through the Windward or Mona passages. Later seamen found that it was easier to follow the Trades as far west as the Yucatan Strait. Then they tacked north until the Gulf Stream carried them through the Florida Channel and into the Atlantic far enough north to pick up the Westerly Winds. The Spanish quickly realised the importance of controlling the Florida Channel.

5 Spain's American Empire

Ovando

What had Columbus achieved for Queen Isabella? He had promised her a way to the wealth of the Indies but all he produced was the conquest of the unfortunate Arawaks on Hispaniola and a Spanish colony where only 300 Spaniards were still alive in 1502. To the Queen and Juan de Fonseca, who had become her chief adviser on the Indies, the lesson was plain. The affairs of the Indies could not be left to private adventurers such as Columbus; in future they would have to be the responsibility of the government in Spain. Their first task was to choose a royal official to be Governor of Hispaniola who would bring order to the island and develop it as a base for further exploration.

The man chosen was a nobleman, Nicolas Ovando. He arrived in 1502 and in the next seven years governed the island in a way which became the model for the Spanish Empire which grew up in the Indies. His first aim was to make it produce enough food for a larger number of Spanish settlers, and to do this he experimented with different crops. It was soon found that olives and vines which flourish in Spain would not grow in the tropics, although orange and lemon trees would do very well here. European wheat and barley were quickly seen to be unsuitable, although it was not long before the Spaniards discovered that Indian corn, or maize, could be made into bread, and rice could be planted in the wetter districts. Two crops which became very important in the history of the Caribbean, bananas and sugar cane, were brought from the Canary Islands. Sheep could not survive easily in the climate, but meat could be obtained from pigs, goats and chickens, which soon roamed freely over the island.

The new foods made it possible for Hispaniola to support ever increasing numbers of Spanish settlers. Ovando had brought 2,500 with him in 1502, to add to the 300 remaining from Columbus' day; only four years later a steady flow of emigrants from Spain had raised the number of settlers to 12,000. Some of the Spaniards were drawn to the Caribbean by the news that Ovando had organised mining for gold on Hispaniola. Others saw a chance of owning land where they could produce goods for export back to Spain. Of the food crops sugar was the most important, but not until the first crushing mills were built, which was probably in 1508. Most Spaniards found cattle ranching more profitable than sugar. The cattle were not kept for their meat, but for the hides and tallow which both fetched a good price in Europe. Some ranchers also bred horses, which were sold to Spanish settlers or to explorers setting out for other islands.

Encomiendas

The Spaniards who were wealthy enough to own mines, ranches or plantations did not come to the Caribbean to work themselves. They were from hidalgo families and came with the hope of being granted encomiendas over the Indians, like those given to the men who had taken part in the conquests of the Moors and the people of the Canary Islands. To set up the encomiendas Ovando carried out a distribution, or *repartimiento*, of the Indians in Hispaniola, parcelling them out into groups of thirty. A Spaniard was then granted encomiendas over one or more of these groups of Amerindians.

After the first repartimiento by Ovando the task of sharing out the Amerindians became the responsibility of the members of the *cabildo* or council of each town on the island. Each cabildo was responsible for the countryside around the town and its members came from the richest and most powerful families in the district. Thus, the successful Spanish in Hispaniola settled down to a life which was a copy of that in Spain, where landowners and merchants used the cabildos to protect their wealth and to control the lives of the local peasants.

A man who had been given an encomienda became the Amerindians' *encomondero*. In theory, this meant he was their protector, with the duty of seeing that they were cared for and taught to become more 'civilised' – from the Spanish point of view. Becoming more 'civilised' really meant nothing more than giving signs that they accepted the Spanish as their masters, covering their bodies as Europeans did, speaking Spanish and accepting the Christian faith. The Amerindians, for their part, had no doubt that it was the cruel and murderous Spanish who were uncivilised. In return for Spanish 'protection' the Amerindians were to give service in the fields or mines of the encomenderos, but they were to keep their homes and farms and to remain free men. Indeed, Queen Isabella had prohibited slavery among Amerindians and set free those sent back to Spain by Columbus.

In practice, the encomienda system was nothing more than a means of obtaining forced labour for the encomonderos. No wages were paid for the work done; churches or schools were not built in Arawak villages. Very often the Arawaks' own farms were ruined by herds of cattle or swine belonging to their encomondero. In any case they rarely had time to grow their own food for the forced labour left them neither time nor strength. Arawaks were not free to leave the encomienda and those who fled were hunted down by men on horseback and dogs. The results were disastrous. The death rate among Arawaks shot up as a result of hunger, weakness and despair among people whose traditional village and family life was completely destroyed. Further epidemics of smallpox helped to complete the total destruction of Amerindian life on Hispaniola. After thirty years of Spanish settlement there were hardly any left alive.

The Spanish made desperate attempts to find new labour and soon turned to Amerindian slavery, although it was officially forbidden except for prisoners taken in a just war. Slaving raids were made on the Bahamas, or Lucayos as they were then called, but the Amerindians brought from these islands died just as rapidly as those from Hispaniola itself. For another source the Spanish turned to African slaves. Such labour was not new to them; for more than a hundred years small numbers of Africans had been taken to Spain itself and later to the cane fields on the Canary Islands. The few thousands brought to the Americas at this time were but the first of some twenty million transported by the end of the eighteenth century.

Fig 5.1 *Amerindians being forced to mine for gold, watched by Spanish soldiers.*

The conquests

The island could only give the chance of a prosperous and comfortable life to a small number of colonists. Their own ill-treatment of the Amerindians meant that there was not enough labour to produce great profits from farming or mining; and, in any case, it was clear that the mines contained only small amounts of gold. So, to most Spanish, Hispaniola became simply a base from which they could go on to seek great fortunes further west. In his seven years as governor Ovando laid the foundations for a wave of exploration and conquest. He organised voyages of exploration to Cuba, which proved that it was an island, and to the Panama coast where a small Spanish settlement was set up. But, more important for the future, was his success in building up Hispaniola's agriculture so that it could supply expeditions with food and horses. It was under the next Governor, Diego Columbus, the son of Christopher, that all the Greater Antilles became Spanish colonies.

The spread of the Spanish Empire was carried out by private adventurers. Yet the government took good care to see that it kept control of newly conquered lands and that a share of the profits went to the royal treasury. Before he could set out, the leader of each expedition had to sign a contract known as a *capiculacion*. This gave him the title of *adelantado* and made him governor of the new territory with the right to own land there and collect customs duties on all fishing and trading. But, the capiculacion laid down that other taxes, and especially a fifth of all precious metals, were to go to the royal treasury. It was made clear that the people of conquered lands would become subjects of the Spanish King and Queen. The capiculacion also stated whether the adelantado or the government would pay for work such as building towns, protecting the colony, bringing new settlers and converting the Amerindians.

In 1509 two adelantados set out to conquer neighbouring islands. One was Ponce de Leon who had lived in Hispaniola for some time. The year before he had made a voyage to Puerto Rico and had returned with some gold. Now he was going with a capiculacion which made him governor of the island with the right to share out its land among his party of *conquistadores*, or fighting men, some of them from Hispaniola and some from Spain itself.

Puerto Rico and Jamaica

The Spanish conquest of Puerto Rico followed the same pattern as in Hispaniola. In 1509 there were probably as many as 30,000 Borequino Amerindians on the island, living in wood and thatched huts grouped in villages near the sea or rivers. Their food came from fishing or trapping birds and small animals and their only weapons were bows and arrows, hardwood swords and stone axes. Like the Arawaks of Hispaniola, these Borequinos were the victims of a repartimiento among the Spanish and were shared out among the conquistadores who became their encomonderos. As in Hispaniola, the result was a desperate revolt in which thousands of Borequinos were slaughtered by the Spanish. In a census taken in 1514 it was reckoned that only 4,000 remained. Yet, from the Spanish point of view, the island prospered for a few years. San Juan and other towns were built to control the countryside where mines, sugar plantations and cattle ranches replaced the villages.

The second expedition of 1509 was more disappointing. Juan d'Esquivel led his party of conquistadores to Jamaica, but they were dismayed to find no precious metals. Esquival himself was happy enough to become the island's governor and share out the island between cattle ranchers and a few sugar planters. But Jamaica offered nothing to the more adventurous and greedy conquistadores such as Panfilo de Narvaez. In 1511, he left the island to join in the

Fig 5.2 *A propaganda picture from the late sixteenth century showing Amerindians being burned alive by Spanish raiders.*

conquest of an island that would become a more important part of Spain's American Empire – Cuba.

Cuba

The adelantado who led the Cuban expedition was Diego Velasquez, who had been Deputy Governor of Hispaniola. The Amerindians on Cuba did not wait to fight until the Spaniards had begun the repartimiento; they probably knew what to expect from the Amerindians who had escaped from Hispaniola and Jamaica. War broke out immediately and for three years Narvaez led his mounted soldiers against the ill-armed Amerindians, who retreated further into the mountains. Most battles were no more than simple massacres with the Spaniards slaying their enemies in thousands. At the same time, Velasquez was carrying out a repartimiento and building the island's first towns which included Santiago, the capital, and

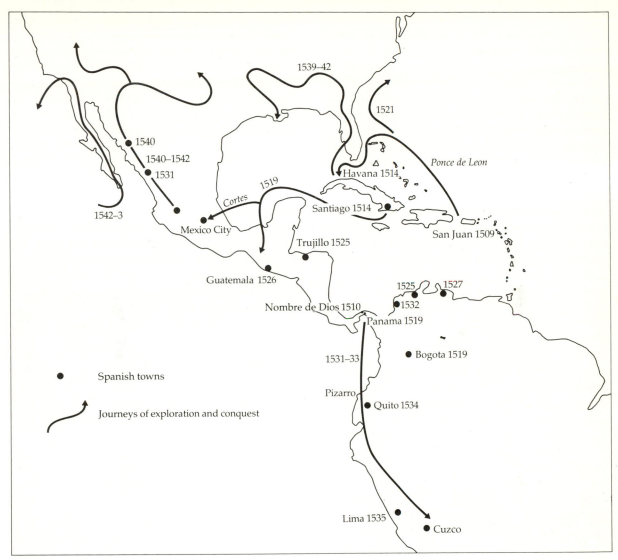

Map 10 *The Spanish conquests.*

Havana, a smaller town on the north coast. Two of Velasquez's followers were Bartolomé de Las Casas, and Hernán Cortes.

Cuba turned out to be a richer conquest than the other islands. Like them, the shortage of Amerindian labour made cattle ranching the main form of farming, but the island had more gold than Puerto Rico or Hispaniola. Yet, to ambitious and ruthless men like Velasquez and his young secretary, Hernán Cortes, the island was only a stopping place in the movement west in search of even greater wealth. Cuba now replaced Hispaniola as the base for Spanish exploration in the New World.

The mainland

Voyages of exploration from Santiago found the coast of Mexico and returned with enough loot to prove that the land held great riches. Velasquez looked for leaders to conquer Mexico and defeat the Aztecs who ruled over the peoples there. Velasquez's first choice was Cortes, but he found that his secretary had been plotting against him. He cancelled the appointment but, by then, Cortes had slipped away taking the 600 best fighting men on Cuba, most of the island's stock of weapons and eleven ships. That was in February 1519; by September 1520 he had conquered the Aztec

Empire and totally destroyed its capital, Tenochtitlan. In 1522 Cortes was made Governor of Mexico which was renamed New Spain.

Mexico was not the first part of the mainland to be discovered by the Spanish. Not long after the discovery of Hispaniola a small Spanish settlement had grown up on the Panama coast. It was from here that Vasco Nunez de Balboa had made the journey which made him the first European to see the Pacific Ocean. But, like the Caribbean Islands, the Panama area gave little profit to the Spanish, who found it difficult to make a living because of hostile Amerindians and the many diseases they caught in the marshy lands. So the settlements became the base for restless adelantados who took their bands of conquistadores towards the great empire of the Incas in Peru. The conquest of this

distant empire with its strongholds in the Andes took longer than the capture of Mexico. There were two failures and much quarrelling among the conquistadores but, by 1535, Francisco Pizarro had captured the Inca capital of Cuzco and replaced it with a new Spanish town, Lima, built on the coast. The land of the Incas became the Spanish Viceroyalty of Peru, the richest part of the Spanish Empire.

Decline of the Caribbean Colonies

Hundreds and then thousands of Spaniards who first settled in Hispaniola, Cuba or Puerto Rico moved on west towards Mexico and Peru. The first were the conquistadores who went for the plunder, but close

Fig 5.3 *Spaniards forcing Amerindians to carry loot taken from the Inca Empire in Peru.*

behind went men who hoped to own mines or cattle ranches larger and richer than those on the islands. The mainland mines produced vast amounts of gold and silver, far more than those on Cuba and Hispaniola which were worn out by the 1530s. On the mainland there were not only thousands of square kilometres of grassland for ranching but still millions of Amerindians to be forced into encomiendas.

So the Greater Antilles, the starting point of the Spanish Empire, became important only as ports of call for Spanish ships on their way to the mainland. Two towns became well known to sailors, merchants and officials from Spain. Those travelling to Panama and Peru called in at Santo Domingo to repair their ships and take on supplies. It was still the Spanish headquarters in the Caribbean and by far the largest island town with perhaps 1,000 people in 1540. Some were Spanish government officials; others were merchants and craftsmen who supplied the ships and their passengers. Next in importance was Havana which was used by ships on their way to Mexico. Because it lay on this route it became more important than Santiago on the south coast and replaced it as the capital of Cuba. Yet in 1540 there were only 200 Spanish families on the whole island; there had been several times that number before the riches of the mainland were discovered.

Peoples of the Spanish Caribbean

The fall in the numbers of Spanish took place throughout the Caribbean. At its time of greatest importance, Hispaniola had a population of 14,000; by 1574 there were only 500 households. Jamaica and Puerto Rico never had more than a few hundred Europeans until the mid-seventeenth century. Further south, there was a pearl gathering settlement on Margarita, but only a few dozen Spaniards remained as a result of over-fishing by the first men on the scene. Most of the Lesser Antilles were never occupied, although the Spanish Government claimed them as part of the empire. There was a settlement on Trinidad but it numbered only seventy Europeans in 1593.

The small population on the islands quickly became very mixed. In an effort to increase the numbers of European colonists the Spanish government allowed non-Spaniards to emigrate. Portuguese farmers,

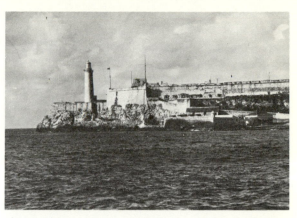

Fig 5.4 *The entrance to Havana harbour guarded by Morro Castle, which has a modern lighthouse on top. The castle was built in 1589 to protect the town from pirates.*

mostly from the over-crowded Azores, were offered land in the Greater Antilles. Among the armies sent out to the New World were many Italian soldiers as well as German craftsmen who made and repaired weapons and equipment. After their army services, many settled on the islands, glad of a chance to start a small business or farm while the Spanish conquistadores were driving further into the mainland.

By the mid-sixteenth century the greater part of these European people in the Caribbean were born here and not in Spain. Many were 'creoles', a word used by the Spanish only for American-born people of European parentage. Others were of mixed parentage. So few women came among the early settlers that many men took Amerindian women, sometimes as wives but more usually for a short time. Many of the children of these unions became accepted in local society and helped to widen the differences between those born here and *peninsulares* – men who came from Spain to work for a time in the Empire.

For creoles outside Santo Domingo and Havana, the main occupation was ranching. On all the islands there were so few landowners that it was possible to allow the cattle to roam freely without the expense of fencing. The hides and tallow fetched good prices from European leather and candle makers, and they would not suffer if they had to be stored for months waiting for a ship. Ranching did not produce as much money as sugar planting, but few creoles started plantations because of the cost of crushing mills and the shortage of labour. The government helped with loans but it was still difficult to make a profit, especially when their sugar had to compete with that grown on the much larger plantations in Brazil, Mexico and the Canary Islands. After sugar and ranching there was a variety of products grown on a small scale, including fruits, tobacco, cassava and maize, but none were very important particularly when a farmer had hardly any neighbours to sell them to.

The centre of creole life in each district of the Spanish colonies was its town, or *villa*. Some, like Santo Domingo in the Caribbean and Lima and Mexico on the mainland, grew into European cities with many stone buildings. But throughout most of the Caribbean the towns never grew much beyond a dusty main square, or *plaza major*, around which stood a few wooden buildings, a church, a town hall, a prison, and perhaps a school. The leading creole families had their homes here, too, for they did not live in great houses on the plantations as later English colonists did. The Spanish villa was more than a market town; it was the centre from which the countryside around was ruled by the cabildo, made up of the heads of the leading creole families in the district. Usually there were twenty-four councillors or *regidores*, but small towns could have as few as four. The first regidores were conquistadores, but as time went on wealthy ranchers or planters could buy a seat on the cabildo, often with the right to pass it on to their sons.

To become a regidor gave a creole a voice in controlling matters in which he had an interest. The cabildo was in charge of sharing out the land in the district, and arranged the repartimiento of Indians so that it controlled the supply of labour. The price of goods in the town was fixed by the cabildo whose regidores owned the land on which most of the goods were produced. The same regidores elected one of their number to be *alcades*, or magistrates, who dealt with crime and legal cases in the area.

Peninsulares

Creoles had control of local affairs but the work of running the Spanish Empire and controlling its trade was done by peninsulares sent out by the government to serve for a time as officials. The royal government ruled its American lands in the same way as the Kingdoms of Castile and Aragon, where its aim was to make the power of the crown greater than that of any group of subjects. To do this they had the aid of the Council of Castile and the Council of Aragon. Each council was made up of a bishop, senior civil servants and lawyers, and was responsible for making laws and regulations. But it was difficult to see that these were obeyed, especially in districts where local noblemen had become wealthy and powerful enough to ignore royal officials. To keep respect for the law was the work of *audencias*, which were courts of lawyers who examined complaints of unlawful behaviour and heard appeals against the decisions of local judges.

Only slight changes were made to this system of government in the American colonies. At first the control of exploration and the government of newly conquered lands were given to the Council of Castile. After a few years the task became so huge that a separate Council of the Indies was set up in 1524. By 1635 this Council had made more than 400,000 laws controlling life in the colonies down to the last detail. It had set up law courts and founded new cities, schools, churches, hospitals and monasteries. But it also dealt with lesser matters, laying down what dress colonists should wear, which Spanish dialect should be taught to Amerindians, and even the order in which officials should enter church.

Audencias

To make sure that those laws were obeyed in the Americas a chain of audencias was set up. The first was at Santo Domingo in 1524, but as the Empire on the mainland grew new audencias were created. In the Americas an audencia had more power than in Spain for it not only judged legal cases but could make its own enquiries into whether the Council's regulations were being obeyed. To back up the judges there was a staff of lawyers, officials and clerks who became the real rulers of the colonists.

When the Empire had grown to its fullest size each audencia supervised an area which contained officials of many ranks. Larger districts were in the charge of presidents and each presidency was divided into several provinces each with its own governor. The more remote or scattered areas were in the charge of captain-generals. Below these senior officials were thousands of lesser government servants. All were peninsulares and could be dismissed and sent back to Spain if their work was found unsatisfactory.

Commandancy General Audiencia of Guadalajara

VICE ROYALTY
OF NEW SPAIN

Captaincy General Audiencia of Havana

Audiencia of Mexico

Captaincy General of Santo Domingo

Captaincy General
Audiencia of Guatemala

Captaincy General
Audiencia of Caracas

Audiencia of Bogota

Guyanese Colonies

VICE ROYALTY OF NEW GRANADA

Presidency Audiencia of Quito

Portuguese Brazil

Audiencia of Lima

Audiencia of Cuzco

Presidency Audiencia
of Charcas

VICE ROYALTY OF PERU

VICE ROYALTY
OF LA PLATA

Paraguay

Banda
Orientale

Captaincy General Audiencia of Santiago

Audiencia of
Buenos Aires

Map 11 *The Spanish Empire showing its administrative divisions.*

Viceroys

At the head of all the officials stood the viceroys. In the sixteenth century there were only two, governing the Viceroyalties of New Spain and Mexico. Later, the boundaries were changed and there became four: the Viceroyalties of Mexico, La Plata, Peru and New Granada. The viceroy was the representative of the King and Queen; he was a great nobleman and given all the honours and luxury of royalty. He was also commander of the Spanish armies in his viceroyalty. But despite the magnificence of his position, his powers were carefully limited. The work of his officials was examined by the audencias and his financial records were inspected by a *visitador*, who came unannounced from Spain to check that the viceroy was not using his position for his own profit. At the end of his term of office the viceroy had to hold a *residencia* when his work could be questioned by people in public.

The Church in the colonies

In Spain the Church was immensely powerful and its bishops and priests had great privileges such as being free from taxes and having the right not be accused in a royal court. Ferdinand and Isabella did not want the Church as a rival to their power in the New World and negotiated with the Pope for the right to control the Church here. In 1508 this was agreed in a Bull, or proclamation, by the Pope which gave the Spanish rulers complete patronage over the Church in the American colonies. Patronage meant that no bishop or priest could be appointed to a cathedral or church except with royal permission. It also meant that tithes, or money paid to the Church by people living in its parish, were collected by royal officials, not by priests.

The New World settlements developed into copies of Spanish society as a result of the activities of the Church. It provided all the teachers and ran all the schools from the smallest mission class up to the universities in Mexico City and Lima. Priests and nuns staffed orphanages, poorhouses and hospitals. Social life was controlled through special Church courts which dealt with matters such as marriage and the inheritance of property. The spread of new ideas was checked by the Church courts which dealt with here-

tics – men who spoke or wrote in a way which the Church said was false. The most famous of these courts was the Holy Office of the Inquisition, whose permission was needed for any book to be published. It is best remembered for hunting down heretics (people who didn't believe in the Catholic Church), including Protestant Dutch and English sailors who came into Spanish ports in the Americas.

The Church and the Amerindians

The leading part in the Church's work among Amerindians was taken first by the orders of friars, especially the Franciscans and Dominicans. In Europe the first friars had been 'mendicants' or beggars, that is monks who had left their monasteries to live, without any personal belongings, among the poor. From these beginnings had sprung up the great organisations, or orders, of friars who provided schools and hospitals across Europe. The Spanish branches of the Dominican and Franciscan Orders saw a great opportunity in the discovery of the Americas. Here were millions of Amerindians, simple, ignorant people who could be cared for and cured, taught the word of God and baptised into the Catholic Church. Unfortunately there was not one but two views of the purposes of the conquests. As one conquistador said, they were to: 'serve God and His Majesty and to give light to those in darkness, and also to get rich'. It was the second view which was held by the Spanish settlers who forced the Amerindians to labour for them. Queen Isabella, a very religious woman, was troubled by the ill-treatment and, in 1500, ordered Amerindian slaves to be set free. On the other hand, she believed the encomiendas were a way of carrying out God's work by giving the Indians protection and a chance to learn the teachings of Christianity. The truth was far different, and it was a Dominican friar, Antonio de Montesinos, who spoke out loud in 1511.

Antonio de Montesinos

The place he chose was the main church in Santo Domingo, the capital of the empire in America. Many encomonderos sat in the congregation and heard Montesinos say: 'Are these Indians not men? Do they not have rational souls? Are you not obliged to love them as you love yourselves?' He ended his sermon by calling on the encomonderos to end the 'cruelty and tyranny you use in dealing with these innocent people'.

The congregation was outraged and so were most wealthy Spaniards on Hispaniola. They tried to silence Montesinos by sending reports to Spain that he was threatening the peace of the island. So Montesinos himself went back to Spain where his views were listened to by a Church council. This wrote the thirty-two Laws of Burgos which King Ferdinand signed in 1512. The laws attempted to make the encomienda system work without such evil effects and laid down the exact hours of labour and food which each worker and his family should have. The Laws of Burgos were completely ignored in the Spanish colonies, but the campaign for fair treatment of the Amerindians was taken over by another friar.

Bartolomé de las Casas

Las Casas had first come from Spain to Hispaniola and then joined Velasquez's expedition to Cuba. There he had owned an encomienda but became convinced that the system was evil. He travelled to Spain to argue that the Amerindian could be converted to Christianity without being brought under encomiendas. He claimed they would work much more willingly if they were settled on their own lands. Eventually, the new ruler of Spain, Charles V, made Las Casas 'Protector of the Indians' and gave him the chance to try his 'social experiments'.

The first was in Hispaniola. A few Amerindians were taken to gold mines and asked to work in return for food, clothing and shelter. They could not understand the point of such work either as free men or under force. The food was eaten but no gold mined. A few years later, Las Casas tried to prove that the Amerindians could be taught to work alongside Spaniards. He took Spanish farmers and Amerindians to a remote place on the Venezuelan coast, but this experiment also ended in disaster. Spanish colonists from Hispaniola wanted to discredit Las Casas and attacked the settlement, carrying off several Amerindians. Those remaining blamed their Spanish neighbours and slaughtered them.

Las Casas tried once more, in Guatemala. He had ballads written which told the Christian story in Amerindian language. These were taught to Amerindian traders who sang them on their visits around the villages. Then priests began to accompany the traders and to win the confidence of the village people. This experiment alarmed the Amerindian priests. In 1552 they led a rebellion in which three Christian priests were murdered, one being sacrificed before a local idol. So Las Casas failed in his efforts to protect the Amerindians from the evil consequences of the encomienda system. His work did have some influence, however, for his ideas were copied by priests, especially the Jesuits, who worked among Amerindians on the frontiers of the Empire away from the main centres of Spanish settlement. But that was mostly in the seventeenth century; in the sixteenth century the creole settlers were so desperate for labour that they refused to accept laws which protected the Amerindians.

Such laws were made with the encouragement of the Pope, who declared in 1537 that Amerindians were: 'not to be deprived of their liberty or the possession of their property even though they may be outside the faith of Jesus Christ . . . nor should [they] be in any case enslaved'.

This forced Charles V, king of Spain 1516–56, to issue the New Laws of 1542 which forbade new encomiendas to be granted and ordered that Amerindians should be freed on the death of their encomendero. But the Laws could not be enforced. The Viceroy of Peru was murdered for trying to introduce them; the Viceroy of Mexico never even published the Laws. The authorities in Spain decided to risk the displeasure of the Pope and allow the encomienda to continue rather than be faced with revolts from the colonists.

The wealth of the Empire

From the government's point of view the wealth of its Empire in the Americas existed solely to increase the power of Spain. This meant close control over buying and selling by colonists. All goods produced in the New World had to be exported to Spain and to no other country; everything the colonists bought had to be imported from Spain itself and be brought in Spanish ships. The ideas behind this economic system have been called mercantalism. Mercantalists held that the key to a nation's wealth lay in keeping a monopoly over all its trade and excluding foreigners.

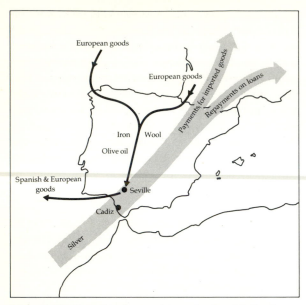

Map 12 *The flow of trade to and from the Spanish Empire.*

This would benefit not only merchants and seamen but also the shipbuilders, the industrialists and the craftsmen who made goods for the new overseas markets. It would also increase the income of the government which could tax all the goods which passed either way between the mother country and the colonies. If the tax were collected in precious metal, gold or silver, it would provide the funds to pay for the armies and navies which would make the nation more powerful than its rivals.

The Casa

To enforce Spain's monopoly of trade with her own colonies the *Casa de Contratación*, or House of Trade, was set up at Seville in 1503. The Casa served as a customs point where all ships bound for the colonies were checked; no other port could send ships to the colonies. All goods arriving from the Americas had to complete their journey at Seville. Here Casa officials took one-fifth of all precious metals as the king's share and charged customs duties on all other goods.

The Casa was also responsible for granting licences, or *asientos*, to foreigners who wished to ship goods to the colonies. The African slave trade first began with an asiento granted to Portuguese merchants. The Casa also maintained a school, to train map makers, sailors and geographers, and set up special courts to deal

with disputes that arose over trade.

The Casa was successful in controlling trade from Spain and in keeping unlicensed foreigners from taking part. In the New World it was much less easy to keep a check on either the colonists or on foreign ships which slipped in to sell goods to the Spanish settlements scattered over thousands of kilometres. To stop the smuggling, cruiser fleets patrolled the seas from bases at Santo Domingo, Havana and Cartagena. South American colonists could receive supplies only through Cartagena and Nombre de Dios and, later, Portobello.

Effects of the monopoly system

How well did the monopoly system work? The royal treasuries certainly received large quantities of silver from the Americas, but in some years this was not enough to pay for the costs of government, and the Spanish kings had to borrow from foreign bankers. Some Spanish industries benefited, especially those connected with shipbuilding and textiles. Some estate owners found profitable new markets in the New World for their olive oil, wine and grain. Seventeenth-century laws forbade colonies to produce their own wine and oil or to buy it from another colony.

Yet there were probably more weaknesses than strengths. Spain never managed to keep more than a fraction of the silver from the New World; most of it was shipped out to other European countries to buy supplies, so that merchants in Holland, England and Germany prospered at the expense of Spaniards. The great flow of silver had other disadvantages. Between 1503 and 1600 the Spanish American mines increased the amount of silver in Europe by three times. But such an increase had the same effect as a modern government printing more bank-notes; it simply put up prices. All European countries suffered from inflation at this time, but Spain most of all.

The greatest weakness of Spain's mercantile system was that it failed to develop the colonies. Part of the trouble was that it placed too many restrictions on the Spanish settlers. Sometimes these were absurd; one Spanish governor noted that as no Spanish ships were calling at Trinidad the settlers there were selling their tobacco to English and Dutch vessels; this was clearly breaking the regulations and the governor's solution was that the King should forbid tobacco growing on the island! Mostly, the fault of the restrictions was that they led to costly delays and shortages; not surprisingly when it is remembered that every ship to and from the New World had to make the 115 kilometre journey up a narrow river behind the port of Cadiz to be checked at the Casa in Seville. Nor did the Spanish ever have enough ships to carry all the goods required by the colonists, yet they refused to allow other nations to supply them. Colonists continually complained that asientos given to the Portuguese only licensed them to carry a fraction of the number of slaves they needed.

The colonies which suffered most from these weaknesses were those in the Caribbean. All the settlements were small; in the Greater Antilles the Spanish populations were measured in a few hundreds, on Trinidad and the Guyana coast only a few dozens, and on most of the Lesser Antilles there were none at all. So it was in the Caribbean that two forces challenged the Spanish monopoly. One was the willingness of the settlers to disobey the regulations and trade with other nations for supplies and slaves. The other was the determination of seamen from European nations with larger navies to break the monopoly.

6 Sixteenth-century warfare in the Caribbean

The Treaty of Tordesillas

After Columbus' first voyage Isabella and Ferdinand acted quickly to make an international claim to all the lands in the area discovered by Columbus. Their first move was to ask for the support of the Pope, whose judgements were held to be binding by most European Christians. Pope Alexander VI was a Spaniard by birth and an ally of Isabella and Ferdinand so he was very willing to back up their claim. In a decree he divided up the world outside Europe into two zones, one each side of a line which ran 100 leagues (about 640 kilometres) west of the Azores. All lands discovered in the western zone were to belong to Spain and those in the east to Portugal.

Portugal objected that the division was unfair and refused to recognise Spanish claims to the New World unless the line was moved to 370 leagues (about 2,400 kilometres) west of the Azores. Spain agreed and the new dividing line was written into the Treaty of Tordesillas which the two countries signed in 1494. It gave Portugal a piece of the New World as Brazil was discovered on her side of the line.

Of course, no other European nation would accept Spain's claim that she ruled all of the world west of the Treaty line. England and France soon sent explorers to North America. In 1497 the King of England sent the Italian, John Cabot, who landed on the shores of Newfoundland. In 1524 the French King provided ships for another Italian, Giovanni de Verrazano. Verrazano mapped the North American coastline from Carolina to Nova Scotia. Ten years later the Frenchman, Jaques Cartier, made the first of several journeys which took him down the St Lawrence River into the interior of the North American mainland.

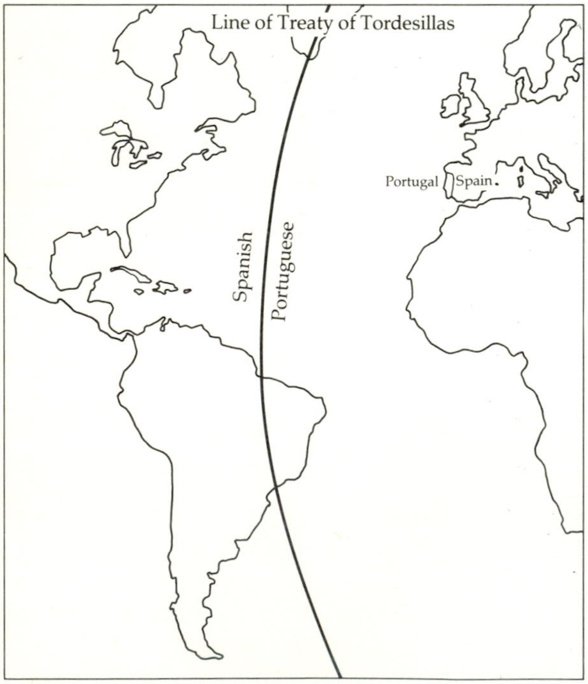

Pirates

But for a long time these North American discoveries interested Europeans less than the chance of sharing in the wealth of the Spanish Empire in the Caribbean and the lands of Central and South America. To do this they had to defy the regulations which forbade Spanish settlers to deal with foreign traders. But more than regulations were needed to stop the pirates who attacked ships and raided Spanish settlements for any loot they could carry away.

One of the first pirates was Palmier de Gonnville who led his crews across the Atlantic to Brazil and returned by way of the Caribbean. Here his men seized small quantities of logwood and hides from the surprised Spanish but found that they did not sell in France for enough to cover the cost of the voyage. De Gonnville never returned to the Caribbean because the booty was not worth the risk. Pirates caught by either the Spanish or French navies would have been hanged.

Map 13 *The Treaty of Tordesillas*

Privateers

Pirates were not the only threat to the peace of the Caribbean. For nearly three centuries after Columbus' arrival European nations fought wars here. Most of them had their cause in purely European affairs or perhaps a quarrel in another part of the world, but this did not stop the fighting from spreading to the Caribbean. In the sixteenth century most of the ships which fought in these wars were privateers. Privateers were private ships, some belonging to pirates, others to men who were legal merchants in peacetime. When war broke out their captains were given 'letters of marque' which authorised them, in the name of their government, to attack enemy ports and ships. They had to hand over part of any booty to their government but could sell the rest on the open market. A great advantage to pirates was that their letters of marque gave them the rights of soldiers; if captured they would be made prisoners rather than hanged as outlaws.

France fights Spain

The first important war in which Spain had to defend her claims to the Caribbean was fought against France between 1521 and 1559. A French merchant, Jean D'Ango, organised a privateering fleet which, in 1523, came upon a Spanish convoy carrying loot which Cortes had stripped from the Aztec temples and palaces in Mexico. Two galleons were taken with holds full of gold and precious objects. Once the wealth of America was known, other owners of mer-

Fig 6.1 *Pirates raiding the Spanish settlement at Cartagena in 1555. This is a French drawing made in about 1600.*

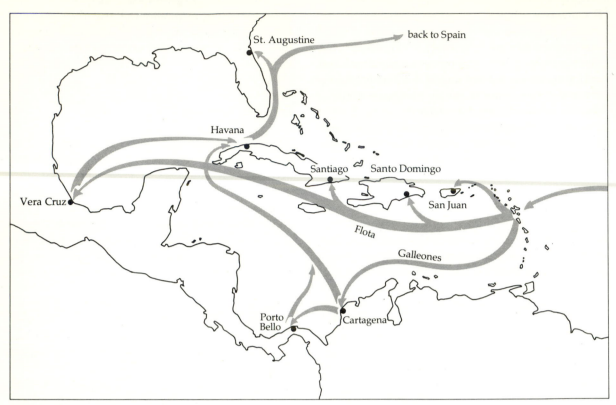

Map 14 *The convoy system.*

chant ships were eager to join the privateering fleets.

In 1531 D'Ango brought together thirteen ships and 3,000 men to attack Havana and Nombre de Dios. So many prizes were taken on the outward voyage that the ships turned back before reaching America. But the fleets soon returned. By 1536, French privateers, called *corsaires*, were regularly plundering Spanish ships in the Florida channel and boldly attacking settlements in Cuba, Hispaniola and Puerto Rico. In 1543 the corsaires reached the mainland and sacked New Cadiz and burned Santa Marta to the ground. Even more brutal were the raids led by François le Clerc, nick-named 'Pie de Palo' by the Spaniards on account of his wooden leg. One of le Clerc's most ruthless raids took place in 1553 when his squadron captured Havana. For eighteen days the citizens were tortured to make them reveal where they had hidden their money. One by one the inhabitants of the town confessed. When the last copper coin had been extracted the French methodically destroyed the city. A French fleet which arrived two months later could not find one whole bucket to carry fresh water to the ship's barrels, so complete had been the devastation.

Convoys and castles

The government in Spain took strong measures to defend the treasure fleets from smugglers and pirates. In 1543 ships passing to and from the Americas were ordered to sail in convoys. Further orders, between 1564 and 1566, laid down the convoy pattern which was followed for the next 150 years. There were to be two annual fleets. The first, the *Flota*, left Seville in April or May and sailed to the West Indies where it divided. Some of the ships stopped at West Indian ports and the rest continued to Vera Cruz in Mexico. In August another fleet, the *Galleones*, sailed from Seville. Part sailed to the central American ports while the other ships turned south to Colombia and Venezuela. Both the Galleones and the Flota reassembled in Havana in April or May. After refitting and taking food on board the combined fleet, under heavy protection from guard ships, sailed through the Florida Channel and across the Atlantic to Spain.

The convoy system was remarkably successful. In its long history the whole fleet was captured only four times, although one or two ships were lost every year in storms or to pirates. However, the need to wait until convoys were ready limited the number of goods and slaves which could be carried to America. As a result the system was very unpopular with colonists, who frequently used the excuse that they could not obtain Spanish goods to justify dealing with illegal French, English or Dutch traders.

Spain also strengthened her forces in the Caribbean itself. In 1562 Pedro Menéndez de Aviles was sent to the colonies to hunt down pirates. He rebuilt the coastal towns they had plundered, adding walls and fortifications. Havana was rebuilt in stone and the Moro castle constructed at the harbour entrance to protect the fleets assembling for the homeward voyage.

De Aviles launched an attack on Florida where French corsaires had bases for their raids on the homeward bound convoy. The French sailors were brutally slaughtered in the so-called 'Florida Massacre'. It was a terrible example of Spain's determination to defend her claims. A new Spanish fort was built at St Augustine where a permanent squadron kept guard over convoys in the Florida channel.

The English

After the war against France, English sailors became the most active challengers of the Spanish in the Caribbean. A seaman, John Hawkins, thought that Spanish settlers would pay good prices for African slaves to replace the Amerindians they had destroyed through ill-treatment. In 1563 he arrived on the north coast of Hispaniola with three ships carrying 400 slaves from West Africa. The colonists eagerly paid for the slaves with hides and sugar. Hawkins claimed he was a peaceful trader and paid all Spanish taxes and customs. He insisted that local Spanish officials give him letters stating that he had traded peacefully and obeyed the laws. Two additional caravels were hired from the colonists to carry the overflowing cargoes which were sent direct to Seville. However, the Spanish government confiscated the ships and imprisoned their crews for breaking regulations which forbade foreigners to trade with Spain's colonies.

The following year Hawkins made another voyage, this time to the mainland settlements where he hoped to take on more gold and pearls and less cheap hides

Fig 6.2 *A nineteenth-century picture of the defeat of Hawkins at San Juan de Ulloa.*

and sugar. He was not disappointed. The settlers were keen to pay gold for his slaves.

Back in England Hawkins gave a profit of 60 per cent to the merchants who had paid for the expedition. Money flowed in to pay for a third voyage, despite Spanish warnings that the trade was illegal.

Hawkins should have noted the warnings. In September 1569 his fleet was driven before a hurricane to seek shelter in the Spanish American harbour at San Juan de Ulloa. While the English were refitting their ships, the annual Flota arrived from Spain with the new Viceroy of Mexico on board. In the battle that followed no quarter was given. One hundred of the three hundred men under Hawkins' command were killed or captured. Only three ships, one of them commanded by Sir Francis Drake, escaped and made their way back to England.

English privateers

The profits made by Hawkins' voyages encouraged many more English merchants to take part in direct trade with the Spanish colonists. But events at San Juan de Ulloa convinced some bands of adventurers to drop any pretence at honest trading. Hawkins and many like him obtained privateering commissions from the Dutch and French who had united in a new war against Spain. While some English tried to trade openly and fairly with colonists, men like Sir Francis Drake looted, burned and stole. Officially the English government disowned the privateers, as Spain was

Fig 6.3 *Drake's fleet outside Santo Domingo in Hispaniola. The picture shows the town's defensive walls surrounding streets laid out on a rectangular plan with a cathedral in the centre.*

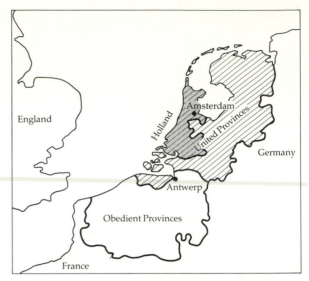

Map 15 *The Netherlands. The United Provinces revolted under the leadership of William of Orange. The Obedient Provinces remained under Spanish rule, and in 1839 became Belgium.*

still a European ally and merchants did not wish to lose the legal trade through Seville. Yet officials of the English court, and Queen Elizabeth herself, helped finance the privateering raids.

Open war finally broke out in 1585 and lasted until 1604. It was mainly a privateering war with English naval captains such as Sir Francis Drake, Sir Anthony Shirley and Sir Walter Raleigh, making daring raids on Spanish American strongholds. The attacks involved much senseless brutality and destruction; there was usually no real military gain and often not a great deal of loot. As the years passed it became clear that those English who peacefully traded with the colonists had done far more to open up the Spanish Empire to foreign trade than the privateers.

The Dutch

In the 1580s another nation's sailors had joined in the effort to break into the Spanish trading empire. They were the Dutch people from the Netherlands in northern Europe. Since 1519 the Netherlands had been ruled by the kings of Spain. Holland and the other provinces were a great gain to Spain for the Dutch people were far more experienced than the Spanish in shipbuilding, sailing and trading. It was not long before Dutchmen were managing the re-export to other European countries of goods sent to Seville from the Americas. By 1560, there were more Dutch than Spanish merchants in Seville; and the bankers and traders in the Netherlands towns of Antwerp and Amsterdam were leading figures in arranging exports and imports to and from the Spanish Empire.

Despite the wealth they made for his Empire, the Spanish king's rule of the Netherlands was harsh. He limited the power of their noblemen and city councils, and several leading Dutchmen who opposed him were executed. Persecution was especially severe against Protestants in the Netherlands. Under the Spanish Governor, the Duke of Alva, Protestant churches were closed and their worshippers had their property seized by the Spanish. Thousands fled to Germany and France. The final straw was a 10 per cent sales tax which the Duke brought into force in 1572.

The Sea Beggars

A revolt broke out under the leadership of a Dutch prince, William of Orange. His first supporters were the Protestants who had fled from the Netherlands, who gave themselves the name of 'Beggars'. William of Orange was an admirer of the French privateering leaders, and he hit on the idea of creating a force of Dutch privateers with the name of 'Sea Beggars'. Merchant vessels were armed and turned into warships and William issued letters of marque to their captains.

Within months the Sea Beggars drove the Spanish occupying forces away from the coast of the Netherlands. In an effort to crush the revolt, the Spanish king tried to ruin the Dutch merchants. He ordered the closing of their trading buisiness in Spain and Portugal (which had united with Spain in 1580). To avoid ruin, merchants from Holland simply sent their ships direct to the Caribbean. They found the colonists eager to trade with them, for their goods were cheap and could be bought on easy terms. The Dutch were also forbidden to load salt for their herring industry from the salt pans in Portugal. Instead, herring fishermen crossed the Atlantic to the salt pans on the coast of Venezuela and at Punta Arya. But they called first in Africa to collect slaves who were sold to the Spanish colonists and Portuguese planters in Brazil.

After a century of war

As the sixteenth century ended and the seventeenth began the Caribbean sailing routes were controlled for most of each year by Dutch, English and French sailors.

Spanish convoys still sailed to collect the precious metals from the mainland, but their rivals had the strongest grip on trade with the agricultural settlements in the Caribbean basin. Years passed without a Spanish ship calling at places like Trinidad. One governor of the island pointed out that it was easier and cheaper to take passage from Europe on a Dutch than a Spanish ship.

Most Spanish officials simply did not bother to complain; they were happy to grow rich themselves from taking part in illegal trade. In 1602 the Spanish King sent an agent to find out how loyal his colonial governors were. He found those in Puerto Rico, Cartagena and Havana guilty of trading with the Dutch rebels and returned with the disturbing news that Dutch ships in the Caribbean outnumbered the Spanish by five to one!

Spaniards welcomed foreigners who provided goods which could not be obtained from Spanish traders; some were even allowed to open shops in the colonies. In 1604 the new Spanish Governor of Jamaica, Don Fernando Melgarejo, was dismayed to see colonists buying from Englishmen and joining them in friendly games of bowls. When he tried to enforce the law and drive the English traders out, the colonists revolted and threatened to hire a hundred Englishmen to kill him. The Governor quickly backed down, using a phrase which all Spanish officials had to use often: 'Obedezo pero no cumplo' – I obey the law but I do not insist on it.

'Effective Occupation'

The government in Spain would not recognise the facts. In the treaties which ended her war with France in 1559 and England in 1604, Spain refused to accept any French or English claims to land or trade in the Americas. On the other hand, England and France refused to accept that Spain had any rights over places which she did not 'effectively occupy'. The Spanish clearly had enough soldiers, officials and settlers on parts of the mainland to say that she effectively occupied them, but this was much less true of the western Caribbean islands, and not true at all of those in the east. In the seventeenth century this question of 'effective occupation' was put to the test when Spain's rivals began to build their own colonies in the Caribbean. This story is told in the next chapter.

El Dorado

No-one ever found El Dorado, the golden man, but for many Spanish adventurers his kingdom was a real place, as rich in gold as Peru or Mexico, waiting to be discovered by the traveller who dared to make the journey up the Orinoco River. Several made the attempt but none tried so hard as Antonio de Berrio whose third journey, made when he was seventy, lasted for eighteen months. After many disasters he turned back with only a handful of his 120 men still alive, believing that he had come to within four days march of El Dorado. The tiny group finished their journey by crossing to Trinidad in rowing boats, and de Berrio decided that the island should be the base for his next attempt to reach El Dorado.

Trinidad

Trinidad had been visited four times before de Berrio. Columbus had sailed round the southern coast in 1498 and named the island after the Trinity. In 1520 a

Fig 6.4 *Sir Walter Raleigh with a group of followers in Trinidad. This is an imaginary scene drawn in the nineteenth century.*

Spanish slaving raid took off 200 Caribs for slavery in Puerto Rico and Santo Domingo. In 1530 a conquistador arrived with a capiculacion from the King to build a new colony. His small force was quickly destroyed by the warlike Caribs. The same fate probably met the two small groups of priests who came to convert the islanders. It was only from de Berrio's time that Europeans managed to stay permanently on the island and then only in tiny numbers. In 1592 de Berrio sent a soldier of fortune, Domingo de Vera, to conquer Trinidad as a 'point of entry for the River Orinoco and the very rich provinces of Guinea, Dorado and Manoa'.

With twenty-eight soldiers, a friar and a lawyer, de Vera set out to take possession of an island inhabited by nearly 40,000 Amerindians. He landed at the spot which became Port of Spain and marched inland to pace out the boundaries of the future city of St Joseph, the first capital of the Spanish colony on the island. The Amerindians drew back from these places. By the next year the number of soldiers had reached a hundred, and de Berrio ordered de Vera to take thirty-five of them to seek El Dorado. He returned with only some gold ornaments but falsely claimed to have discovered the golden land.

Dudley and Raleigh

Letters describing the conquest of Trinidad and the 'discovery' of the land of El Dorado were captured by an English privateer and the news reached England before Spain. Two English expeditions were fitted out to surprise the weak Spanish forces and seize Trinidad and El Dorado. The first, led by Sir Robert Dudley, landed on Trinidad and claimed the island for Queen Elizabeth I. Dudley kept well clear of the Spaniards and managed to frighten the Amerindians with musket fire. From Trinidad he led a party to the Orinoco, where they got hopelessly lost and were lucky to return alive. After another march across Trinidad, Dudley returned empty-handed to England, just before Sir Walter Raleigh set out with high hopes of discovering El Dorado and setting up a rival

American Empire to that of Spain. The key to the scheme was the capture of the Spanish garrison on Trinidad. Raleigh easily took Port of Spain and St Joseph and made de Berrio his prisoner. Shortly afterwards, Raleigh was the first European to see the pitch lake and to use some of the substance to stop leaks in his ships.

Raleigh was now ready to search for El Dorado, but he turned out to have less courage than some of the earlier Spanish explorers. After only a few days on the Orinoco he turned back to the Caribbean. He tried to make good his failure by a raid on the Spanish town of Cumana, but even here things went wrong. The Spaniards were warned and ready, and most of Raleigh's men were killed in the raid.

Raleigh's exploits brought Trinidad and Guyana to the notice of the government of Spain. In 1597 it sent de Vera to the area. His force of twenty-eight ships and 1,500 men recaptured the tiny settlements in Trinidad and set up a few new ones in Guyana. But within a few months most of the soldiers were dead because, curiously enough, their numbers were too large. They had not planned to grow their own food or build their own shelters; they expected to be supplied by the Amerindians. But the Amerindians of Trinidad and Guyana simply melted away from the Spanish camps, forcing them to go further and further afield in their search for food. Soon the whole expedition collapsed from starvation, misery, desertion and quarrelling among the hungry Spaniards.

With the failure of de Berrio, de Vera and Raleigh, the dream of finding El Dorado began to fade, although there was a final episode in 1617. In that year Sir Walter Raleigh returned to try once more. He was going to almost certain death because King James gave permission only on condition that he did not clash with Spaniards as the two countries were at peace. But there was fighting, the Spanish protested to James, and seven weeks after Raleigh returned to England – still without gold – he was beheaded in the Tower of London. He was the last of the gold-seeking adventurers; by the time of his death men were already making fortunes from another commodity which Guyana certainly did produce – tobacco.

7 English, French and Dutch colonies

Tobacco

In 1609 Robert Harcourt wrote a pamphlet in support of a scheme to set up a tobacco plantation on the Guyana coast. He wrote:

> I dare to presume to say and hope to prove within a few years that only this commodity, tobacco, will bring as great benefit and profit as ever the Spaniards gained by their richest silver mine in all the Indies.

Tobacco had been brought back to Europe by the early explorers, but for many years it had been used mostly by sailors. In the later sixteenth century, however, pipe-smoking came into fashion in England, especially among the well-to-do. Some tobacco was grown in the country, but nowhere near enough to meet the growing demand. From England the pipe-smoking habit passed to Holland and then quickly into Germany and Central Europe and on to Turkey. At the same time the Spanish were learning to like cigars and the Irish were known for taking snuff. Demand for tobacco soared, despite the efforts of some rulers to prevent the habit. For a time it was banned in Turkey and had to be smuggled there by Italian sailors, while in England King James wrote a pamphlet in which he called smoking 'a custom dangerous to the eye, hateful to the nose, harmful to the brain, dangerous to the lungs'.

But these efforts could not slow the demand. In 1614 an Englishman wrote:

> There has been a catalogue of all those houses that have set up that trade of selling tobacco in London, and near about London; and if a man may believe what is confidently reported, there are found to be upward of seven thousand houses that live by that trade.

Supplying shopkeepers in almost every European town was very profitable. The English started their own tobacco plantations in Virginia on the American mainland, but its production nowhere equalled that collected from lands in the Spanish Empire. In 1615–16 fewer than 1,360 kilograms of Virginia tobacco was landed in England, while more than 26,300 kilograms came from the Spanish Americas. Similarly large quantities passed through Dutch warehouses in Amsterdam. Thus, the largest profits could only come from illegal trading inside the Spanish Empire. For many reasons Trinidad and Guyana, or Guinea as it was known to Europeans of the time, seemed the most suitable area.*

Guyana

Provided they were peaceful there was little risk that the Dutch, English and Frenchmen interested in tobacco would run into trouble from the very few

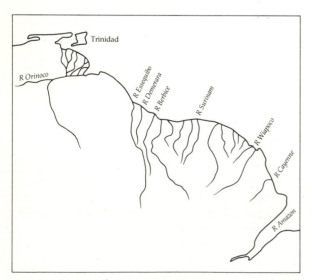

Map 16 *The Guyana coast and Trinidad. In the sixteenth and seventeenth centuries this region was known to Europeans as Guinea.*

*Note that Europeans later came to spell Guyana as 'Guiana'. In this book the modern spelling has been used throughout, except in official titles of the time, eg. Colony of British Guiana.

Spaniards in the region. The largest Spanish colony along the coast was the island of Margarita which had fifty-one houses of which nineteen were said to be the homes of priests or widows; the rest of the population numbered about thirty-five. Numbers on Trinidad were even smaller. The isolated Spanish communities were completely neglected by the government in Spain. After de Vera's fleet in 1597 no Spanish ship called at Trinidad for nineteen years, although in 1611 alone, fifteen French, Dutch or English ships called there, mostly to collect tobacco, which at that time was often known in England as 'Trinidada'. Most of this was grown or simply gathered by Amerindians and it was believed that the trade could be far more profitable if Europeans established their own plantations on the Guyana coast. The possibilities became stronger after England signed peace with Spain by the Treaty of London in 1604.

In that year Captain Charles Leigh borrowed money from his brother and set off with forty-six men to build the first English colony in Guyana. He selected a site for the first crops of tobacco, sugar, cotton and flax on the banks of the Wiapoco River. The colony began well but tropical heat and fever took their toll; nine men died before the provision grounds were prepared. Within two months the ship's supplies had run out and Leigh was forced to exchange his farming tools and even some of his men's clothes for food from the Amerindians. By January 1605 Leigh was dead. In March a Dutch ship carrying slaves to the Spanish colonies stopped at the little colony and fourteen of the settlers agreed to load salt at Punta Arya in return for a passage back to England. A month later, ten more colonists left on a French ship. The remaining men stayed on to harvest a pitifully small crop of tobacco and flax. This they hoarded until 1605 when five survivors traded it for a passage to England on a Dutch merchant ship.

After Leigh, other small bands of French, English and Dutch arrived with high hopes of hacking plantations out of the tangled jungle. The first French efforts were organised by René de Montbarrot who sent his deputy, Daniel de la Ravardière, to select a suitable spot. He chose one on the Cayenne River and in 1607 three ships and 400 Frenchmen arrived to plant tobacco. The month after their arrival most were killed in a fierce Carib raid. The survivors moved south to the Amazon delta but this time were forced to flee by the Portuguese. Of all the attempts only one was success-

ful, when the Dutch managed to start a small colony on the Berbice River.

Joint stock companies

Would-be settlers learned many lessons from these early failures to set up colonies on the Guyana coast. There had to be some way of supporting a colony over the first few difficult years. Money was needed for a good store of provisions, for building materials so that strongholds could be made, and, above all, to bring out more stores, food, ammunition, farming equipment and new colonists to replace those who had died. The English solution to this need for money was the joint stock company.

Before the arrival of the joint stock company, most trading ventures were paid for by one merchant or a group of merchants. Even when the costs were shared, the risks were very great. A sudden raid by Amerindians, a storm or an outbreak of fever meant danger to the sailors and settlers and financial ruin to those who had sent them. The risks, however, could be spread much more widely by setting up a joint stock company and selling shares in the planned colony. In the early days a share usually cost £12.10 shillings which was the estimated cost of 'planting a settler', that is getting one man established in the colony as a grower of tobacco or cotton. The settlers were looked on as the tenant-farmers of the company, which would take his produce back to England and sell it to make a profit from which the shareholders would be paid a dividend. In some cases it was agreed that after the first ten years the land would pass to the settler or to the man who had bought the share which had paid for him to come out to the colony.

One of the earliest joint stock companies was the Amazon Company, started by Roger North in 1620 to plant settlers on the Guyana coast. North led the expedition himself and the scheme began well, but disaster then overtook him, for reasons which later companies did well to remember. A joint stock company needed a licence from the king. This gave it the sole right to colonise in a stated area, but, unfortunately for North, what the king gave he could just as easily take away. In 1620, James I was trying to make an alliance with Spain by marrying his son to a Spanish princess. So, when the Spanish pointed out that North's settlement was a threat to Spaniards in

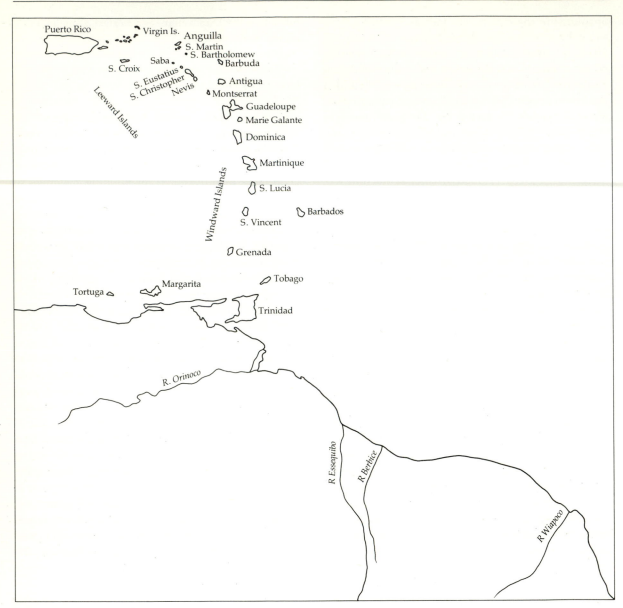

Map 17 *The Lesser Antilles.*

nearby Venezuela, James I withdrew the licence. He had North recalled from Guyana and imprisoned in the Tower of London for three months.

St Kitts

The harsh treatment of Roger North led Englishmen to shift their attention towards the islands of the Lesser Antilles. The Leewards were a favourite stopping place of an English pirate, Captain Painton. After North had been recalled to London, Painton had called in on the Guyana settlement where he became a close friend of Captain Thomas Warner, one of the men left in charge. Warner listened intently as Painton spoke of the healthy climate in the Leewards where the air was always fresh and cool because of the continual easterly trade winds. There were no swamps and the soils were fertile. The only drawback, Warner learned, might be the local Caribs, who had

Fig 7.1 *Thomas Warner's gravestone. It refers to him as Lieutenant-General of the Caribee Company and Governor of St Christophers.*

already massacred a ship load of colonists who had called in to St Lucia on their way to Guyana in 1609.

Still, he did not forget the rest of Painton's glowing account and on his way back to England in 1622 he stopped at St Christophers. He studied the soil and planted a few tobacco seeds which soon sprouted into healthy plants. Before leaving he left gifts with the local Carib chieftain, Tegramond, and promised more, provided he was welcome to return with men to plant on the island. Back in England Warner kept his plans to himself and made a secret arrangement with a merchant, Ralph Merrifield, who agreed to supply money and stores in return for any tobacco that was grown on St Kitts, as the island became known.

In November 1622 Warner set out from England with one small ship, his wife, thirteen-year-old son and fourteen companions. They chose a site on the north coast near the middle of the island, where their first shelter was made by sticking a few branches in the ground and covering them with brush and leaves. All shared this hut while they cleared the ground for the first tobacco crop. The work was slow and hard for so few people. They were unable to cut the trees down so they ringed the trunks with an axe and planted the tobacco between the dead stumps. One of the colonists, Captain John Smith, kept a diary in which he wrote on 20 September 1624: 'By September we made a crop of tobacco; but upon the 19 September came a

hurricane and blew it away'.

The colonists went back to their ruined fields and planted a second crop, which was ready for shipment to England in 1625 when the *Hopewell* arrived with more supplies and colonists sent by Merrifield. Warner himself returned to England on the *Hopewell* to ask for a royal licence for the company he and Merrifield had started in secret. Much to his surprise the plan to colonise St Kitts was warmly welcomed. While he had been away England's friendship with Spain had broken down and she was again preparing for war. The King's military advisers were looking for men to settle islands in the West Indies to serve as naval bases. Many merchants were also pressing for colonies to supply England direct with tobacco and other goods without having to buy them from Dutch, Portuguese or Spanish traders.

Lord Proprietors

Yet the merchants had learned not to trust the King and looked for someone with power and influence at court to act as Lord Proprietor of the colonies. For a price he would protect their interests and prevent the King from changing his mind and granting the charter to someone else. The Lord Proprietor chosen by Merrifield and Warner was the Earl of Carlisle. In 1625 the King granted him a charter to colonise St Kitts, Nevis, Montserrat and Barbados. Carlisle could appoint governors for the island, raise taxes from the settlers and make laws for the colonies. He was made responsible for the defence of the islands and for recruiting new colonists. Each year Carlisle was to pay the King £100 to have the charter renewed.

Carlisle had no personal interest in the colonies. He left the management of them to Merrifield and his fellow merchants who ran the joint stock company. In the Caribbean the real master of St Kitts was Warner, who was made governor by the Earl of Carlisle.

Barbados

Carlisle's charter did not remain unchallenged for long. In 1624, on his way to England from Guyana with a cargo of tobacco, John Powell called at Barbados. On reaching England he suggested a scheme for growing tobacco on Barbados to his employer, Sir

William Courteen, a Dutch merchant living in England. Courteen knew of Merrifield's schemes for St Kitts and hurried to set up a rival company to pay for tobacco planting on Barbados. In February 1627 John Powell led a party of eighty men to the island. He left some there to build shelters and sailed to Guyana where he 'furnished himself with roots, plants, fowls, tobacco seeds, sugar canes and other materials together with thirty-two Indians which he carried to the said island'.

The little colony was growing quickly, but Courteen could make no profits because the King had already granted the licence to colonise Barbados to the Earl of Carlisle. In 1628 Courteen managed to arrange for the Earl of Pembroke to be made Lord Proprietor of Barbados as well as Trinidad and Tobago. Carlisle immediately protested and used his influence with the King to have Pembroke's claim set aside; he himself was granted a new charter making him Lord Proprietor of all the Lesser Antilles.

Carlisle's company then made great efforts to establish colonies on all the islands named in the new charter. Anthony Hilton left St Kitts and began planting tobacco on Nevis. In 1632 settlers began planting tobacco on Montserrat and Antigua.

Problems for English settlers

Carlisle and the merchants in England did not understand the difficulties which the settlers had to face before they could begin a profitable export trade. In addition to clearing the land and facing the natural disasters of hurricane, drought and disease they had to cope with raids from Caribs. A Carib raid on Antigua in 1640 resulted in fifty colonists being killed and the Governor's wife, his two children and three other women being carried off as hostages. It was difficult to force the Caribs away from settlements on the windward side of the island. In their war canoes they could push their way out to sea against the wind and so move freely up and down the coast. Sailing ships, on the other hand, found this difficult to do without being forced back to the shore. So most European settlements were on the leeward of islands.

Occasionally there were raids by Spaniards. In 1629, the Spanish fleet on its way to Mexico turned aside to call at St Kitts. The Spaniards destroyed the few buildings and burnt the crops. The French

colonists fled to nearby St Martin, but most of the English had their homes destroyed and were forced to sail back to England. Within a year they were back and planting in the ashes of the last year's crop.

As the number of settlements grew so did the difficulty of finding men willing to emigrate from England. Occasionally shareholders went out themselves but more usually the companies looked for someone to 'plant' as a tenant farmer. Often these settlers were small farmers looking for more land than they had in England, but others were craftsmen with no knowledge of agriculture. Many were members of non-conformist religions seeking new homes where they could practise their beliefs freely.

Such men were often independent-minded and reluctant to grow export crops for the companies. Many found they could make a much better living as craftsmen, traders or builders. This meant that the shareholders' chances of making a profit lay in the large plantations set aside to be owned by the company as a whole and not let out to tenants. As the Spanish colonists had discovered, the greatest problem on the large plantation was finding a large enough supply of labour. The first English solution was the indenture or bondservant system.

Bondservants

Under the indenture system the companies gave a special contract to poor emigrants who were usually poor agricultural labourers. In return for a free passage to the Caribbean they signed an indenture bond agreeing to work for five years on one of the plantations. When their five year bond ran out they were to be given a few simple farming tools and allowed to take up five acres (about two hectares) of land to begin their own small plantation. Bondservants suffered terribly for this chance to escape from a hard life in England. The journey to the Lesser Antilles took between four and six weeks, with each emigrant sleeping in a space 60 by 180 centimetres and living on cold and raw food. Yet a steady stream of men took up indentures, and the flow of bondservants raised the European population on Barbados from 6,000 to 36,000 between 1636 and 1645, and on St Kitts from 3,000 to over 20,000 between 1629 and 1643. But even the bondservants could not overcome the most serious difficulty, which was that fortunes could no longer be made by growing tobacco on the English islands. Tobacco planters faced competition from the Spanish and French colonies but especially from the English plantations in Virginia which had now gained the largest part of the European market. In 1638, the port of London received 1.1 million tonnes of Caribbean tobacco and 3.4 million tonnes of Virginian. With larger areas of land, Virginia was able to produce tobacco at a much lower cost and its flavour was greatly preferred by European smokers. Even the French bought Virginian tobacco in preference to that produced on St Kitts and the other French plantations in the Caribbean.

At the height of the tobacco crisis, Henry Winthrop borrowed money from his father, sailed to Barbados and bought a small tobacco farm. After receiving the first shipment his father wrote back to say that no profit could be made from a tobacco 'so very ill-conditioned, foul, full of stalks and evil coloured'. He advised his son to find another cash crop. Some planters, faced with the same problem, tried growing cotton, but the European markets were well supplied with cloth that was produced in the Far East. In 1640 one planter reported: 'This year has been so base (poor) a cotton year that the inhabitants have not made so much cotton as will buy necessaries for their servants'.

Quarrels with England

Because of poor profits, merchants in England became less and less willing to risk their money by lending it to Carlisle's company. Fewer ships arrived with supplies and the colonists found themselves almost abandoned and increasingly poor. This was especially true on the smaller islands. 'If you go to St Christophers', said one visitor in 1645, 'you will see the ruins of a flourishing place' and ten years later the island was described as 'almost worn out'.

Not surprisingly the white settlers came to resent the claims of the Lord Proprietor for taxes. When Carlisle sent an agent to collect overdue rents and taxes on St Kitts the planters simply refused to pay and 'took it ill and mutinied'. On another occasion the colonists in Barbados drove out the man appointed as governor by Carlisle. They tore up his letter of appointment under a gallows and elected their own governor in his place.

In 1642 ties between the colonies and England became even weaker. In that year civil war broke out in England between supporters of King Charles I and the armies of Parliament under the leadership of Oliver Cromwell. During the six years of fighting the English neglected the Caribbean colonies, and settlers here were able to ignore the Lord Proprietor. In 1643 settlers on Barbados stopped paying the rents they owed him. The chance for an even more complete break came in 1649 when Charles I was executed and England became a 'Commonwealth' ruled by Oliver Cromwell. The colonists then declared themselves supporters of the dead King's son, hoping that this would mean they need not accept the laws and orders made by the new government in London. In Barbados two royalist soldiers, Colonel Humphrey Walround and his brother Edward, persuaded the settlers to support a new governor, Lord Willoughby, appointed by the dead King's son. Most other colonies took similar action. In Bermuda the colonists condemned 'that horrid act of slaying His Majesty' and drove out all those they suspected of supporting the Commonwealth government. The refugees fled to Eleutheria in the Bahamas and helped to give England a strong claim to these islands. The Governor and most of the colonists in Antigua declared support for the King's son. By 1651 most of the English territories in the Caribbean were free from London's rule.

The French

When Warner had returned as Governor to St Kitts in 1626 he had been greeted by a number of Frenchmen, led by Pierre Belain, who had landed to refit their ship after a fight with a Spanish man-of-war. The English colonists had welcomed the French as they needed help against the Caribs, who had become more and more hostile as Europeans spread over the island. Warner and Belain led a joint expedition in which Chief Tegramond and many of his men were killed and the remaining Caribs driven off the island. In return for their help Warner agreed to divide the island, giving the French the ends and keeping the middle for his company. It was an awkward arrangement which was followed by many quarrels as each side accused the other of taking the best lands.

In 1629, Belain returned to France where he was given support for his new colony by Cardinal

Richelieu who governed the kingdom as regent on behalf of the King, Louis XIII. Richelieu was determined that France should have a share in the New World. He had already claimed parts of Canada and followed this by founding a number of companies to settle Caribbean islands which were not 'effectively occupied' by other European powers. The French companies, like the English, were financed by private merchants, but the government kept much closer control because of the importance they gave to colonies as possible naval bases. The Company of St Christophers was the first to be formed and Belain returned to the island as Governor of the French colony there.

Company of the Isles of America

In 1635 the Company of the Isles of America was founded and given a twenty-year monopoly of all trade between the West Indies and France. In return it had to pay a large rent to the French government in the form of tobacco and cotton. In addition all company ships had to carry a number of *engagés* to the islands. Engagés were French bondservants who had engaged to work for three years on the plantations; they were commonly known as *les trente-six mois*, the thirty-six month men.

The Company of the Isles of America soon settled colonists on four islands: St Lucia, Grenada, Martinique and Guadeloupe. All were occupied by Caribs, so the first years were ones of frequent fighting between the two peoples. In the end the Caribs were driven away from the land most wanted by the French, although it was sometime before they were completely wiped out as the Arawaks had been by the Spanish in the Greater Antilles. But the warfare meant that the colonists were slow to establish plantations and send produce back to France. As a result many French merchants lost interest in the Caribbean. The French government, too, found little use for them after it made peace with Spain in 1648.

The French colonies abandoned

Without support from either merchants or the government, the Company of the Isles of America went bankrupt; for several months it looked as if the colonies would be abandoned altogether. Eventually it was decided that each colony could be purchased privately from the bankrupt company. The King of France kept a small connection with the Caribbean by appointing the French Governor of St Kitts as his lieutenant-governor, but otherwise the French colonies remained neglected for nearly twenty years.

The Dutch

Between 1609 and 1621 there was a truce in the long war between the Dutch and the Spanish. At the end of the truce the Dutch immediately set up the West India Company to fight all-out war in the Americas against Spain and against Portugal which was united with Spain between 1580 and 1640. All Dutch seamen and merchant companies wishing to trade in the Americas or the west coast of Africa had to belong to the West India Company, accept its rules and use its factories as trading bases. The Company had its own army and navy to fight the Spanish and Portuguese forces in the New World.

The war at sea

In a few years the West India Company's admirals cleared the west Atlantic and Caribbean of all Spanish shipping apart from the annual convoys. In 1628 even this life-line between Spain and her colonies was cut when Piet Hein ambushed the homeward bound convoy off the north coast of Cuba. The first nine galleons were captured without a shot. Their cargoes of hides, cochineal, ginger, cocoa and other valuable goods would have satisfied Hein, but behind them came four treasure galleons carrying the year's output from the gold and silver mines in Peru. Hein returned to Holland with nearly 90,600 kilograms of silver, 61 kilograms of gold, a large quantity of pearls and several bags of precious stones. For Spain the loss of such an enormous amount of treasure was a disaster; her soldiers went without pay and ammunition for a year. In the circumstances the Italian bankers who made loans each year to the Spanish government flatly refused to do so any longer. For shareholders in the West India Company there was a fifty per cent dividend and still enough money to pay for an expedition to capture the Portuguese sugar plantations in Brazil.

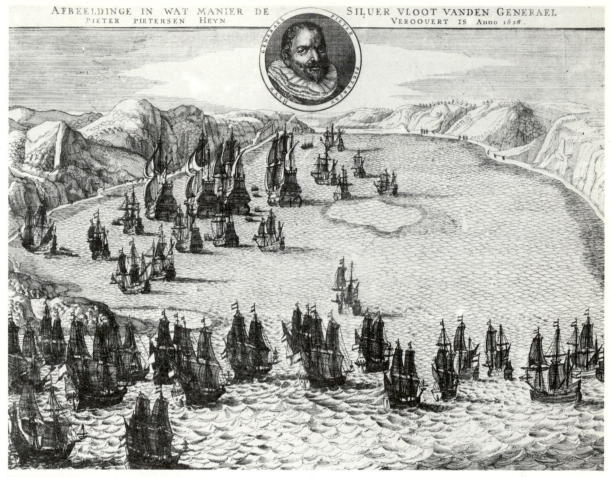

AFBEELDINGE IN WAT MANIER DE
PIETER PIETERSEN HEYN

SILUER VLOOT VANDEN GENERAEL
VEROOUERT IS Anno *1628*.

Fig 7.2 *Piet Hein's fleet comes out of its hiding place in Matanzas Bay to ambush the Spanish treasure convoy in 1628.*

The Dutch in Brazil 1630–54

The north-east of Brazil was the largest supplier of sugar to Europe. Most of the planters there came from wealthy Portuguese families who had been able to meet the heavy costs of starting a sugar plantation, especially the purchase of a mill to crush the cane. There were two kinds of mill: the *trapiche* powered by horses, oxen or sometimes slaves, and the *ingenio* powered by water. The trapiche could handle twenty-five to thirty-five cartloads of cane every day and the ingenio forty to fifty, so that the mill's owner needed a large plantation to supply it. Large plantations meant a large labour force and the Portuguese, like the Spanish, had turned to the use of African slaves. At the time of the Dutch conquest, there were 350 plantations with mills in Brazil, most of them worked by between thirty and forty slaves, although some were much larger.

Between 1630 and 1635 the West India Company conquered 1,600 kilometres of the north-east coastline of Brazil and, for a time, was able to take a very large share of the profits from sugar. Portuguese planters had no choice but to ship their sugar to Europe in Dutch ships and to buy their copper boiling kettles from the Dutch. Most important, they bought their slaves from the Dutch as the West India Company's forces had captured the Portuguese slaving posts on the West African coast. Dutch merchant ships could now call there to load with a human cargo before crossing the Atlantic.

The Dutch Empire in Brazil did not last long. In 1640 the Portuguese broke away from Spanish rule and began a war to drive the Dutch from Brazil. By 1654

Fig 7.3 *A Portuguese settlement in Brazil, drawn in 1628.*

they had recaptured the whole country. But this short period of Dutch control over Brazil was important for the history of the Caribbean. The Dutch had learned from the Portuguese planters about the use of African slaves to work large sugar plantations. They had also found that huge profits could be made by carrying slaves, and also plantation supplies, across the Atlantic and returning with sugar grown on the plantations.

The Dutch in the Caribbean

As well as supplying Brazil, the Dutch also brought slaves and goods to the Caribbean. They showed hardly any interest in planting here, apart from small settlements on the Berbice and Essequibo rivers. Instead they seized two groups of tiny islands suitable as bases for trading with the Spanish colonies. The islands in the southern group of Aruba, Curaçao and Bonaire, were taken because they lay close to the ports of the Spanish mainland. The northern islands of Saba, St Eustatius and St Martin were near to the Spanish colonies in the Greater Antilles.

In 1648 Spain recognised these islands as Dutch colonies in the Treaty of Munster, which ended the war which had been restarted in 1621. The Treaty of Munster was the first in which the Spanish agreed that another nation could own colonies here. However, they still refused to allow her colonists to trade with the Dutch or any other Europeans. But Spain had not the sea-power to prevent the Dutch being the main suppliers of Spanish colonists. At the same time Dutch merchants and ships kept open the link be-

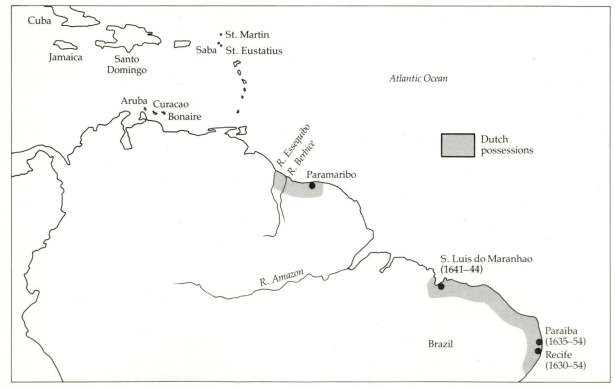

Map 18 *The Dutch Empire in the seventeenth century.*

Fig 7.4 *A Dutch warship of the seventeenth century.*

tween Europe and the abandoned French and the rebellious English settlements in the Caribbean.

The foster-fathers

The Dutch have been called the foster-fathers of the French and English settlements in the Caribbean for the way they kept them supplied in the years when they were abandoned by France or rebelling against England. During these years it was Dutch merchants who carried tobacco and other produce back to Europe and, as one colonist said, brought to the Caribbean 'all things that were in any way necessary for their comfortable subsistence'. Dutch warehouses lined the harbours of the Lesser Antilles colonies. When fire broke out at Basseterre on the French part of St Kitts it destroyed sixty Dutch warehouses and their contents.

It was from the Dutch that English and French settlers learned of the profits which could be made from large-scale sugar planting. A small amount was already grown on Barbados and turned into a strong wine, but no sugar was exported until two Barbadian planters, James Holdip and John Drax, visited the Dutch plantations in Brazil. There, they saw canefields and factories worked by African slaves. Back in Barbados they planted canes and cropped their first harvest, probably in 1643. Very soon sugar was the main export crop on the island.

The Dutch had many reasons for encouraging sugar planting. It brought more work for their ships and seamen; their merchants could lend money to planters to set up mills and buy the copper kettles needed for boiling. Refineries in Holland needed ever increasing supplies of raw sugar. But, sadly, the greatest profits were to be made from carrying slaves across the Atlantic to work on the plantations.

Despite the profits, other English islands were slow to turn from tobacco to the new crop, and Barbados was the only prosperous English island for twenty years. However, the Dutch also encouraged sugar planting by the French in Guadeloupe and Martinique in the 1640s. In some cases Dutchmen fled to these islands when they were driven out of Brazil in the years between 1640 and 1650. A thousand came to Martinique and 300 to Guadeloupe, bringing their knowledge of sugar and slavery with them.

For a few years in the 1640s and early 1650s, the Dutch profited from being the only European people carrying regular trade to and from the Caribbean. But they were too successful not to attract the attention of rivals and, soon, the merchants of England and France were pressing their governments to take a new interest in the Caribbean. The first to move was the English government, as the following chapter shows.

8 Colonies and empires

Barbados retaken

In the early months of 1651 settlers in the Lesser Antilles were enjoying freedom from British rule. They and their Dutch trading partners seemed able to look forward to a time of prosperity without interference from proprietors or the English Government. But the rebel colonies were greatly mistaken. Victory in the civil war brought Oliver Cromwell to power at the head of a far stronger government than that of Charles I. The merchants of London and Bristol were among the most powerful supporters of Cromwell and pressed for firm action to recover the lost rebel colonies in the Caribbean.

Their main interest was in the profits to be made from sugar. It was already Barbados's most valuable crop and there was every possibility that it would grow successfully in the Leewards. British merchants saw no reason why Dutch traders and refiners should have these profits. Under their pressure Parliament passed an Act in 1650 which aimed to starve the rebels into obedience, by forbidding other nations to trade with Bermuda, Antigua and Barbados. The Act was, of course, ignored by the royalist 'governors', such as

Fig 8.1 *Casks of sugar being unloaded at Bristol.*

Willoughby in Barbados, and the rebels went on trading with the Dutch. A soldier such as Cromwell saw only one answer: an expedition to recapture the islands.

It set out in August 1651 led by Sir George Ayescue. On arrival at Barbados, he immediately confiscated twelve Dutch ships and blockaded the ports to stop all incoming and outgoing vessels. Ayescue had too few men to capture the island but the blockade was effective. Lord Willoughby slipped away with some followers to start a colony in Surinam. The rebellion in Barbados was over and, soon after, planters on the Leewards also changed their loyalty to Cromwell's government.

The Barbados Charter

Ayescue was careful not to lose the goodwill of the recaptured colonies. So the peace terms allowed the English settlers to keep the system of government which had grown up under the Lord Proprietors. They could continue to elect an assembly to make laws, although the British Parliament would have to approve them. Article 3 of the peace stated that 'no taxes, customs, imports, loans or excise shall be laid nor levy made on any of the inhabitants of this island without their consent in a general assembly'.

Because it stated the European colonists' right to control their own financial affairs and make their own local laws, the peace came to be called the Barbados Charter. The system of locally elected assemblies continued for two hundred years in the British West Indies, while the Spanish and French Empires were under direct rule from Paris and Madrid.

The colonists, of course, were not in complete control of their islands. The power of the assemblies was balanced by that of the governors who were appointed in London. Governors could call and dismiss assemblies when they wished. They could also demand taxes to meet the costs of an island's govern-

Fig 8.2 *A view of Bridgetown, Barbados, in 1695.*

ment and defence. This often led to conflicts with the assemblies, which had the right to disagree with taxes but could not dismiss a governor. However, the greatest check on the colonists' freedom were the English laws which controlled trade and industry in the colonies.

The Navigation Act

Just how little freedom the West Indian colonists were to have was made clear in the Navigation Act passed by the British Parliament in 1651. This ordered that no produce from a colony could be carried to England or any English colony, except in ships owned by Englishmen or English colonists and with a crew which was at least three-quarters English. Goods made in a European country could be carried to the colonies only in the ships of that country, or those belonging to England or her colonies. They could not be shipped by vessels of another nation acting purely as a carrier. The Act aimed first and foremost to prevent the colonists dealing with the Dutch, who carried goods from many European countries, as well as slaves from Africa, to the English colonies, and took their tobacco and sugar back to Europe. Both the English government and the merchants were determined to make London, not Amsterdam, the greatest warehousing and shipping centre for colonial goods and trade. One mark of this determination was that 200 ships were added to the British navy between 1651 and 1660.

The First Dutch War 1652–4

The Dutch immediately refused to accept the Navigation Act and in 1652 declared war on England. This First Dutch War was fought almost entirely in European waters where armed English ships tried to prevent Dutch vessels from leaving port and sailing to the colonies. The blockade was never complete but it did make regular Dutch sailings impossible. Those ships which did get through to the colonies found Cromwell's governors in control and ready to prevent English settlers from trading with the enemy. The colonists had no choice but to use English ships, borrow money from London merchants and accept English manufactures, however expensive. They were particularly annoyed by being forced to buy English woollen cloth; even the most finely woven caused terrible itching in the tropical climate.

From the London point of view, however, the war was a huge success. Colonial sugar, cotton and dyewoods were pouring into English warehouses and a busy trade in re-exporting them to the rest of Europe was growing up. Cromwell and his supporters were not ready to listen to the colonists' complaints or to give way to the Dutch. In 1654, the Dutch put their desire for peace first and agreed in the Treaty of Westminster to accept the Navigation Act.

The Western Design

For the moment the Dutch were no threat to the English

in the Caribbean. Cromwell then turned his attention to the 'Western Design', a scheme for forcing Spain to recognise Britain's right to own colonies in the Caribbean and trade with Spanish settlers here. The Western Design was to begin with a surprise attack on Hispaniola. Once captured, it would be settled with Englishmen already living in the eastern Caribbean and become a supply base for raids on Spanish settlements in Central America.

An army of 2,500 men, commanded by General Robert Venables, set off from Plymouth in December 1654. Its first call was made in Barbados where Venables offered freedom to any bondsmen who wished to join the expedition. This roused the anger of planters who had paid for the bondservants' passage, and who were seriously short of labourers. The bondservants, of course, were eager to take the chance of freedom and land of their own. When the Barbados assembly refused to grant funds to buy arms for the new recruits, Venables issued them with sharpened sticks.

His next call was to the Leewards, which were already overcrowded with European small farmers living on the edge of poverty. Four thousand of them were attracted by the chance of a larger plantation on one of the western islands. They, too, were not a serious addition to the fighting strength of Venables' force, for they came on board with their wives, children and slaves and even herds of animals and flocks of geese and chickens.

The attack on Hispaniola was a disaster. Admiral Penn put the men ashore in the middle of an unhealthy swamp, about fifty kilometres from Santo Domingo. The untrained troops lacked the food and water for a fifty kilometre march and were easily scattered by a force of Spanish lancers. They fled in confusion to the ships, where they refused to listen to Venables' pleas to face the Spaniards again. General Venables and Admiral Penn were faced with mutiny in the Caribbean and the certain anger of Cromwell at their failure. To repair the damage as much as possible they decided on the capture of Jamaica, the least wealthy and worst defended of the Spanish islands.

The capture of Jamaica

The total Spanish population of Jamaica was no more than 1,400 and the Governor surrendered the island without a fight. Yet the English forces who landed on the south coast suffered terrible hardships. Food was scarce and could only be obtained by hunting the wild cattle and swine. Men who strayed only a few kilometres in their search for food were killed in the hills, either by Spanish guerillas led by Cristoval de Ysassi or by bands of maroons. Yellow fever struck them down in their hundreds, so that starvation and disease in one year killed more than 5,000 of the 7,000 in Venables' expedition. But Cromwell was deter-

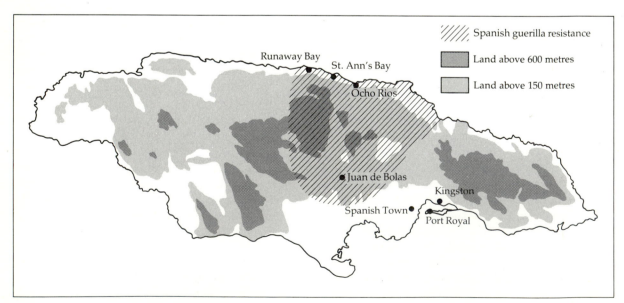

Map 19 *Jamaica in the mid-seventeenth century.*

mined to make the most of the island.

The Military Governor, Edward D'Oyley, was ordered to press ahead with building forts at Port Royal and around the coast. Troops were sent out from England and ordered to grow their own food, open new roads and build towns. To build up the population Cromwell ordered a thousand Irish men and as many women, mostly prisoners taken in his wars against the Irish, to be deported to Jamaica. From the island of Nevis, Luke Stokes brought 1,600 farmers hoping for grants of land.

By 1660 the first stage of Jamaica's settlement was completed. D'Oyley had built forts along the shore to house troops of soldiers. All male settlers served in local militia bands which helped the regular soldiers to drive the last of Ysassi's bands from the island. The first plantations had been opened to begin the transformation in most of the island from ranching to crops. In 1660 small quantities of sugar were first exported through Port Royal. This peninsula which protected the magnificent harbour at Kingston had grown, thanks to D'Oyley's work, into a naval base from which attack after attack was launched against the Spaniards.

The first attacks from Jamaica had little success. In 1655 a raiding party destroyed the small Spanish settlement at Santa Marta, but the plunder did not 'pay for the powder and shot spent in the service'. In 1656 an attack on Rio de la Hacha in Cuba led to the capture of only 'four great brass pieces of ordinance of near 4,000 pound (about 1,800 kilograms) weight each'. After similar failures in 1657, D'Oyley hit on the idea of inviting the buccaneers to come to Jamaica and join the British fleet's campaign against the Spaniards.

Buccaneers

The first buccaneers were runaway bondservants and men fleeing from the law. They had found safety on the north-west coast of Hispaniola which the Spanish had abandoned because of Dutch raids in the 1630s. The living they made was a poor one, hunting wild cattle and swine for their hides and montego, which were then bargained for powder and shot from passing ships. The hard life and raids by Spaniards from Santo Domingo led the buccaneers to move to Tortuga, a few kilometres away, and join bands of pirates already there. With these pirates the buccaneers

Fig 8.3 *A drawing from a seventeenth-century French book illustrating the life of a buccaneer.*

formed bands to raid shipping and defenceless settlements in the Caribbean.

Most of the bands were made up of men from the same nation, England or France or the Netherlands. Each band had its own rules. Profits were shared out among all those who had taken part in raids, and compensation was paid to injured men. The rule was that the most severely wounded received the largest payments. Buccaneers clearly understood that they lived by a system of 'no prey no pay'. Their leaders understood this too, for they could keep their position only so long as they led their ruffian followers to the prey. The most usual victims of the buccaneers were the Spanish but, from time to time, vessels and villages belonging to French, English and Dutch colonists were attacked.

From time to time an Englishman or Frenchman would try to unite all the bands but they never succeeded in bringing foreigners under their rule. When Governor D'Oyley called on the English buccaneers to move to Jamaica they left behind the French, who were usually known as *flibustiers* (pirates).

The English fleet working from Jamaica was immediately helped by the buccaneers' skill in navigating the Caribbean currents and shoals, and by their knowledge of Spanish shipping movements. In 1659 the fleet returned from an expedition which had destroyed Campeche, Coro, Cumana and Puerto

Cabello and captured loot valued at over £300,000. The regular fleet was then recalled to England. But D'Oyley increased the number of buccaneering ships under his command and their raiding of Spanish villages increased. Loot from these raids poured into Port Royal which, for a time, became the fastest growing town in the British Empire. The wild spending of the buccaneers also made it the most lawless port in the Americas.

More Navigation Laws

By then Cromwell was dead and England was again ruled by a king, Charles II. But the change made no difference to the policy of driving the Dutch from a now tightly controlled English trading empire. The government gave itself new powers over trade by the Navigation Act of 1660 and the Staples Act of 1662. Under the Navigation Act valuable goods were 'enumerated' or placed on a list of those which could be exported only to England or another English colony. Among enumerated goods were sugar, tobacco, cotton, indigo, ginger and dye woods, none of which could be carried direct to the ports of England's trading rivals. They had first to be taken to England and re-exported, thus increasing the profits of British merchant companies and the industries which manufactured or refined the colonial raw materials. The royal treasury also profited from increased custom duties. Another section of the Act closed all colonial ports to foreign vessels apart from certain free ports, such as those in Jamaica, where Spanish ships were allowed to buy English manufactures and slaves.

The Staples Act was passed to strengthen British trade and industry at the expense of other Europeans, especially the Dutch. It laid down that all non-British goods could be sent to the colonies only after they had been first landed in England so that both import and export duties had to be paid. These extra customs charges made foreign goods more costly in the colonies than those manufactured in England. The only items to escape the Staples Act were those England did not herself produce such as wine and slaves.

Slaves

To gain control of the Dutch business of supplying slaves to the colonies, the Company of Royal Adventurers Trading into Africa was set up in 1660. In 1663, Captain Robert Holmes was sent to Africa with a fleet to arrange for slaves to be supplied to the Company's ships from the Portuguese trading factories on the coast. The Dutch tried to prevent Holmes's activities. In 1664, acting without orders, he seized several Dutch trading factories and used them as bases for supplying slaves to the Company of Royal Adventurers. In the same year the British captured the town of New Amsterdam, which later became New York, These British captures signalled the start of the Second Dutch War.

The Second Dutch War 1664–7

The Dutch struck the first blow in 1665 with a surprise attack on Barbados. Although unable to land, they destroyed several English merchant ships before sailing on to plunder Montserrat and Antigua. In reply the new Governor of Jamaica, Thomas Modyford, called on the buccaneers to attack the Dutch islands. St Eustatius and Saba were sacked but quarrels between the buccaneers over the division of the booty meant that there was no raid on Curaçao as planned.

In 1666, the English faced new dangers when France joined the war on the side of Holland. The quarrelling English buccaneers were no match for the disciplined French fleet which soon arrived on the scene. St Kitts, Montserrat, Anguilla and Antigua fell to the French and their English settlers were deported to Nevis. Governor Modyford reported that they had been plundered 'to their very shirt tails'. In 1667 only Nevis, Barbados and Jamaica were in English hands. In the fighting the buccaneers had refused to follow orders; those who had been sent to defend St Kitts sailed off at the height of the battle to attack Spanish settlements. The British Government realised that buccaneers could not be relied on and sent a fleet with trained soldiers and sailors in the spring of 1667. Within a few short months Montserrat, Antigua and Anguilla were retaken. The war was then brought to an end by the Peace Treaty signed at Breda.

Treaty of Breda

All colonies were returned to their owners, except that

Fig 8.4 *An artist's impression of the burning of Panama City by Morgan's pirates.*

the British allowed the Dutch to keep Tobago, and the colony founded by Lord Willoughby in Surinam, in exchange for New York. The treaty's greatest importance, however, was that it marked the end of the Netherlands' position as chief supplier to the Caribbean settlements. Not only had they been driven from trading with the English islands; the way was now open for the British themselves to replace them as the main carriers of slaves and manufactured goods to the Spanish colonies.

The end of the buccaneers

The buccaneers had failed against the fighting navies of France and Holland but they still plundered and terrorised the Spanish settlements. The most famous among them was Henry Morgan, an escaped indentured servant who had won a name for cruel and murderous treament of captives. Sailing under a privateer's commission from the Governor of Jamaica, he continued with his cruel career until 1670 with a round of attacks on Cuba, Hispaniola and Central America. His last expedition was a march across the

isthmus to fight a fierce battle to seize and pillage Panama before withdrawing with £10,000 worth of loot. But, even before he set out, Spain had signed a treaty which recognised the British right to own territories in the Caribbean. In return, Britain agreed to cancel all privateering commissions and bring pillaging by the buccaneers to an end.

Morgan had known about the Treaty before he sailed from Port Royal for Panama. He had probably gone with the good wishes of the Governor, but on his return he was arrested and sent back to England to stand trial for piracy. However, anti-Spanish feeling was high in England, and Morgan was welcomed as a hero. He was acquitted in court and soon after knighted and sent back to Jamaica as lieutenant-governor.

For a few years Morgan played a double game; officially his task was to suppress the buccaneers, but secretly he helped finance more raids against the Spanish. Yet buccaneering no longer received support from the most powerful merchants in Jamaica or England. The raiding made the Spaniards reluctant to grant them legal trading arrangements. Planters, too, objected that privateering took away the labourers they needed. In 1685 the British Government sent the first of several naval forces to suppress buccaneering. Within four years most of the English buccaneers had fled from the Caribbean to the mainland around Carolina or Virginia. Others gave up sea-roving altogether and settled as planters or sailed to Campeche to cut log-wood. A last blow was the destruction of their main base, Port Royal, in an earthquake in 1692. By then, legal trade with the Spanish was growing fast. Before 1700, £1½- million worth of English goods were sold to Spanish America each year, bringing valuable profits to merchants in both Britain and Jamaica.

The French

While the British Government was building an empire out of the Caribbean colonies, the French islands had remained in private hands. Under their proprietors, the French settlements had increased in number and in wealth. There were three distinct types. In the eastern Caribbean lay the colonies on Martinique, Guadeloupe, Marie Galante, Desirade, the Saintes, Grenada and part of St Kitts. As in the English colonies, the first tobacco farms had given way to sugar plantations; African slaves had been imported and profits were increasing yearly. For their slaves and for the shipment of produce back to Europe, the French settlers relied on the Dutch.

The second group of French settlers were those who had moved on from the Lesser Antilles to the deserted parts of the western Caribbean. In Western Hispaniola, or St Domingue, which had been abandoned by the Spaniards, flourishing sugar plantations had grown up. Nearby, the flibustiers still had their base on Tortuga. The third group were plantations in the Cayenne region of the Guyana coast.

For years there was no official communication between France and her colonies, even though the Governor of the French colony on St Kitts had the title of Lieutenant-Governor to the King. But the growing wealth of the colonies attracted the notice of French finance officials who began to argue that France should take advantage of them as her European rivals were doing. In 1658 the Finance Minister, Nicholas Fouquet, wrote to the Council of State:

> The great number of vessels which Dutch merchants send to the French islands is proof that trade with these islands is very profitable, for otherwise they would not send 100 or 120 large ships there every year. In order that the French may profit from this commerce, it is necessary to exclude all foreigners from privileges of trade there, as the Dutch, Spaniards and English have done in their colonies.

Six years later in 1664 Colbert, the French Minister for Trade, purchased the colonies back from the Proprietors and, at the same time, set about strengthening French trade with them. To increase the supply of slaves he ordered the small French fort of St Louis on the Senegal River to be enlarged and had new ones built in Gambia and Sierra Leone. In the West Indies he planned a trading base on Granada to hold slaves and manufactured goods for sale to the Spanish colonists. A new lieutenant-governor was sent to the Caribbean with the difficult task of forcing French colonists to trade with the French West India Company and not the Dutch.

A French West India Company was set up and soon given the task of managing trading depots and collecting customs while the ships of private merchants actually carried goods to and from the Caribbean.

The new arrangement increased the flow of trade but the colonists on French islands continued to deal with the Dutch. So, in 1670, Colbert sent a naval fleet, commanded by the Sieur de Gabaret, to drive the Dutch from the French islands. Within a year de Gabaret had cleared the Dutch from the eastern Caribbean, but he was faced by revolts of French colonists and Dutch merchants in western Hispaniola. One by one, its towns refused to obey the French Government. De Gabaret succeeded in regaining control but the lesson was not lost on Colbert. The Dutch, he said, had to be crushed once and for all.

The Third Dutch War 1671–8

The First and Second Dutch Wars had arisen from the English determination to drive the Dutch from their Empire. The Third was started by Colbert's intention to do the same thing. During the first two years France had the support of England, but from 1673 she fought on alone against the Dutch who had some help from the Spanish. The combined Dutch and Spanish forces were no match for the well-armed French fleets and armies, and in 1674 the Netherlands withdrew all her ships from the Caribbean to fight on for a while in European waters. In 1678 she admitted defeat, agreed to accept the French monopoly of trade and to with-

Fig 8.5 *Jean-Baptiste Colbert.*

draw all Dutch agents from French West Indian colonies. The Dutch also recognised France as owner of Tobago and the Cayenne settlements.

The war finished the effort begun by the English to break the Dutch hold on American trade. The great Dutch West India Company, which had opened the Spanish Indies to English and French settlers, collapsed into bankruptcy.

France, like England before her, still had a quarrel with Spain who refused to accept her claims to western Hispaniola or to an open door for her trade with the Spanish settlements. As the English had done, Colbert now turned to the buccaneers.

The last Buccaneering War

In 1679, Colbert sent Le Comte d'Estrees with eleven ships and orders to enlist the aid of the flibustiers in a round of attacks to persuade the Spaniards to allow French ships into their American ports. The first raid was on Santo Domingo in 1680; in the following year Cartegena, Santa Marta and the coast of Venezuela were plundered. In 1683 the flibustier bands com-

bined for their greatest success, the capture of San Juan de Ulloa. The town was taken without the Spaniards firing a single shot, and for two weeks a fleet of fourteen Spanish ships lay outside the harbour not daring to interfere while the flibustiers plundered and burned the churches and public buildings. Once back in Hispaniola the loot was found to raise enough cash to pay off 1,000 shares at 800 pieces of eight each.

The raid on San Juan, the chief port of the Viceroyalty of Mexico, was proof of how helpless the Spaniards had become at defending their possessions. But, instead of following up this military success, Colbert made a truce with Spain. Buccaneering would bring far less profit to France than building up St Domingue into a vast sugar producing colony.

St Domingue

Immediately after the truce, the Sieur Tarin de Tracy was sent to St Domingue with orders to suppress the buccaneers. He cancelled the flibustiers' commissions and encouraged them to use the loot from raids on the Spanish to set up sugar mills and purchase slaves. He continued the schemes of the previous governor of bringing women from France and auctioning them as wives; he reported that the wives had been more effective than the King's fleet in stopping the flibustiers. Flibustiers' leaders were given pensions or made officers in the French navy. One, de Grammant, was appointed a Lieutenant-Governor of St Domingue.

Both the Spanish and English were opposed to the French settlement on St Domingue; Jamaican planters complained loudly about the competition from such a near neighbour. In 1689 France and England went to war and the Spaniards made an alliance with the English to get their help in driving the French from St Domingue. The French, however, were determined to remain. In 1690 the Governor of St Domingue led a raid on the Spanish part of the island and burned St Jago de Los Caballeros. In 1695 a new governor led the French in a last great privateering raid against Jamaica. For more than three weeks they pillaged the south shore carrying off slaves, mills, livestock and even trees to their new plantations in St Domingue.

The war, known to the English colonists as 'King William's War' ended with the Treaty of Ryswick in 1697. The Spanish and English finally recognised St

Domingue as French. Already it was on its way to becoming the largest and most prosperous sugar colony in the Caribbean.

Brandenburgers and Danes

At the close of the Third Dutch War, merchants from Holland were faced with ruin unless they could find some way of continuing their trade in the Caribbean. Many of them hit on the plan of sending goods to the West Indies on ships registered in Denmark or Brandenburg, the small German state which had Berlin as its capital. Denmark and Brandenburg were neutral nations and there was a chance that their ships would be ignored by English and French customs officials. The scheme was successful enough for several Dutch merchants to move their entire businesses to Denmark or Brandenburg.

These men put money into the Danish Guinea Company so that it would open two new slaving stations at Anamabo and Christiansborg near Accra. A year later they financed a Danish West India Company which opened a trading base on St Thomas in the Virgin Islands. St Thomas had a fine harbour and was close to the slave markets in Puerto Rico and the Leewards. In 1682 Dutch merchants were behind similar Brandenburg schemes. A Brandenburg-Guinea company was set up and a fort, Gross Fredericksburg, was built on the Gold Coast. In 1685 the Dutch got the Danes to agree to allow Brandenburgers to build a warehouse and slave compound on St Thomas.

The combined Dutch, Danish and Brandenburg enterprise had only short-lived success because of the opposition of the English and French. After only thirty years the new companies had dwindled into bankruptcy. The Brandenburgers completely disappeared from the scene although the Danish settlement at St Thomas survived. It was too small to be a threat to any of the other colonies, and it served as a useful shelter for merchant ships in times of war and for men

		1697	1713	1748	1763	1783	1815
British Empire		Antigua					
		Barbados					
		Jamaica					
		Montserrat					
		Nevis					
		St Kitts (part)					
		Virgin Islands					
French Empire		Cayenne					
		Desirade					
		Granada			To Britain		
		Guadeloupe					
		Marie Galante					
		Martinique					
		St Bartholomew				To Sweden	
		St Domingue					Independent
		St Kitts	To Britain				
Spanish Empire		Cuba					
		St Domingo					Independent
		Puerto Rico					
		Trinidad					To Britain
Dutch Empire		Aruba					
		Berbice					To Britain
		Bonaire					
		Curacao					
		Demerrera					To Britain
		Essequibo					To Britain
		St Eustatius					
		Saba					
Danish bases		St John					
		St Thomas					
Neutral islands		Dominica			To Britain		
		St Lucia			To France		To Britain
		St Vincent			To Britain		
		Tobago			To Britain	To France	To Britain

escaping the laws in their own colonies. In 1685 its numbers were swollen by Protestant French who were driven from their own colonies. As the number of refugees increased, the little colony spilled over to include the neighbouring St John and, after 1733, St Croix.

French and British empires

The last war of the seventeenth century ended, as we have seen, with the Treaty of Ryswick in 1697. By that time Britain and France had both created large Carib-bean empires. Away from the American mainland they had no serious rivals. The Spanish colonies held few settlers and the Dutch had ceased to be a major power in the area. There were only four unclaimed or neutral islands left in the Caribbean.

The European empires remained very little changed from 1697 until recent times. The most important changes were to the advantage of Britain who took over some French, Spanish and Dutch colonies as a result of the wars of the eighteenth and early nineteenth centuries. The chart opposite shows the European empires in 1697 and the later changes in ownership.

9 *Imperial control*

Economic controls

Both French and English Governments thought of their colonies in the light of the economic ideas which later historians have described as mercantilism. As the name suggests, at the heart of the mercantile system stood the merchants and the merchant companies of the metropolitan countries. Growth of their trading activities would have several important advantages for the economy of England or France. Obviously there would be an increase in employment in shipbuilding, seamanship and so on, as well as in industries which processed imported raw materials and food or made goods for export. In the days before income tax, customs duties on traded goods were the most important source of money for government treasuries. Large treasuries meant the money to pay officials and strengthen the government's power within its own country, as well as building up strong armies and navies for the defence of the growing empires.

But a successful mercantile system would not come simply from settling overseas colonies. There would be a drain on profits and employment away from France and England if the settlers started manufacturing their own cotton goods or refining their own sugar. There would be no profit for merchants in the mother country if colonials built their own ships and traded with each other – for example if Jamaican settlers sold sugar to New England in exchange for iron goods made there. Colonies were costly to protect and govern, and would not be profitable if their goods were shipped on vessels belonging to a rival country or ended up as cheap raw materials for the factories of another nation. So the mercantile system had to be enforced by laws which tightly controlled the trade and economic life of the colonies, and these laws had to be backed up by strong navies. In the later seventeenth century the French and British governments issued the regulations that created the mercantile system.

Plantation Duties Act

At the heart of the English government's mercantile system were the Navigation Acts of 1651 and 1660 and the Staples Act of 1663. These aimed at excluding foreign rivals from trade with the colonies and had to be enforced by warfare. The mercantile system was completed by tax and customs regulations which limited the colonials' freedom to trade and manufacture. The Plantations Duties Act of 1673 placed a high duty on a list of enumerated goods if they were shipped from one colony to another. This made it very expensive for West Indian planters to send their goods to a North American colony in exchange for food and supplies for their plantations. Heavy taxes on all West Indian sugars, except wet unrefined Muscavado, meant that the colonists could not refine their own produce; instead the industry grew rapidly in Britain especially near the port of Glasgow.

Of course, there were colonial protests and many petitions were sent to England complaining of the high price of manufactured goods and slaves carried in English ships, and the high costs of exporting goods to London. Whenever possible planters ignored the Acts and traded with Dutch, Danes, French or Portuguese. If they were brought to trial they were usually acquitted by a jury made up of fellow colonials. It was to prevent this that the Consolidating Duties Act of 1676 was passed. It summarised all the laws on colonial trade and set up in each colony a separate Admiralty Court which worked like a court martial, without a jury, to deal with those who broke the regulations.

The French 'exclusive'

The French had a similar system of economic control over their colonies, generally described as 'the exclusive'. It was the work of Colbert and continued long after his death in 1683. The exclusive was made up of a series of laws, such as the Ordinance of Marine in 1671 and the Ordinance of Commerce in 1673, which excluded foreigners from trade with the French colonies. Colbert was firm in allowing no breaks from this rule. He refused to allow Guadeloupe and Martinique to send molasses and rum to the British colonies in North America even though there was no market for these products in France. This was because the rum and molasses would have been exchanged for salt meat from the British colonies and not from France.

The exclusive also prevented French colonists competing with industry in France. Sugar refining gave work to many colonists but it was banned in 1684. When the colonists continued to refine their own sugar, a duty was placed of 22 livres a hundredweight (about fifty kilograms), while unrefined sugar was allowed into France at only 1 livre a hundredweight. This completely strangled the colonial industry.

In 1698 a general decree brought all the many regulations together and laid down harsh penalties for those who broke them. Foreign smugglers would have ships and cargo confiscated while French colonists who traded illegally could be fined, imprisoned or sent to work in the galleys.

Political controls

To make the mercantile system work, close political control of the colonies was essential. In England this became the task of the Council of Trade and Plantations, set up in the reign of Charles II. It soon became the Board of Trade and Plantations, whose President was an important member of the government. The Board underwent many changes in the eighteenth century as the Empire grew, and in the nineteenth century it became two government departments, the Board of Trade and the Colonial Office.

One early achievement of the council was to end for all time the proprietory system. It had been ended in Barbados when the islanders made their peace with Ayescue, but there was still quarrelling over the ownership of the other Antilles islands which had been granted by Charles I at different times to the Earls of Carlisle and Pembroke. The heirs of these two men were each trying to get the English law courts to agree that they had the rights to the profits from the colonies. The government stopped the squabble by making its own arrangements with the colonies. Each

was to have a council and elected assembly which could make laws which had to be confirmed by the English Parliament within two years. In return for this freedom from the proprietors the colonies had to accept British governors and pay a 4½-per cent duty on all exports.

The Lesser Antilles

To save money the Leewards were placed under the same governor as Barbados. This first attempt to build a small federation of West Indian colonies did not last long because of the rivalry between them for the biggest share of the English sugar market. After they had suffered from raiding in the Second Dutch War, the Leeward planters complained in a petition to the King that the Barbadians were pleased that their people had been driven away and their export trade damaged:

> It is in the interest of the Council and Assembly of Barbados that these islands be no more settled, for one pound of their sugar will be worth as much as two before these islands were lost, and petitioners can prove that several Barbadians have wished these islands sunk.

In 1671 the Council of Trade gave in to the demands for a separate administration in the Leewards. A Governor-in-Chief was appointed for St Kitts, Nevis, Montserrat, Antigua, Barbuda, Anguilla and 'all the other of the Leeward islands which His Majesty has thought fit to separate from the Government in Barbados'.

Fig 9.1 *The Court House in St Johns, Antigua, drawn in 1823. Note the contrasts between the lives of blacks and whites.*

Jamaica

When Charles II came to the throne, D'Oyley was still Military Governor of Jamaica. But the new plantation owners complained that the time for military rule was over; the last Spaniards had been driven away and the island was well protected by the forts at Port Royal and around the coast. They wanted a system of local government similar to that in the Lesser Antilles. In 1662 the Council of Trade gave in to this demand and sent a new Governor, Lord Windsor, with instructions to set up a council and call elections for an assembly. The island was divided into twelve parishes. The leading figure in the parish government was the custos, a title which came from the old English official of the Custos Rotulorum or Keeper of the Records. Each custos had a seat on the council and the landowners in each parish also elected two members of the Jamaica Assembly.

The governors

The first responsibility of colonial governors was to act as representative of the king. As such they had to enforce all laws and regulations, such as the Navigations Acts, take charge of the defence of the colony and collect taxes and customs owing to the king. In the name of the king they could summon and dismiss assemblies and call for elections to new ones. They were responsible for enforcing the local laws made by the assembly as well as for overseeing the work of the many officials who were appointed in England to serve in the colonies; chief justices, lieutenant-governors, customs inspectors, tax collectors, clerks of the court and so on.

The councils

Members of the council of each colony were appointed by the governor, who chose them from among the most prominent merchants and planters. Councils had the duty of advising the governor and supporting him in enforcing regulations which came from the imperial government in England. A councillor who did not do this would be almost certainly dismissed. The council was also the upper law-making body in the colony and laws suggested by the elected assemblies had to be agreed by them as well. This, of course, meant that laws which the governor wished to see brought into force could be passed by the council and then passed down to the assembly to seek its approval. Finally, in most colonies the council acted as a court of appeal against decisions made by magistrates and judges.

The assemblies

The right to vote in elections to the assemblies was held only by the wealthier freeholders – men who owned property and were not tenants. In most of the Leewards, for instance, to claim the right to vote a colonist needed to own ten acres (four hectares) of land or property which could be rented for £10 a year. If he actually wished to stand for election to the assembly he needed forty acres (sixteen hectares) of property worth £40 a year to do so. These property qualifications meant that assemblies represented the interests of the wealthier colonists, the men who made up the group sometimes called the plantocracy.

The greatest power of the elected assemblies lay in their control of the local revenue. They alone, without the council, had the right to vote taxes for the running of the colony's government. Sometimes an assembly used its control of local taxes to blackmail the governor and king into accepting laws which they did not wish to agree to. In 1677 the English Government attempted to challenge the power of the Jamaican Assembly in a way which would have given them grounds for ignoring other islands' assemblies in the future. Thirty-seven Acts concerning the island's affairs were prepared in London and sent to the island with a new governor. His orders were to have the laws passed by the local legislature to establish that the assembly must accept laws already decided in England. Not only the Jamaican Assembly but also the Council flatly refused. Indeed they emphasised their independence by leaving the king's name off all future laws which were always passed in the name of 'the Assembly, the Council and the Governor'.

Such quarrels between the English Government and the local assemblies were common. Often, too, there were the same conflicts between creoles and peninsulares in the Spanish colonies. The wealthy, locally-born planters and businessmen considered they could run their colony far better than the gover-

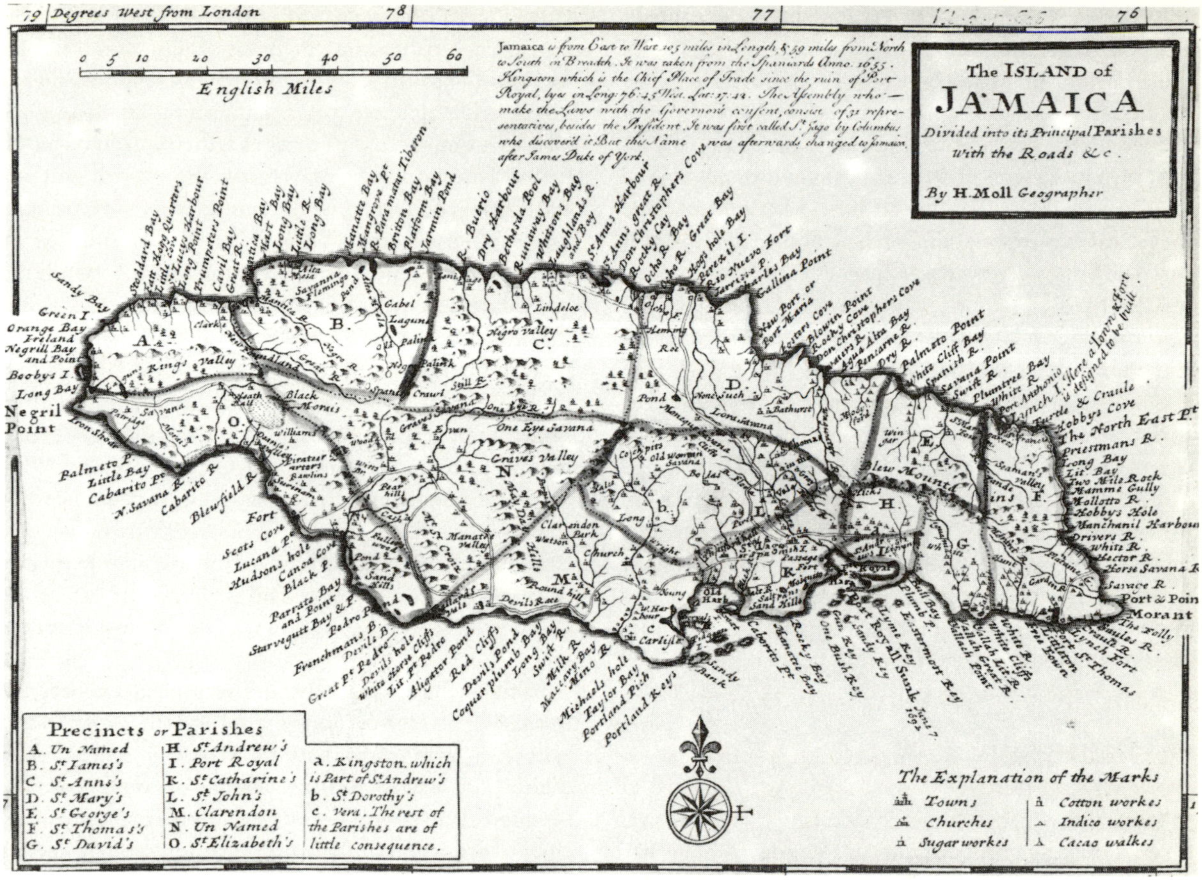

An eighteenth-century map of Jamaica with decorative title cartouche reading:

> *Jamaica is from East to West 165 miles in Length, & 59 miles from North to South in Breadth. It was taken from the Spaniards Anno 1655. Kingston which is the Chief Place of Trade since the ruin of Port Royal, lyes in Long 76.48 West Lat 17.44. The Assembly who make the Laws with the Governors consent, consist of 33 representatives, besides the President. It was first called St Iago by Columbus who discover'd it But this Name was afterwards changed to Jamaica after James Duke of York.*

> **The ISLAND of JAMAICA**
> Divided into its Principal Parishes with the Roads &c.
> By H. Moll Geographer

Precincts or Parishes

A. Un Named	H. St Andrew's
B. St James's	I. Port Royal
C. St Anns's	K. St Catharine's
D. St Mary's	L. St John's
E. St George's	M. Clarendon
F. St Thomas's	N. Un Named
G. St David's	O. St Elizabeth's

a. Kingston, which is Part of St Andrew's
b. St Dorothy's
c. Vera. The rest of the Parishes are of little consequence.

The Explanation of the Marks

Towns — Churches — Sugar workes — Cotton workes — Indico workes — Cacao walkes

Fig 9.2 *An eighteenth-century map of Jamaica showing that it then had fourteen parishes. Twelve parishes were initially created on the island in the 1660s.*

nor and the officials, judges and bishops appointed in England. But the balance of power was clearly tipped in favour of the imperial government in London. It frequently refused to give its agreement to laws made by the local assemblies; it tried to keep control over the appointment of officials and, from afar, it could decide on the prosperity of the colonies by the taxes and duties it placed on their goods.

Later it was seen that the greatest weakness of this system was that neither the imperial nor local governments gave attention to the need to develop the colonial territories. The English Government was interested chiefly in supplies of raw materials and food, as well as ports of call for the Royal Navy. Beyond that it was not prepared to spend money on colonial development. The assemblies, because they represented the interests of rich colonials, were reluctant to vote taxes to be spent on roads and bridges, hospitals and schools. The roots of the underdevelopment of the colonies at the point of independence lay in the mercantile and political systems of the seventeenth century.

Parishes

All Caribbean colonies were divided into parishes. They were based on the English system of the time where the whole kingdom was divided into parishes which were run by committees or vestries elected by all free-holders – men who owned their land and were not tenant farmers. The vestries supervised tasks such as road building and appointed constables to keep law and order and control beggars and vagabonds. This method of managing local government in the countryside was brought to the colonies, where many of the seventeenth-century parish names have lasted to the present day.

In England the most powerful men on the vestries were usually the wealthiest landowners. Some of them became magistrates or justices of the peace, who held courts to try all people accused of small or 'petty' crimes, those not serious enough to be passed on for trial by a judge and jury. This system, too, developed in the colonies. The wealthiest planters became magistrates, responsible for law and order in their district. But, whereas magistrates in England controlled the lives of labourers and tenant farmers, in the colonies they dealt mainly with the enforcement of the slave laws made in the assemblies.

One of the duties of a parish magistrate was to see that the militia was always in readiness. The militia was a force of volunteer soldiers who could be called out to deal with any riot or disturbance or to hunt down runaway slaves. Although occasionally coloureds served in the militias, they were usually made up of whites – planters and their sons, overseers and bookkeepers and any others likely to be willing to defend the planters' property.

The French system

Whereas power in seventeenth-century England was shared by king and parliament, France was governed by an absolute monarchy with all decisions taken by the king's personal ministers. Also, instead of allowing local affairs to be managed by magistrates and parish committees, the districts of France were ruled by royal officials known as *intendants*.

Colbert placed a centralised and absolute system of government in the colonies. It was headed by the Conseil d'Etat (Council of State) in France which appointed all officials and wrote all laws for the colonies. Each colony had a governor who was a nobleman and soldier. The governor was responsible for the colony's defence and acted as a figure-head with all the ceremony and privileges which would be given to the King's representative on the island. But his position was checked by the intendant, who was master of all the public officials on the island. As in France, the intendant was responsible for managing public works, such as harbour, bridge and road building; his officials also acted as magistrates and policemen in charge of law and order. The intendants and their officials were not creoles but metropolitan Frenchmen serving a term of duty, and they gave their loyalty to their masters in the Conseil d'Etat.

Creole colonists had far less say in their island's government than the English. Each colony had a local council but it was appointed by the intendant and had no power to make laws. The governor or intendant could seek its advice but he was not bound to follow it.

Each of the local governors was placed under the authority of a governor-general for the West Indies whose headquarters was in Martinique. He could take advice from a *conseil superieur*, or greater council, selected from members of the colonial councils. Yet the governor-general and the greater council had no more legislative power than the colonial governors and councils. They were simply another link in the chain of officials set up to see that laws decided in France by the King and his Conseil d'Etat were carried out. In many ways the governor-general was similar to a Spanish viceroy and the French colonial government was like the Spanish in being highly centralised under the authority of the metropolitan government.

10 *Sugar and slaves*

Sugar

There was an immense demand for sugar in Europe. Most fruits which grow there are cropped between July and September and for the rest of the year are eaten preserved in sugar or made into jam. Sugar was also needed for distilling and brewing as well as making cakes and biscuits. In the sixteenth century Europe's only natural source of sugar came from bees, apart from a few canes grown on the Mediterranean coast and the islands of Cyprus and Sicily. The sugar which came from the early Spanish and Portuguese plantations in the New World sold for good prices and the demand grew as new uses were found, especially as a sweetener for coffee, tea and cocoa.

The idea of planting sugar on a large scale had been

Fig. 10.1 *An early sugar factory in the Caribbean. The cane is crushed by the large roller in the background and the juice boiled in the copper at the front left.*

brought to the Caribbean from Brazil by the Dutch. Barbados had been the first English island to take up the new crop in the 1640s. Guadeloupe and Martinique became the first French sugar islands in the 1650s. With the new crop came a great change, for sugar cultivation went hand in hand with the growth of large plantations. It was generally reckoned that at least eighty to a hundred hectares had to be planted before a farmer could make a reasonable profit on the money he spent on mills, boiling houses, haulage animals and a large labour force. The successful sugar planters were men able to buy tobacco lands from their neighbours and amalgamate them into large sugar estates. According to John Scott, who visited Barbados in 1668, the number of landowners there had fallen from 11,200 in 1645 to 745 in 1667. The amalgamations led to a steep rise in the value of land. In the 1640s land prices in Barbados rose by more than fifteen times and in Nevis by more than ten.

Migrants

Some poorer settlers did not give way to the temptation to make a cash profit by selling their land at the new higher prices. Others sold only land which was suitable for canes and kept the hilly and rocky sections of their plantations. So there were always a few farmers who made a living from growing and exporting tobacco, cotton and indigo. But most of the poor settlers and freed bondservants looked for any chance to escape from the first islands to go over to sugar. Many of the early settlers in Jamaica came from Barbados, Nevis and Antigua; some first joined the buccaneering bands before turning to farming. Poor French settlers from Guadeloupe and Martinique moved to St Domingue. Other migrants from the over-crowded islands started the first colonies on the smaller territories such as the Bahamas, the Virgin Islands and Surinam. Many Englishmen left the Caribbean altogether and moved to the British colonies in North America. In the later years of the seventeenth century, British settlements developed along the whole eastern coastline of the modern United States. Not all the migrating settlers were farmers; some were craftsmen or small peddlars who lost their livelihood when the large estates began to keep their own carpenters and builders and to buy their supplies in bulk from large overseas merchant firms.

Bondservants and convicts

The profits of the sugar planters depended on increasing the supply of labour for the yearly cycle of planting, hoeing, cutting, hauling, crushing, boiling and packing. Yet the spread of large plantations meant that it became more difficult to recruit European labourers. The first English bondservants or French engagés had found the chance of a small farm after three or five years labour worth the terrible conditions of the Atlantic crossing. But these men had been brought to the Caribbean to work as craftsmen or as labourers on small farms, whose owners may have treated them no worse than their masters in Europe had done. On the sugar plantations there was nothing but the most grinding toil. In 1659, bondservants in Barbados were described as:

> Grinding at the mills and attending the furnaces or digging in this scorching island; having nothing to feed on (notwithstanding their hard labour) but potato roots, nor to drink but water with such roots washed in it . . . being bought and sold still from one planter to another . . . being whipped at the whipping post (as rogues) for their masters' pleasure, and sleeping in sties worse than hogs in England.

No wonder that there were outbursts of rebellion. When Richard Ligon visited Barbados in 1647 an island-wide revolt of bondservants had just been put down. Eighteen ringleaders had been executed but the planters feared more trouble, and Ligon noted that they were frantically rebuilding houses 'in all manner of fortifications', adding bulwarks and bastions from which they could pour boiling water on mutinous workers. Such measures could not stop bondservants taking the first chance to run away.

Obviously only the most desperate Europeans would leave home for such plantation work, so that the planters came to rely for their labour on dishonest recruiters who travelled through the country districts of Europe. They signed up simple youths who had no idea where the 'sugar islands' were and what future to expect. Ships' captains found it a profitable business. In Jamaica they were paid £6 or £7 for every bondservant they brought to the island. Catholic priests complained about the methods of French captains:

> Some have been mean and knavish enough to entice children aboard their vessels under various pretexts and force them to go to the islands where they were sold to masters who fed them poorly and made them go to work so exces-

sively and treated them so inhumanely that many of them died in a short time.

Some European suppliers used kidnapping raids in seaside towns where unsuspecting sailors and fishermen were 'barbodised'; that is seized, often when drunk, and hustled on board ship. Labourers recruited by these methods never received proper indenture papers. Many did not survive their years of bondservice but, for those who did, there was usually no grant of land at the end. In Jamaica freed bondservants were given 136 kilograms of sugar. This was worth just £2, which was the sum paid in cash to freed bondservants in Barbados in the 1690s.

Prisoners

Not all European labourers in the sugar fields were bondservants. After about 1650 many were convicts or prisoners of war. European courts sentenced men to be transported to the colonies for the time of their prison sentence. Many of them were petty criminals from the cities and turned out to be disorderly and bad farm workers. Perhaps the saddest groups of all were the Scots and Irish sent to the Caribbean by Oliver Cromwell. Some were prisoners taken in the wars he fought to spread his rule in Scotland and Ireland. Nearly 8,000 men were sent from a Scottish army he defeated in 1651. Others were simply rounded up after his army had won a victory, like the 2,000 Irish men and women ordered to be sent to Jamaica in 1656.

Measures such as bringing convicts and prisoners to the Caribbean did not at all meet the huge and growing demand of the English and French planters for more labour. Increasingly, they turned to the use of Africans. For more than a century and a half the prosperity of the planters and the comfort of sugar-using Europeans depended on a particularly inhuman form of the age-old evil of slavery.

Slavery

Slavery in the Caribbean had begun in the earliest days of colonisation. As chapter three shows, the Spanish had enslaved Amerindians before Queen Isabella had ordered them to be placed in encomiendas which were different from slavery only in name.

But, as early as 1501, slaves were brought across the Atlantic, mostly from Spain itself. Some were Moors, taken prisoner in the reconquista, some were black Africans captured earlier and taken to Spain or Portugal as slaves; others were European prisoners. It was in 1518 that the first ship-load of slaves was brought here direct from the African coast and soon the Spanish Government placed the evil trade on a regular footing. Few slaves were brought in Spanish ships; instead the government gave an *asiento*, or licence, to merchants usually from Portugal. The Portuguese were well placed to carry on the slave trade because they had forts and trading posts down the coast of West Africa. The Spanish had agreed in the Treaty of Tordesillas that trade and exploration in this area should be carried out by the Portuguese.

By the end of the sixteenth century, the Portuguese had built up a regular trade both to the Spanish colonies and to Brazil, where large sugar plantations had been opened. Most of the trade then fell into the hands of the Dutch, who captured several Portuguese trading posts in Africa and were masters of Brazil between 1630 and 1654. Up to the 1640s, when the Dutch became the 'foster-fathers' of the English and French colonies, African slavery had not been introduced on a large scale to the new settlements started by Englishmen and Frenchmen. Tobacco was mostly grown by European smallholders with the help of a few bondservants. But, in a few years, the Dutch persuaded their fellow Europeans of the advantages of sugar planting and the use of African labour. Very few men of the time considered the morality of the question; what mattered to most Europeans in the sixteenth and seventeenth centuries was the fact that slavery seemed to answer *their* labour problems and brought profits to the slavers. Dutch slavers pointed out to likely buyers that the cost of an African slave compared favourably with that of a European labourer. True, in 1650, an African sold for between £15 and £20, whereas the price of a European convict was between £10 and £15, but the buyer had to pay transport and take the risk that the condemned man would not escape or die on route to the plantation. The planter also expected his labour supply to increase from the birth of slave children, whereas the sons and daughters of bondservants were not bound by their parents' indentures. Owners of both slaves and bondservants could raise money by mortgaging them to a lender, but the servant with a five-year indenture was

Fig 10.2 *A shop for the sale of slaves in Brazil.*

poorer security for a long term loan than an African enslaved for life. Finally, the Dutch could guarantee a steady supply of African slaves, whereas the flow of bondservants was uncertain.

But it was more than costs which made the planters favour African slaves. In 1640, the Barbadian planters who visited the Dutch plantations in Brazil were impressed by the ease with which a few Dutch overseers managed large gangs of African slaves; a sharp contrast to the rebellious conditions on the plantations worked mostly by Europeans. The Africans were no less hostile to their masters but, when torn away from their homeland, resistance had less chance of success. Bondservants knew their master's culture, language and weaknesses too well to be easily subdued. It was easy for them to escape by mixing with the thousands of other Europeans who came and left the islands each year; because of his colour the African could not disappear into the crowd. The Dutch also pointed out that the Africans' death rate in the tropics was about one third less than that of Europeans, although death rates in their first few months

in the Caribbean was still terribly high. This gave rise later to racist theories that blacks were physically better suited to work in the tropics. Such theories are not absolutely true; both Africans and Europeans could survive the work and heat as the Europeans who cleared the first farms and plantations did. But the Africans did come to the West Indies with immunities to several diseases common to both West Africa and the Caribbean and it took Europeans several generations to build up the same resistance. The visitors noted one other important value of African slaves; they were usually more skilful at agriculture than bondservants. Nearly all Africans came from agricultural societies used to hoe cultivation, whereas most bondservants and convicts were brought from cities and port towns.

African and European labourers

The switch from European bondservants to African slaves took many years to complete. The table shows

	1678		1700		1774	
	Black	White	Black	White	Black	White
Nevis	3,849	3,521	3,676	1,104	10,000	1,000
Antigua	2,172	2,308	12,960	2,892	37,808	2,590
St Kitts	1,436	1,897	3,294	1,670	23,462	1,900
Montserrat	992	2,882	3,570	1,545	10,000	1,300
	8,449	10,406	23,500	7,211	81,370	6,790

the gradualness of the change in the Leeward islands. In 1678 whites outnumbered blacks everywhere except Nevis, and by 1700 there was still almost one white for every three blacks. The greatest change took place between 1700 and 1775 when the ratio became one white to every twelve blacks. On all the sugar islands white bondservants and black slaves at first worked side by side, but by the 1770s the only whites were owners or overseers.

The evil of slavery was present throughout the Caribbean, but the number of Africans was smaller on the Spanish islands where sugar was not the main crop. Cuba in the 1770s still depended mostly on tobacco and cattle ranching, and there were more whites than blacks on the island. In Trinidad, cotton, coffee and cocoa were grown but not sugar and, in 1783, although there were 310 slaves to 126 Europeans, there were also 295 free people, probably *mestizos*. It is interesting to note that, because the island was then still not fully developed by European farmers, there were 2,032 Amerindians, more than the Europeans and Africans together.

11   *The Africans*

The African background

Many planters wrote books on the economics of slavery and the management of plantation gangs. Other books of the time looked at the question of how the laws on property could be fitted to slaves. In them the slave was described as a chattel, the legal term for a piece of property which the owner could buy and sell as he wished. Very little was written about the slave as a person with a culture and a home or with hopes, fears, strengths and weaknesses which are seen in every human being. The planters had no real interest in the background of their slaves, although they were ready to explain their behaviour in over-simplified and inaccurate ways. Thus, owners were advised to avoid Igbos, because it was said that they often became depressed and committed suicide, and the Angolans, who had the greatest weakness of all – laziness. They would do better to buy Popos or Ibibios for they were cheerful and hardworking.

Today we can read much better informed and unbiased accounts of the African peoples and understand how each of them had a place in the rich history of their continent. Seventeenth-century slave owners would certainly have been surprised to read that twentieth-century scholars believe that the first true men appeared in Africa. Remains of such early men with their pebble tools have been found by archaeologists digging in Tanzania and Ethiopia. The pebble tools gave way to simple shaped hand-axes and for hundreds of thousands of years more of these were made in Africa than in any other part of the world.

The peoples of Africa

The ancestors of modern Africans appeared towards the end of the old stone age. The best clues to this distant past of between 50,000 and 10,000 years ago can be found by studying African languages. These can be divided into three main groups. One is the family of languages spoken by Hamite and Semite people of the north and north-east. These light-skinned Africans probably have people from Asia among their ancestors. The second group are the Bushmen and Hottentot languages spoken in some parts of the west and south-west. The speakers of these tongues are usually smaller than the other African peoples. They are the only group out of the three to fall in number since the old stone age.

Finally, there are the Negro and Bantu languages. The speakers of the first languages in the Negro-Bantu group lived in West Africa, but their descendants spread into the centre and south. The names given to them are European. Negro is a European word which means 'black' while Bantu does not describe appearance but is the name given to some of the languages.

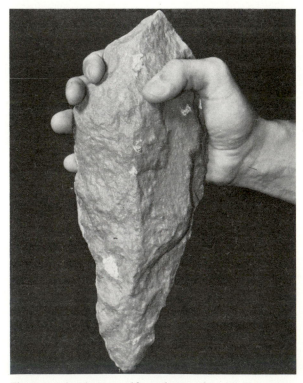

Fig 11.1 *A hand-axe, used by early man, found in Tanzania.*

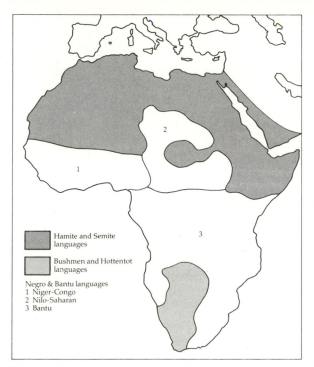

Map 20 *The main language groups of Africa.*

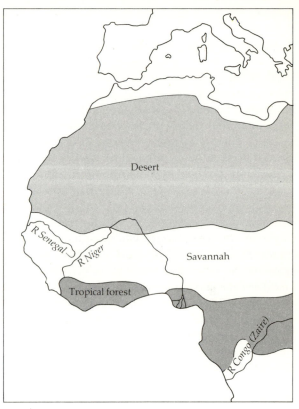

Map 21 *Vegetation zones in West Africa.*

The word 'Negro' is rarely used today except to describe a language. It is seen as an abusive and racist term which should be avoided. There are other good reasons why it has become thought of as incorrect. Firstly, it is now known to be untrue that 'Negroes' are a separate race; they were certainly related to other African peoples in very early times. Secondly, it is obvious that all the black African peoples have had separate histories for thousands of years, so that it is quite inaccurate to talk about any one type of 'Negro' society. As we look at the background of the enslaved Africans we find lands and societies which differ greatly.

Map 21 above shows these lands. Most of the slaves brought to the Americas came from a section of West Africa which stretches in an arc from the Senegal coast to southern Angola. Within this there is a smaller section between the Senegal and Congo Rivers where the Africans shipped to the Caribbean came from. The northern part of this section is a region of savannah, open grasslands which stretch for hundreds of kilometres. As the traveller moves south he passes through a zone of mixed grass and woodland until he reaches the tropical forests of the Guinea coast. The savannah and forest regions of West Africa each pro-

duced very different types of African society. First, we will look at the societies of the savannah.

The savannah

Crops of peanuts, millet, yams and many green vegetables grow on these fertile grasslands. The savannah people also reared goats, cattle and sheep, not only for meat but also for the leather which they sold to handicraft workers. Most of these lived in the towns which lay across the northern edge of the savannah: towns such as Kumbi Saleh, Walata, Jenne, Timbuctu, and Gao. These towns became important as the starting points of the trade routes which led to North Africa across the Sahara Desert. From them, caravans of laden camels set off with finely worked cloth and leather articles from the savannah as well as goods collected in the forests to the south. These included gold, ivory, kolanuts, ostrich feathers and slaves. On the return journey the caravans brought salt, grain and many luxury items from North Africa.

Ghana

Armies could move swiftly over the open grasslands or along the rivers and there are few mountains to shelter rebels. This made it possible for powerful warriors to control empires which stretched for thousands of square kilometres. Between the eighth and the sixteenth centuries there were three especially powerful empires: Ghana, Mali and Songhai. The empire of Ghana arose in about the eighth century and was ruled by the Soninke, a Mandingo-speaking people. Like the other savannah empires, the wealth of Ghana was built on control of trade across the savannah. Gold was mined in the river valleys of the Senegal and Niger and brought through Ghana on its way to the North African coast. The most important product crossing the other way was salt, which merchants could sell at a very high price to the forest peoples in the south. The treasuries of the emperors were enriched from the taxes paid by these merchants.

Much of the emperor's income was spent on keeping peace and order throughout the empire, for this was why the merchants used the routes across Ghana rather than making risky journeys through the territory of nomadic peoples beyond the control of the empire. But there was enough left for emperors to live in magnificent style, which made travellers marvel at their wealth. Arab merchants reported banquets at which thousands were fed, and described how those who approached the emperor at his court were expected to fall on their knees and sprinkle their heads with dust.

Towards the end of the eleventh century Ghana was attacked by Muslim Berbers from the north and from that time on fell into decline.

Mali

In the thirteenth century an even greater empire arose ruled by another group of Mandingo-speaking people, the Malinke. Their empire was known as Mali and it was described by one traveller as stretching as far in length and breadth as a man could travel in four months. An Arab traveller, Ibn Battuta, spoke in praise of its people, who:

> possess some admirable qualities. They are seldom unjust and have a greater abhorrence of injustice than any other

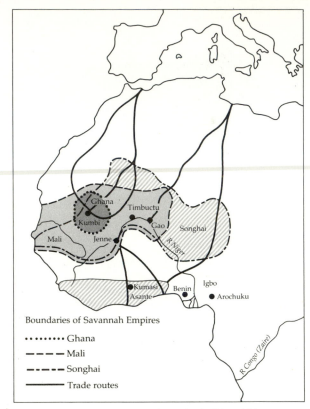

Map 22 *Important empires and peoples in West Africa.*

> people. Their Sultan shows no mercy to anyone guilty of the least act of it. There is complete security in the country. Neither travellers nor inhabitants in it have anything to fear from robbers or men of violence.

Ibn Battuta described the Mali emperor as a 'sultan', and we know that by the thirteenth century the emperors had become Muslims and encouraged the Islamic religion among their people. Mosques and other buildings in the Arab style were built in the trading cities. Islam helped to expand trade and introduced new trading techniques. Muslim priests, scholars and advisers at court helped the rulers of Mali to modernise the administration and thus retain effective control over a rapidly expanding empire. Islamic systems of writing and numbering were used in the Empire and, at Timbuctu, an Islamic university was opened with a staff of scholars from north Africa.

Songhai

At the end of the fifteenth century Mali gave way to a

Fig 11.2 *The Sankoré Mosque at Timbuctu. It was originally built at the time of the Songhai Empire.*

still larger empire, Songhai, which had its capital at Gao on the bend of the River Niger. During the fifteenth and sixteenth centuries the rulers of Songhai conquered many territories and brought many different peoples into their huge and immensely powerful empire. In spite of quarrels between later rulers and revolts from conquered peoples, Songhai remained strong until it was conquered in 1591 by a large Moroccan army whose soldiers had the advantage of possessing guns.

The forest

In the dense tropical forests the only links between villages were footpaths. The cascading rivers were too dangerous for canoes, and work animals were of little use in the tangled undergrowth. Poor communications kept the African peoples separate from each other and as many as 500 different societies grew up in the two main areas. Those who lived in the forests facing the Atlantic included the Mende and the Temne. The forests facing the Gulf of Guinea were the homes of the Edo, Ibibio, Igbo and many others.

The difficulties of travel meant that many of the Africans of these 500 societies lived in separate villages, although as time went on common links developed, such as those which united the Igbo people of eastern Nigeria.

Igbo society

The Igbo had no centralised government, no kings and no famous leaders. The village was the basic political and social unit, and the inhabitants of each Igbo village grew up in the belief that they were all direct descendants of one common ancestor and were distinct from the people of other Igbo villages. Each village managed its own affairs and had a council of elders, headed by a chief or headman who was considered the direct descendant of its founder. But, in contrast with the majority of centralised states, Igbo society was highly democratic and the power of the elders was limited. Every man had a right to voice his opinion at the village assembly, and the elders had to accept the will of the assembly.

Igbo settlements were made up of several single-roomed thatched buildings which served as sleeping quarters. Most daily activities took place outside, under pavilions, where uncles, aunts, and children talked, cooked, ate and took part in celebrations. Around the cluster of homes there was a hardwood stockade and a few yards further out would be a barricade of matted thorn bushes. The space between served as a pen for guinea fowl, pigs, goats and chickens. Food crops such as yam, plantains, groundnuts, and peppers were grown beyond the outer barricade.

Occasionally over-crowding or family quarrels would lead some members of the community to set up a new village in the forest. But they would respect their common ancestors and work with the other villages of their relatives as part of a village group. All business of the village group, or clan, was dealt with by a united council under a senior headman, the Ofo.

Although the Igbo clung to their village groups they understood that they belonged to a wider society. All Igbos shared a common language as well as other links. Igbo men selected wives from outside their village group and the villages were connected by a complex trading system. For example, some villages

Fig 11.3 *A painting of the Asante yam festival at Kumasi in the late days of the Asante Empire.*

produced a surplus of foods such as yams which they traded with others specialising in particular skills such as iron working. Disputes or crimes were normally dealt with by the village community, but in difficult cases which could not be resolved, the Igbo turned to oracles through which they could communicate with their gods or ancestors. The most powerful oracle was at Arochuku. Here there was a shrine where Igbo people brought their quarrels about trading bargains and so on to be judged by a very powerful god. First they made offerings and then a priest, acting as the god's mouthpiece, gave judgement. Igbos believed that the god would use supernatural powers to kill those who disobeyed his verdict.

The Asante

The Asante of the Gulf of Guinea went a step further than the Igbos in their political organisation. They too, began with independent villages which grew into a village-group or clan society. But these clans became larger than those of the Igbos and grew into states, each with its own paramount chief or *Omanhene*. These states became wealthy from taxes on the gold trade. Soon they joined together in a federation. Its capital was at Kumasi which stood in the strongest and wealthiest of the states and at the centre of the gold and kolanut producing region.

The paramount chief of the state became the *Asantehene* or federal emperor. At first the Asantehene's power was limited by a council of chiefs of the other states in the federation. They recognised the Asantehene's right to call on them to provide warriors in an

emergency, and Asante people could seek justice from the high court at Kumasi if they were dissatisfied with their own chief's judgements. Yet in all other matters the Omanhene had complete power in their own states. This check on the Asantehene's power was there for all to see in his symbol of authority, the golden stool. This stool, which was said to have been 'conjured from the sky' symbolised the supremacy of the Asantehene over all the other states of Asante. But, although the golden stool was always carried before the Asantehene, he never sat on it to show that he had not taken over those powers personally.

In the eighteenth century the Empire became less of a federation and more of a centralised state ruled by the Asantehene from Kumasi. People living on the borders of the Asante Empire were conquered and forced to pay tribute directly into the Asantehene's treasury. The purpose of these conquests was to give the Asantehene control of the trade routes both north to the sources of gold and kolanut and south to the coast. Some merchants carried gold and other products towards the savannah cities of Timbuctu and Jenne and, of course, paid taxes on them. But there were also routes used by African slavers taking their captives south to Europeans waiting in their factories at Elmina and Accra. All routes passed through Kumasi where a high tax had to be paid on each slave before they were allowed forward to the coast. Throughout the years of the slave trade the Asantehene was powerful enough to keep Europeans out of the interior of his empire. After the trade was ended in the nineteenth century the British, who feared the power of the Asantehene, began to encourage rebellions in the small states conquered by the Asante.

Between 1870 and 1900 several battles were fought between the British and the Asante. The Asante resisted the attempts of the British to colonise them. Eventually the Asante were defeated and brought under British rule as the colony of the Gold Coast, today the modern state of Ghana. The office of Asantehene was restored during the 1930s, but without the power that it had wielded before the time of colonial rule.

Benin

Eight hundred kilometres east of Asante the Edo of Benin created an empire in the forest zone which was centralised from the start. Its government was headed by the *Oba*, a semi-divine king. Although there was a council made up of Edo chiefs it had no real power over the Oba. The chiefs were forced to live permanently in the capital, Benin, and their peoples were ruled by overlords appointed by the Oba.

Benin lay just west of the Niger Delta and was the southern point of trade routes which passed north into the savannah cities, where they were linked with the trans-Saharan trade. In the early days the Edo sent large quantities of ivory, pepper and ebony to the northern markets, but easier trading opportunities came when the Portuguese arrived on the coast in the fifteenth century. There was a great European demand for ivory, ebony, pepper, jasper stones, coral, leopard skins and slaves. Yet, like other West African rulers, the Oba wished to retain his position as middleman in the trade, and would not allow Europeans to enter the interior to trade directly and thus weaken his position.

Europeans, however, were allowed to visit Benin and returned home to report that it was a grander city than those of their own countries. In 1602, a Dutchman, Olfert Dapper, wrote of Benin's thirty main streets, some of them over thirty six metres wide, which made a sharp contrast to the narrow twisting alleys of European capitals. Dapper was especially impressed with the Oba's palace, which was a collection of buildings with many wide airy rooms and galleries, supported by 'wooden pillars encased in copper where their victories are depicted'. Each roof was crowned with a 'small pyramidical tower, on the point of which is perched a copper bird spreading its wings'.

Fig 11.4 *A bronze sculpture from sixteenth-century Benin. It shows the Queen Mother and is one of Benin's finest works of art.*

The Portuguese were so impressed with Benin that they invited the Oba to visit their kingdom. For a time Portuguese soldiers travelled to Benin to serve in the Oba's army. But, above all, Benin became famed in Europe for the work of its craftsmen who produced beautifully carved ivory and wooden sculptures, finely woven and dyed cloth, and exquisite jewellery in gold, ivory and copper. In the fifteenth century, Benin sculptors produced bronze objects, particularly models of human heads, which are among the world's finest works of art. The sculptors were employed by the Oba, and their carvings, in which the Oba was invariably represented as a god-like figure, served to enhance his power and prestige.

Benin was at its height during the fifteenth and sixteenth centuries. After this the empire was weakened by struggles between rivals for the Oba's position, and by dishonest and inefficient government. Nevertheless the Obas retained sufficient power and wealth to be able, like the other West African emperors, to keep control of the supply of slaves to Europeans on the coast until the trade ended. Then, in the nineteenth century, the Benin Empire, along with the lands of the Igbo and other peoples, fell to the greater fire-power of Europeans and became part of the British colony of Nigeria.

The world of the West African

Slavery tore each group of West African slaves away from its homeland and threw them together haphazardly on the Caribbean plantations. Here the different African peoples found that they shared many beliefs and explanations for the experiences which are common to all men: birth and death, the sense of belonging to a family, a clan and a wider group, the benefits of rain and the disaster of flood or drought. An explanation of these mysteries was found in the belief of the existence of gods. Many West Africans believed that their ancestors had been brought into being by a creator god. He was far removed from their daily lives and so could not be worshipped as a being who controlled men's moral behaviour and expected them to be good rather than evil. Sharing a belief in the god was a powerful way of helping people to understand what it meant to say 'I am one of the Edo people' or 'I live in the land which was given to the Yorubas at the beginning of time'.

Tales of the gods often described how they had taught ancestors to farm, fish, use iron, discover the best season for sowing and planting and so on. These stories were acted out in dances and the drummers at the god's shrine would beat out the rhythms which reminded people of their common ancestry.

Social bonds

In many African societies it was accepted that there were three groups of people in a village; the living, the ancestors whom the living joined at death, and those waiting to be born. These bonds between the living and dead, between temporary humans and spirits, helped explain the sense of belonging to a family, clan or village group. The shrines of ancestral spirits in village compounds were a practical way of reminding the living of the importance of rules and customs which had helped them survive in the past, and which must be kept if those about to be born were to have a secure home. The dead were not thought of as separate from the community and were often called on to give advice, especially in times of trouble. For many African peoples, burial ceremonies were a way of handing down these traditions. When an Edo elder died it was his eldest son's duty to see that he was buried with the equipment he would need to join the other spirits of the clan and become a spirit-elder. At the same time a shrine was set up so that the living could give respect to the leadership and guidance he had given when alive. The ceremony also showed that, while the father was being accepted by his dead spirit-relatives, the son was being recognised as the new family elder.

Like most African peoples, the society of living Edos was grouped into grades according to age. In this case there were headmen and elders and below them the younger men who were warriors and organised the villages' farming and trade; finally there were the youths who were the village workers. Some African people had even more age-sets; there were seven among the Tiriki people of north-west Kenya. Sometimes entry into the different ranks and age-sets was controlled by societies whose elders had kept alive the traditions and rules of an African people for many centuries. The societies organised the times of initiation for men ready to move from one age-set to the next. The lives of the people of several African societies in the area which is now Sierra Leone and Liberia were regulated by the Poro society. Elders of the society took boys of about fourteen to a sacred area of bush away from their village. The boy was now said to have been eaten by the spirit *namu*, whose priests wore wooden masks fringed with strands of raffia straw. Inside the sacred bush, he was taught the history of his people and the skills he would need in the future: farming, crafts, house building, fighting and the use of medicines. He had to undergo tests of physical strength and was given harsh punishments to train him to accept the authority of the society's elders. After this initiation, the boy was said to have been reborn and returned to his village with a 'bush name' and with scars on his back and chest to represent the teeth marks of the spirit which had eaten him and then given him new birth. The scars were a public sign that he had undergone the training to play a full part as an adult in the affairs of his people.

Dealing with nature

The human world was explained through the existence of gods and spirits, but so was the natural world of water, earth, plants, animals and the seasons. The African needed to understand, as all men do, why the cow can support life and the snake can take it away, why steady rain helps crops and a thunder-storm destroys them. The explanation was to be found in the spirits which lived in the beasts and trees or controlled the forces of nature. Europeans often scoffed at the complicated spirit world seen by the Africans and accused them of 'worshipping' stones and trees; they said the wooden or stone carvings of gods were nothing more than idols. In fact, Africans were not idol-worshippers. The many dances and ceremonies and the sacrifices at god's shrines were much more a way of showing that mere men have no real control over the forces of nature. They were part of the education of the young who learned to fear the dangers of certain forest paths or streams and to understand the anxiety of their elders that they could do nothing to stop a god, such as Shango – the Yoruba god of lightning – striking at their homes or their livestock.

The gods and spirits had to be served by priests, men who understood them and could explain their power over humans. Priests were thus important in African societies, and respected for the years of study

Fig 11.5 *A Benin bronze statue of the Oba's horn-blower.*

which brought them the wisdom to keep alive traditions or give help in times of trouble. Many priests were also medicine men. The best of these had great skill in curing illness with medicines made from herbs and plants, a skill which could only be learned after a long apprenticeship. The African's belief in a spirit world also meant that medicine men had to be able to drive out spirits. A young man with a snake bite would not believe it had happened accidently but that he had offended a mischievous spirit. So his cure would not be complete if the medicine man did not drive away the spirit.

A rich heritage

In African societies the individual was regarded first

and foremost as a member of a community. From earliest childhood the African learned to know the sounds and rhythms of the many drums beating out from the shrines or playing for the village dances. He learned to take part in the dances, or to play the drums and other musical instruments, and through them to learn the history of his people, their rules of good citizenship, their techniques of farming and the way they counted time – whether by the seasons or the phases of the moon. He was surrounded by carvings which told him the same stories in a different way.

Many of the Africans who came to the Caribbean were far more highly skilled than Europeans realised. Some were farmers used to the hoe or lonely cattle-watching, but others had learned the craft in which their village specialised: they could produce salt from sea water, make metal or wooden tools, work leather, or lead other men along trade routes with the aid only of the sun and stars. On the slave ships and in the slave compounds were men who could cure illnesses which baffled Europeans, headmen and princes who had led villages and clans through war or time of great disaster, brave warriors, and artists capable of making the most beautiful carvings and sculptures.

12 The slave trade

Development of the trade

The story of the connection between sugar and African slavery began in the twelfth century when Italians planted cane fields on the island of Cyprus. They employed African slaves, skilled in cane cultivation, from Arab suppliers. By the fourteenth century sugar cultivation had spread westward to Crete, Sicily, southern Spain and Portugal. More slaves were brought from North Africa but, by now, it was to work as unskilled labourers rather than skilled artisans. Most were still black Africans bought from Arab traders. In the fifteenth century many of these captives were shipped from Spain and Portugal to work the cane fields in their colonies in Madeira, the Azores and the Canary Islands. By the close of the century, Portuguese traders shipped slaves there direct from their new forts along the West African coast. In the sixteenth century they brought them still further west to the new colonies in the Americas.

In the Americas sugar planters remained the greatest users of slaves. By 1700, sugar and slavery had moved across the Caribbean from Barbados and the Leewards to Jamaica and St Domingue. A century later the cattle ranches in Puerto Rico and Cuba were changed by African slave gangs into cane fields. In the United States the close link between sugar and plantation slavery ended in Louisiana, for most of the millions of Africans in the rest of the southern United States were put to labour in the tobacco, cotton and rice fields.

Numbers of live slaves taken from West Africa 1451–1870

British Caribbean	
Jamaica	747,500
Barbados	387,000
Leeward Islands	346,000
St Vincent, St Lucia, Tobago & Dominica	70,000
Trinidad	22,000
Grenada	67,000
Other places	25,000
French Caribbean	
St Domingue	864,300
French Caribbean continued	
Martinique	365,800
Guadeloupe	290,800
Louisiana	28,000
French Guiana	51,000
Dutch Caribbean	500,000
Danish Caribbean	28,000
Brazil	3,646,800
North America	399,000
Spanish America	1,552,100
Europe	175,000
San Thomé	100,000
Atlantic islands (Madeira and Canaries)	25,000
	9,566,100

Averages per year

1451–1600	1,800 each year
1601–1700	13,400
1701–1810	55,000
1810–1870	31,600

(Adapted from P. D. Curtin, *The Atlantic Slave Trade: A Census*, University of Wisconsin Press, 1972.)

The table gives the destination and estimated total of African slaves brought to each part of the Americas. It lists only the live arrivals. For every African who arrived alive at least one other perished in the slaving raids, on the trek to the coast or during the trans-Atlantic crossing. So, it has been calculated that, over a period of 400 years, about twenty million Africans fell victim to the Atlantic slave trade.

Europeans and the slave trade

The four hundred year history of the Atlantic slave trade can be divided into three main stages. First, in the sixteenth century small shipments to Portuguese and Spanish colonies were carried at a comparatively low cost. The second stage began in the early seventeenth century with the rapid growth of sugar plantations and a resultant increase in slaving. To make this possible ships had to be built or hired; forts, warehouses and slave pens set up on the African coast; and payments made to local slavers. The Dutch were the first to spread the cost over many investors by setting up their West India Company in 1621. In 1660 the British Government followed their example by giving the sole right of selling slaves in English colonies to the Company of Royal Adventurers trading into Africa. In 1672 this became the Royal African Company with backers from rich merchants, noble landowners and members of the royal family. In 1664 the French West India Company was founded with similar government encouragement.

These companies and the smaller ones of Denmark and Brandenburg were expected to enrich their nation by trading according to the mercantilist ideas of the time (see pp. 68–9). Each was to be the sole supplier of slaves to its own country's colonies, and it aimed too to take a large share of the trade to colonies of rival nations. The natural result were the seventeenth-century wars. In addition to the struggles in the Caribbean and Europe there was also fighting between Europeans to seize control of the main forts on the African coast.

By the beginning of the eighteenth century each nation controlled separate sections of the West African coast. The French were the leading traders in Senegal, the Ivory Coast, the Cameroons and part of the Congo, while the English were strongest in Gambia, the Windward Coast and the Niger Delta. The Portuguese still had a large trade in Angola and parts of the Congo. Scattered in-between were the Dutch, Brandenburgers and Danes, who owned very few colonies but were active in the trade with the Spanish colonies and the southern United States.

The government-sponsored companies never made large profits. One reason was the cost of the coastal trading stations. Each was protected by a fort with a garrison of soldiers paid by the company. Another reason was the large number of company agents in Africa and the Americas. They often cheated by tricks such as selling slaves who they reported as having died on the crossing, declaring a lower price than that actually received, or simply disappearing with company funds.

Private trade

These difficulties brought about the third stage in which the British Royal Africa Company gave way to

Fig 12.1 *A modern photograph of the fort at Cape Coast, Ghana, which once guarded a slaving station. Cape Coast was owned by Spanish, Dutch, Danes and, after 1664, by the British.*

large numbers of private companies. Planters preferred to deal with them because their slaves were cheaper as African slavers had sold to them direct, by-passing the company trading posts. The British Government accepted the change and granted licences to the private companies to trade in return for a small payment towards the upkeep of the forts. The new traders greatly increased the number of slaves brought to the Americas. Between 1680 and 1688 the Royal Africa Company delivered an average of 5,155 each year; in 1708 English private companies, using over 100 ships, carried 25,000. Most of the trade was in the hands of well-organised merchants who directed their ships from offices in Liverpool, Bristol and London. After 1720 merchants from Boston and Charleston also took part.

The French and Dutch Governments continued to support government companies and during the eighteenth century their share of the trade fell as that of the

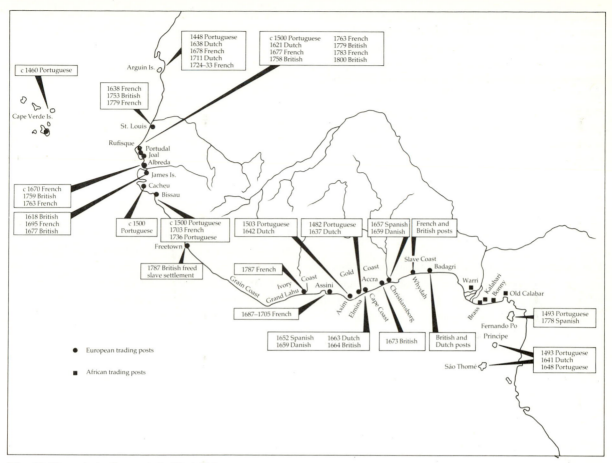

Map 23 *The main trading posts in West Africa.*

British private traders rose. In 1768 approximately 96,100 Africans were shipped to the Americas. Of these, British vessels brought 53,100 and British American ships a further 6,200, while the French carried only 23,000, the Dutch 11,300, the Portuguese 1,700 and the Danes 1,200.

Africa and the slave trade

The African slaves were traded for consumer goods from Europe such as brandy, iron, wine, guns, powder, silks, brocades, laces and velvets. But the import of consumer goods and the export of labour had serious effects on the economies of many African societies. Local industry stagnated or declined. African merchants exchanged slaves for these foreign goods either with Europeans waiting in the coastal factories or directly with ships' captains. In both cases

the captives had been first taken through an inland market town where taxes had been paid to an African ruler. These taxes often made up the biggest part of a chief or king's income. This was true of the King of Dahomey, a small but warlike forest state, even in the late nineteenth century. At that time the British sent envoys to seek the king's help in stamping out the last remnants of the slave trade. They offered him a large annual payment and help in setting up a palm oil industry if he would forbid slaves to pass through his land. The king refused, stating that this would not replace what he got from taxes on slaves. Later, as the slave trade declined, he was forced to introduce palm oil plantations in order to survive. Ironically, these plantations used slave labour.

Slavery was not new to African society, which traditionally recognised four ways in which a freeman could become a slave. First, in cases of famine, parents could place their children as domestic slaves in the care of a wealthy man who would prevent them starving. Secondly, people could be sold into domestic slavery as payment for their debts. Once the debt was paid they could regain their freedom. Thirdly, freemen could be enslaved for serious crimes such as witchcraft, adultery and murder. Finally, prisoners of war and people seized in raids were regarded as their captors' slaves. They were not considered as chattels and could not be sold unless they were found guilty of a serious crime. Indeed they were usually treated as well as freemen and many rose to high positions in their master's household.

New forms of slavery

The Atlantic trade altered these traditional forms of slavery. Slaves became a source of wealth which could be sold to Europeans like any other goods. To meet the European demand, new means of acquiring slaves grew up. One group would invent a cause for war against a neighbour, solely to collect slaves. Frequently European traders encouraged such slaving wars by supplying one people with guns in return for the slaves; often the other peoples would also be armed if they, too, agreed to deliver slaves. Generally, however, African rulers needed no encouragement to raid their neighbours. John Atkins visited Whydah in 1721 and reported how one of the petty African kings there first bargained with his neighbours for slaves but, if he 'can not obtain a sufficient number of slaves that way, he marches an Army inland and depopulates'. This sort of thing happened all along the coast. C.B. Waldstrom gave evidence against the slave trade in 1789 and stated that, for African kings, 'Public pillage (raiding) is of all the others, the most plentiful source, from which the slave trade derives its continuance and support'.

Few Africans foresaw that the new slavery could lead to the break-up of their stable societies, but one Congolese king wrote to the King of Portugal in 1556 about its effects in his land. He was deeply concerned about the damaging influence of the trade.

> Many of our people are keenly desirous of the wares and things of your kingdoms, which are brought by your people, and in order to satisfy their voracious appetite, sieze many of our people, freed and exempt men; and very often it happens that they kidnap even noblemen and the sons of noblemen, and our relatives and take them to be sold to the white men who are in our kingdoms; and for

this purpose they have concealed them; and others are brought during the night so they might not be recognised.

Slaving raids

No West African was altogether free from the risk of enslavement, but generally the raiders came from the well-organised kingdoms and the victims from inland villages and tiny separated communities. For the majority of our West African ancestors the first step to slavery began with a surprise night attack. The raiders quickly fired the houses and, in the panic, collected the villagers, yoking them two by two with forked sticks around their necks into a slave coffle. Speed was important; the coffles had to be on their way before the fires died down and the villagers regrouped and overpowered the raiders. Quickly they were prodded towards the coast. The strongest and fittest survived; the very young, the old, the weak and sick were cut from the coffles to die along the wayside or make their way back to their ruined village as best they could. After a march, often lasting several weeks and covering three or four hundred kilometres, the coffles reached the slaving markets of the inland capitals at Salago, Oke-Odan, Kumasi, Abomey or Oyo. Here the coffles were broken for the first time and the slaves sold to the dealers who traded directly with the Europeans on the coast. They formed their purchases into new coffles, paid the taxes due on them and marched them down the well-worn routes to the coast.

At the coast

At the coast the slaves were finally sold to Europeans. The chief factor (the agent of a European trading company) at Elmina castle in 1701 was a Dutchman, William Bosman. In a letter Bosman described this final stage.

> When these slaves come to Fida they are put in prison all together, and when we treat concerning buying them, they are throughly examined by our surgeons, even to the smallest member. . . . Those which are approved as good are set on one side; and the lame or faulty are set by as invalids, which are here called Mackrons. These are such as are above five and thirty years old, or are maimed in arms, legs, hands or feet, have lost a tooth, are grey-haired or have films over eyes; as well as those which are affected

Fig 12.2 *A slave coffle on a nineteenth-century plantation in Central Africa.*

with any venereal distemper, or with several other diseases. The invalids and maimed being thrown out . . . the remainder are numbered and in the meanwhile a burning iron with the arms or name of the Company lies in the fire; with which ours are marked on the breast.

Here Bosman paused to offer some excuses for the inhumanity he has described.

> I doubt not this trade seems very barbarous to you, but since it is followed by mere necessity, it must go on; but we yet take all possible care that they are not burned too hard, especially the women, who are more tender than the men.

The middle passage

Captains of slaving ships acquired their human cargoes in one of two ways. Either they cruised along the coast dealing with several small African dealers, or they sailed directly to a trading station and bought their slaves from a European factor. The first method was used mainly by private shipowners who could not afford the overhead charges at the trading stations. As a result they could often sell their slaves slightly cheaper in America. However, they could

seldom load a complete cargo at one point and had to ply up and down the coast for a few slaves here and there. These delays could be costly as additional provisions had to be taken on board and wages paid to seamen for little work. The risk of losing both cargo and crew from disease in the unhealthy coastal swamps increased each day.

The ships of merchant companies who called at the trading stations could take on a full load straight away. The captain, along with his 'surgeon', went ashore to select the slaves and bargain for them with the goods on board. John Atkins describes the procedure at Whydah in 1721:

> The commanders with their surgeons (as skilled in the choice of slaves) attend the whole time on shore, where they purchase in what they call a fair open market. The mates reside on board, receiving from time to time their masters' directions as to the goods wanted, and to prepare the ship for the reception and security of the slaves sent him; where this is a rule always observed, to keep males apart from the women and children, to handcuff the former . . .

The middle passage began with a short trip in open boats to the waiting ship. For the slaves it provided a last glimpse of a homeland few would see again.

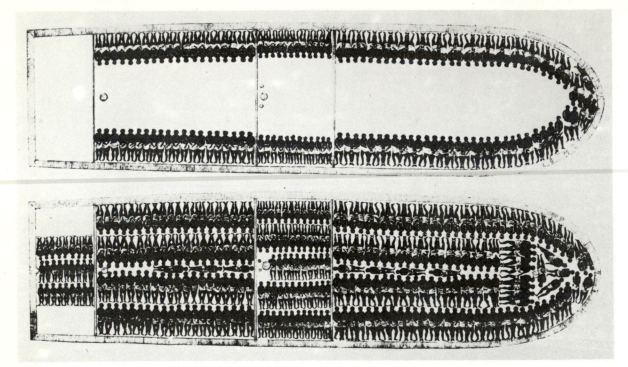

Fig 12.3 *Plan of a slave ship showing the inhuman packing to make use of every centimetre. The bottom diagram shows the lower deck and the top one shows a platform fixed round the sides of the ship's walls between the lower and upper decks.*

Slave ships

The waiting ships were fully prepared for their human cargoes. Along the whole length, under deck, ran tier upon tier of open-ended, box-like trays 150 centimetres long and 50 centimetres wide and high. The men were placed in these with iron shackles around their ankles, joined by chains looped to the shackles of their neighbours. Women and children were crowded below decks in the fore section. The slavers' equipment included feeding bowls, food containers, guns and special chisels to knock out front teeth so that slaves who were determined to starve to death could be forcibly fed. Provisions were simple: rice, yams, oil, a few fresh fruits and water. The ships were horribly crowded as it was reckoned that one-fifth of the slaves would die during the crossing. To offset these losses, one-fifth more of the slaves than the number insured for by the captain before he left his home port were crammed below deck.

When all was ready the hatches were bolted, the sails raised and course charted west from Africa to America. For the first days, until the ship was well out to sea, the slaves were kept below deck. Then a steady routine set in. The ship's doctor made morning rounds attending to the sick and disposing of the dead. Relays of slaves were allowed on deck where they were closely watched while being allowed to exercise and take their meal. In fair weather, women and children were generally allowed to remain on deck and sometimes captains forced groups of men to join in songs and dances.

But such times were rare. Heavy seas often kept the hatches bolted for days on end and few captains considered more than the most basic needs of their cargo. The gloom, stench and sweltering heat below deck brought unbelievable misery. Slaves and crew alike suffered from inflammations, fevers and smallpox; their limbs swelled and bodies rotted from yaws and dropsy. Despair made the possibility of infection and death all the greater. The captain of the slave ship *Hannibal* had taken on 700 slaves. Before reaching American waters 320 had died and he lamented:

> After all our pains and care to give them their messes in due order and season, keeping their lodges clean and sweet as possible, and enduring so much misery and stench among a parcel of creatures nastier than swine . . . to be defeated by their mortality!

The middle passage lasted from six to ten weeks, depending on the weather and destination. The shortest route was to Brazil and the longest to the continental United States. The main slave markets in the Caribbean during the eighteenth century were at Barbados, Martinique, Jamaica and Hispaniola. The Dutch island, Curaçao, also served as a transhipment port for slaves for the mainland colonies of Spanish America. After the British suppressed their slave trade in 1807, the main American trading centres became Havana and New Orleans.

Sales and auctions

Upon reaching port, the ship was washed down and the slaves prepared for sale. Captains tried to make their cargo as attractive as possible. Slaves were stripped and shaved to remove grey hairs which lowered the selling price. Palm oil was rubbed into muscles to give a healthy firm appearance. Some captains tried to conceal wounds and scars by rubbing them with cosmetic mixtures which included gun powder, lime juice and even iron rust.

The final sale to the planters was conducted either by a slave scramble' or an auction. In a slave scramble the Africans were divided into groups for which set prices were fixed. At a signal, the planters rushed on board to assess which group offered the best quality for the least money. The practice was extremely cruel; at the on-rush of the planters many of the terrified Africans flung themselves desperately into the sea. The scramble was eventually outlawed in most colonies and replaced by the auction when planters were allowed to inspect the slaves before the bidding began. After the scramble or auction the slaves were branded again, this time with their new master's mark. They were issued with a set of osnaburg clothes – pants and a hat for men, a petticoat and scarf for women – and taken to the plantation where the long process of converting an African into a seasoned American slave began.

The African heritage

The beginning of the African's journey to America was described in 1700 by William Bosman in a few plain words:

> Their masters strip them of all they have on their backs; so they come aboard stark-naked, as well women as men: in which condition they are obliged to continue.

Most European immigrants started their new life very differently. Even bondservants had their clothes and a little baggage; while the more fortunate came with many possessions, letters of introduction to friends or relatives and perhaps even a farm waiting for them. Perhaps most important of all the European could keep in contact with those he had left behind. The African arrived naked but not completely cut off from his homeland. He had his language, beliefs, skills and a place in society as perhaps a warrior, priest or skilled craftsman. He had a rich store of memories, stories and dances. In time he would use all these to piece together a life in his new American surroundings which owed much to his African heritage.

13 The eighteenth-century plantation

The sugar plantation

It has been reckoned that in 1774 the typical plantation in Jamaica was worth £19,324 – at a time when an Englishman could live very comfortably on a few hundreds of pounds a year and a farm labourer in England earned only a few shillings a week. The value of such a plantation of 240 hectares can be broken down like this:

105 hectares sugar cane	£4,273
135 hectares other land	£1,728
Sugar works	£3,962
Slaves	£7,641
Livestock	£1,380
Other equipment	£340
	£19,324

Of course, not all plantations on the sugar islands were of 240 hectares. Many were much larger, especially in Jamaica where land was used more wastefully and where it was usual to give slaves plots to grow provisions. On Barbados and Antigua estates were rarely more than 120 hectares. But there was less waste or mountain ground and each hectare was used with more care so that plantations on the smaller islands were roughly the same value as those on Jamaica. The figures for Jamaica point to two features which were true for most estates. First, the most valuable property were the slaves, generally worth about two-fifths of all the planter owned. Second, a sugar plantation was a combination of industry and agriculture; the sugar works were worth nearly as much as the canefields.

Sugar production in the ten leading Caribbean islands

	Area in Sq. Km.	Yearly average in tonnes 1741–5	1766–70
St Domingue (Fr)	27,856	43,078	62,227
Jamaica (Br)	11,424	15,827	36,597
Antigua (Br)	280	6,329	10,861
St Christopher (Br)	176	7,345	9,856
Martinique (Fr)	1,105	14,389	8,918
St Croix (Danish)	218	742	8,361
Guadeloupe (Fr)	1,702	8,241	8,024
Barbados (Br)	430	6,746	7,944
Grenada (Br)	345	——	6,657
Cuba (Sp)	110,922	2,032	5,283
Total	154,458	104,729	164,728

Comparison of plantation sizes in St Kitts and Jamaica in the eighteenth century

St Kitts		Jamaica	
Size in acres (1 acre = 0.4 hectares)	Number of owners	Size in acres (1 acre = 0.4 hectares)	Number of owners
1–9	19	0–99	263
10–24	21	100–499	566
25–49	23	500–999	303
50–99	26	1,000–1,999	253
100–149	18	2,000–4,999	153
150–199	12	5,000–9,999	52
200–523	15	10,000–22,999	9
Total	134	Total	1,599

Location and layout

These two features played an important part in the choice of a site for a plantation. Close by a river was ideal as water could be carried by an aqueduct to turn the mill; it was also useful for irrigating the fields. If possible, a place near the coast was chosen so that a small dock could be built to send sugar to the main ports of the island for shipping overseas. It would also be the means of bringing in the plantation's supplies. A plantation was described by one Jamaican as being like a little town which bought goods from all over the world. One estate's account books for the 1780s show that in one shipment from Europe it received 15 barrels of beef, 70 barrels of herring for feeding slaves, 200 lbs (90 kilograms) of butter and four kegs of tallow for making candles and soap. To clothe its slaves it also bought quantities of Osnaburg cloth, made in Germany, and supplies of 'negro hats'.

Most plantations on Barbados ran in narrow strips from the coast, and planters fed their slaves chiefly on

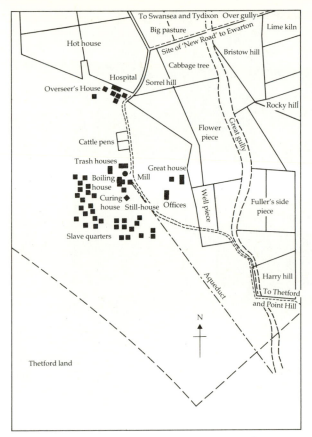

Map 24 *A plan of Worthy Park, Jamaica, in 1794. The estate, situated in St. John's Parish in the central region of the island, covered an area of 614 hectares.*

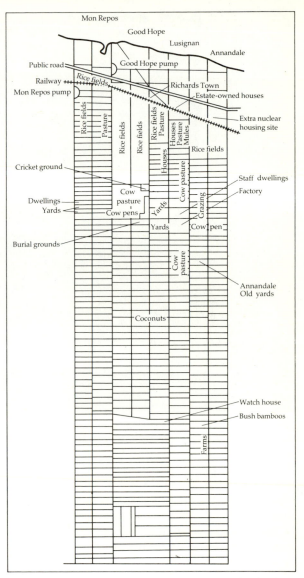

Map 25 *Plantations in Guyana ran from the sea inland in long narrow strips. The layout of eighteenth-century plantations near Georgetown can be seen in the diagram of a modern estate.*

imported foods. In Jamaica this was not always possible as many plantations were opened in inland valleys. Some Jamaican planters built roads to the coast and then paid for their upkeep by charging tolls for other people to use them. But they also found ways of cutting down on the need for transport. Inland plantations were usually larger, in some cases more than 2,000 hectares. More of the land was used for provision crops and often slaves were allowed one and half days per week to grow their own food. The large estate could provide its own timber for building. Owners of these plantations did not need to be such careful farmers. Edward Long wrote in 1750 that they often wore out their plantations by 'incessant cultivation and after throwing it up, pass on to a new piece which is destined to be worked to the bone in the same manner'. The planters with less land to waste, like those on Barbados, were noted for careful manuring which kept their fields fertile.

Fields

Plantation lands were divided into several sections: cane fields, pastures, woodlands, provision grounds, workyards and living quarters for managers and labourers. Most plantations had from three to five cane fields, each surrounded by a closely trimmed hedge or stone wall to keep out wandering cattle. Each year one field was generally left fallow, another grew a second crop of rattoons and the others were planted

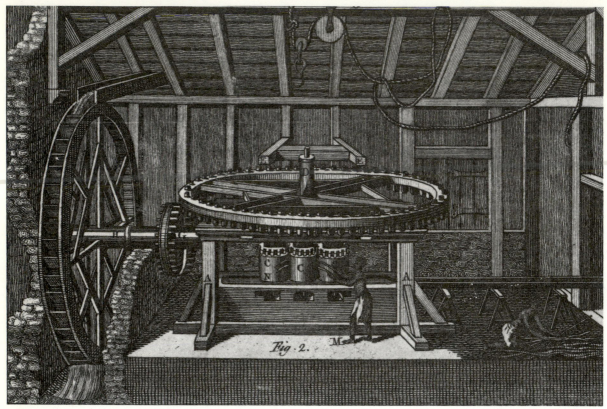

Nig 13.1 *A water-driven mill from an eighteenth-century book. The slave in the centre is pushing cane between the rollers so that the juice will fall into the trough below and will be carried to the boiling house along the gutter leading to the right.*

with new canes. Each field was divided by narrow roads into smaller square plots of six to nine hectares. This made it easier for the overseer to control the rate of the slave gangs' work and to organise the movement of cut cane to the workyard.

The factory

The workyard stood in the middle of the cane fields. It was made up of the mill boiling house, curing house and the blacksmith's and carpenter's sheds. Close by stood the cattle pens, poultry houses and a small 'hospital' which was also used as a jail for runaway slaves. There was sometimes a trash house in which the crushed cane stalks were dried to burn in the furnace.

The mill and boiling house were often built from elaborately cut stone but their mechanisms were not very efficient by modern standards. Juice was taken from the cane by crushing it between three upright rollers made of iron (or wood covered with iron). The power to run the rollers came from animals, wind or water. Animal mills were the simplest and cheapest. Cattle or mules were yoked on to a pole which turned the rollers as the animals walked in a wide circle. Wind mills were possible only in certain places, such as the windward side of small islands where the trade winds blew constantly. They were costly to build but cheaper to run than animal mills. Water mills were the most powerful and efficient. They cost little to run but needed expensive aqueducts to carry the water which drove the huge wheel. Only a few planters could afford aqueducts.

Lead-covered wooden troughs carried the fresh cane juice from the mill to storage cisterns at the head of each furnace in the boiling house. The furnaces were rectangular boxes of brick or stone, with openings near the bottom of one side to stoke the fires and pull out the ashes. Set in the top of each furnace were up to seven copper kettles. Cane juice was taken from the cistern, strained and ladled into the first and largest copper. It was heated and a little lime was added to remove impurities. The juice was then skimmed and ladled down the line of coppers, each smaller and hotter than the one before, until it reached the smallest and hottest, the teache. In the teache the sugar bubbled to a sticky syrup which was ladled into cooling troughs where the sugar crystals hardened around a sticky core of molasses. The raw sugar was shovelled from the cooling troughs into hogsheads which were wheeled away to the curing house. Here, the molasses drained off through holes in the bottom of the hogsheads leaving the muscavado sugar stuck to the sides. After four weeks the holes were plugged and the hogsheads were ready for export to Europe.

The raw muscavado still had to be turned into many grades of fine white powdered sugar, but the Navigation Laws forbade refining in the Caribbean. Refining became an important industry in the chief western ports of Britain: Bristol, Liverpool and Glasgow – as it did in towns in western France supplied by French Caribbean islands.

Planters and attorneys

There were many fewer planter-owners in the Caribbean than there were plantations. It was only on the very small islands such as Antigua that nearly all planters owned and lived on one plantation. Especially on Jamaica and Barbados it became common for the wealthiest planters to own several plantations, but often they had no home on any. At different times up to a third of the planters were absentees living in England, but even in the Caribbean many of the richer planters lived in towns. Absentee planters employed attorneys to be their agents and take care of the plantations. Attorneys inspected the plantation books, purchased supplies and appointed overseers and managers. For this they often received a commission of six per cent of the yearly profits and could share in the privileges of the planter class. Some attorneys lived in the owners' great house and became members of the parish vestry.

Great houses

The richest plantation owners usually lived in Eng-

Fig 13.2 *A modern photograph of a great house. The lower storey and the verandah can be seen clearly.*

land and stayed in towns when they were in the Caribbean. This meant that great houses built in the eighteenth century were not so magnificent as those of the seventeenth century. There were even some planters who chose not to waste money on building a house which would stay empty for most of the year. They would stay in the book-keeper's house if they visited their property. But most built great houses to a fairly simple design. The bottom storey was made of stone and used as a storage shed, storm cellar and a stronghold in case of a slave revolt. The living quarters were on the second floor which was built of wood with a verandah running around. Inside, one large central hall served as the dining room, sitting room, office and occasionally banqueting hall. Around this were the bedrooms. The kitchens and servants' quarters were in a separate building.

The position of the great house showed the planter's desire for comfort but also his fear and suspicion of the slaves. It usually stood on a mound about a kilometre away from the heat and noise of the work-

Fig 13.3 *A painting of slave huts near St Johns, Antigua. The great house stands on the rising ground on the left.*

yard and slave quarters. On the verandah the planter's family and guests could catch the cooling breezes; at the same time they could keep a watchful eye on the slaves at work in fields and factory. For extra safety some planters made their house the centre of a compound which also held the homes of the more loyal workers: the overseers and book-keepers, white craftsmen, occasionally a doctor, and the domestic slaves.

Other whites

The overseer managed the daily work on the plantation. It was his job to keep the plantation books for the planter or his attorney, order the daily work to be done and distribute food, clothing, equipment and stores. He was helped by the book-keepers who, despite their titles, did very little book-keeping. Each day they checked the stock of implements and animals and saw that the slaves got to the fields on time and carried out the day's work set by the overseer. When

there were white mechanics and craftsmen to repair the buildings and machinery they worked under the orders of the book-keepers, although they generally earned a higher wage than him because of their skills. Even when they had been brought out to the colonies as bondservants they had a superior position, and many were given charge over artisan and domestic slaves.

The slaves

Beyond the compound were the slave quarters. These were simple huts made from wattle, daub and thatch, often with a small garden patch at the back and a living yard at the front. Some island assemblies passed regulations that slave quarters could have only one room, one window and one door. Planters preferred to have their slaves do all their domestic work in the front yard where they were in full view. The huts were sleeping, not living quarters.

Plantation owners kept stock books which listed

their slaves in almost the same way as cattle. In the book for Worthy Park Estate in Jamaica you can find entries like this:

Name	Qualifications	Condition
Quashie	Head carpenter	Able
Nero	Field labourer	Able
Waller	Head boiler	Sickly
Grace	Driver	Elderly
Little Dido	Field labourer	Weakly and runaway

These books remind us that the first thing an African lost when he arrived on the plantation was the name he came with. It was replaced with one which the planter could pronounce and which pleased him in some way. Africans were named after Roman emperors, like Nero on this list. In the same stock book there are slaves with the names of European poets such as Pope and Homer, European countries such as Russia and Germany. Scottish planters often gave their slaves the names of clans in Scotland, such as Mackenzie and Macdonald.

Field slaves

Slaves on a plantation were classified according to the work that they did. Most slaves spent some of their lives as field labourers working in one of the two or three field gangs. It was the great gang which contained the strongest, and especially newly arrived slaves whom the planter wanted to 'season' before deciding whether they had the skill for other work. The stock books show that some of them rose out of the field gangs to specialised positions such as boilers and carpenters. But as they became weak and elderly they often became field labourers again, this time working at the lighter tasks given to the second or third gangs.

In the fields the gangs were commanded by a slave who had risen to the position of driver. His task was to see that the day's work ordered by the overseer was completed. As fields were divided into squares it was easy to see which men or women moved more slowly than the others along the lines to be dug, weeded or manured. The driver had permission to use the whip and some could call on another slave, known as the 'jumper' or 'Johnny Jumper', to carry out the whippings.

Artisans

The most valuable group of slaves were the artisans in the work-yard. The head man of each section had the help of journeymen slaves and younger apprentices. Of these artisans the head boiler was the most important. He had to decide how long the sugar should boil in each copper to produce the best quality. Whether the plantation made a good profit or not depended on his skill and judgement. Planters recognised the value of their artisan slaves by giving them special privileges such as extra allowances of clothing, food, drink and more comfortable quarters. When they were not needed on the plantation they were given the chance to 'job away' for another planter or perhaps to work in a nearby town. They paid their owner a percentage of their earnings.

There was also a group of less skilled specialised slaves which included cattlemen, mulemen, mid-wives and watchmen. Nor were slave children free from plantation work. Between the ages of four and ten they had to work in the 'pickney' gang, under the care of an old slave lady who was usually greatly respected by the others. Under her supervision the children moved around the plantation picking up sticks, stones and trash. They carried water and food to the field gangs and fed the poultry. The oldest children were sometimes divided into a separate 'grass gang' to go out and collect feed for the animals.

Domestic slaves

Each planter had domestic slaves to serve his family as maids, cooks, butlers, gardeners, coachmen, valets and nursemaids. Sometimes the domestic slaves were looked on as more fortunate than their fellow Africans in the fields and workyards but, in fact, it was rarely so. Living close to the master and his family they were more often the victims of the white man's anger and in the worst households were punished very frequently. Many of the tasks they had to do were humiliating, especially when they were serving one of the planter's children. One young mistress was described as having three slaves attending her when she took her afternoon nap; two to fan her face and one to lightly scratch her feet. To add to the difficulties of their position they usually had to live in a compound near the great house and away from the other slaves who

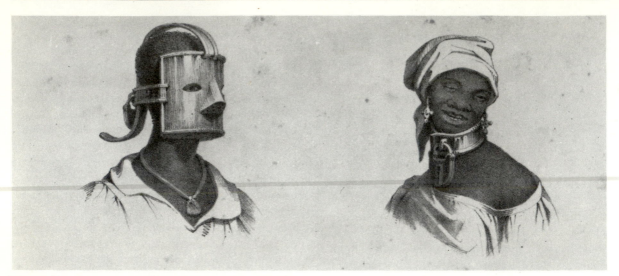

Fig 13.4 *Two ways of punishing slaves, taken from an old British guidebook to the West Indies.*

often treated them as outcasts. Unfairly, they became thought of as 'Uncle Toms', that is slaves who took the master's side against their own people.

Like the artisans, the domestic slaves were faced with the likelihood that they would be returned to the plantation as field labourers if they displeased their master or if he no longer had a use for them. Sometimes the women slaves who were kept in the houses of overseers and managers succeeded in avoiding this fate, but not always. The Worthy Park stock book tells the story of the slave, Dolly. In 1787 she was described as 'in the overseer's house' with a baby, Mulatto Patty. A few years later there are two more coloured babies against her name but Dolly had become a field labourer, presumably because she was too old to be attractive. Whether the father freed the children is not known.

Hired slaves

Between 15 and 20 per cent of the slaves were not attached to a plantation. They belonged to a master who rented them out. The most fortunate were artisans who paid their master for a ticket of leave which allowed them to travel about on work such as carpentry, tailoring, fishing, piloting, higgling and catching rats. Many could earn a fairly comfortable living. A skilled rat-catcher, for instance, could catch sixty to a hundred each week at a ½-cent per rat.

Perhaps the least fortunate of all slaves were those in the unskilled jobbing gangs, which belonged to slave contractors, small landowners or occasionally to a group of planters who shared the use of their labour. They were hired out to do extra work which could not be handled by regular plantation slaves. Sometimes this involved hard and dangerous tasks which the planter feared might cause injury or death to his own slaves. The jobbing slaves had no permanent homes, or regular rations. At night they slept chained together wherever they happened to be working. It was reckoned that a jobbing slave had a life expectancy of about seven years.

The yearly cycle

The slave's sixteen and a half hour working day began at 4 a.m. when the driver rang a bell or blew on a conch shell. Work like feeding the poultry and cleaning the cattle pens had to be done before daylight. At sunrise all assembled for the roll-call by the overseer. The day's tasks were given and work began again until 10 a.m., when there was a half-hour for breakfast. The slaves were given a two-hour break at 12.30 p.m. to attend to their personal chores. Some went to their food plots and others to clean out and feed their pigs and poultry. Work began again at 2 p.m. and continued until sunset. Only after another roll-call were the slaves allowed to go back to their quarters until 4 a.m. the next morning. This routine was broken on Sunday mornings when slaves were

Fig 13.5 *Cutting cane. The picture was drawn in Trinidad after emancipation.*

allowed to go to market to sell the small animals and provisions they had raised. Holidays were given during Christmas week and for a few days after crop time.

The yearly cycle of cultivation began in spring with the planting of new canes. The great gang had to open up the soil to a depth of fifteen centimetres for at least a hundred canes a day. Failure led to whippings. The task was doubly difficult if old rattoons had to be pried out by the roots. Dr Tullideph in Antigua estimated that his field slaves wore out 'near half a ton' of hoes each planting season. Once the field was planted the great gang was kept busy weeding, thinning, hoeing and replanting with the help of the second and third gangs, whose members also undertook the task of manuring the cane holes.

When the crop was growing well the gangs were put to work at other tasks. Provisions had to be planted, fences repaired and roads built. Towards the end of March there was a rush to complete work which could not be done during crop time. The provisions were reaped and stored, staves were cut and piled ready for the coopers to make hogsheads, and cane trash was collected for the boiling house.

During the five months of crop time the working day lengthened to eighteen and a half hours. Most plantations worked a shift-system which allowed each shift only four hours sleep every twenty-four. The shifts alternated between cutting canes and working in the factory. Both were monotonous and backbreaking. The last field shift of the day had to cut enough canes to keep the mill running all night. Artisans had to be on duty night and day to fix breakdowns. The slaves dreaded work in the mills more than cane cutting. The factory work was hot and dangerous as canes had to be fed into the rollers by hand. There was an axe hanging by to cut off tired fingers which became caught up in the rollers. In the boiling house slaves suffered terribly from burns while stoking the furnaces and ladling the boiling sugar from copper to copper.

14 Slave islands in the eighteenth century

Restrictive laws

At the centre of the history of the eighteenth-century colonies is the life of the plantation slaves. What they endured then has been the most important influence on the development of the free Caribbean societies of today. But, at the time, it was not the slaves who controlled colonies even though they outnumbered whites everywhere by about twelve to one. Undoubtedly, power in the eighteenth century rested in the hands of a small section of whites, the plantocracy. In turn, it was only a small number of these, usually the wealthiest, who sat in the island assemblies and wrote the laws. Others, however, held positions of local power through the parish vestries. A planter could serve as a custos, magistrate, justice of the peace, collecting constable and an officer of the militia. The Antiguan planter, Samuel Martin, wrote that gaining a seat on the vestry was 'the proper qualification' for a successful planter to aim for.

The greatest fear of the planters in the assemblies and vestries was that their numbers and strength would fall to dangerously low levels. The plantocracy on the larger colonies already lived with the threat from Maroons in the interior (see pp. 146–7). On all colonies there was an ever-present anxiety about black rebellion.

Deficiency Acts

As we saw in Chapter 10 (p. 77) it was in the early eighteenth century that the ratio of whites to blacks began to fall rapidly. To try to stop this most island assemblies passed a Deficiency Act. This usually stated that a planter must hire one white servant for every ten slaves on his plantation. In fact the Deficiency Acts actually led to a fall in the number of white settlers. The reason was that planters kept their own doctors, storekeepers, carpenters and masons, and so men with private businesses had to close their shops

and leave the islands. In time, too, the planters found that it was cheaper to train a slave than to pay a white craftsman. The fine for breaking the Deficiency Act was not more than £10 whereas it would cost between £40 and £50 a year to employ a European.

The failure of the Deficiency Acts meant that whites on the sugar islands were everywhere in a tiny minority. In Jamaica in 1774 there were only 18,420 compared to 205,261 slaves, a proportion of about 1 to 11. But the whites were not evenly spread. Most of them lived in Kingston and other island towns, or were soldiers in the garrisons. In the countryside there were only a few to each plantation and most of these were men. Lady Nugent, the governor's wife, travelled from Kingston to Port Antonio in 1802 and met only one white woman. The result was fear of the African and strong measures to keep him under control.

Police laws

Each colony passed a series of police laws controlling the movement and behaviour of slaves. Some dealt with the capture and punishment of runaways.

Fig 14.1 *Late eighteenth-century guns at the garrison on Brimstone Hill, St Kitts.*

Movements were controlled and slaves were forbidden to travel away from the plantation without a ticket from their master giving the destination and time of return. Other laws made it illegal for slaves to carry weapons, to blow horns, beat drums or assemble together in large numbers. They were not allowed to inherit land or to own private property without their master's permission. A master could punish slaves for minor offences; for more serious ones they were tried by a Justice of the Peace and three freeholders, who would all be white property owners. At these trials slaves could not speak in their defence. No slave was allowed to give evidence in a trial for a freeman, which meant that there was no evidence to convict a white who had ill-treated a slave. In Nevis a planter, Edward Huggins, was brought to court for cruelty in whipping slaves after he had given 365 lashes to a man and 292 to a woman. The jury found him not guilty. The woman died a few days later and the coroner's jury certified that she had died a natural death.

Another section of the laws tried to prevent masters from treating their slaves so harshly that they would be driven to revolt. The slave codes on each island laid down the minimum of clothing, food and housing that should be supplied. A Montserrat law of 1693 said that all planters should set aside one acre (just under half a hectare) of provision ground for every eight slaves. Old and useless slaves could not be turned out of the plantations. All slave codes forbade masters to kill their slaves or use cruel and unusual punishments. The Barbados law laid down a fine of £15 on the planter who killed his own slave. Yet few masters were ever found guilty as they were always tried by a jury of fellow planters.

Other controls

In the case of a serious slave disturbance or revolt the planters could call on the local militia, a force of part-time soldiers made up of whites and free coloureds. But they were not often called on. The greatest security against trouble came from the way the slaves were treated. Newly arrived Africans went through long periods of training called 'seasoning'. Arriving at the plantation they were put in the charge of slave families who helped them to build houses, prepare provision grounds and taught them the ways of the plantation. If they rebelled or ran away they were severely punished; if they worked hard they were rewarded with extra rations or better jobs. It was useful for the planters to divide their slaves into different grades with different privileges, since this was one way of preventing the Africans uniting against their master.

There were other ways. Slave gangs were mixed to include Africans from different backgrounds and languages. Marriages were not encouraged and male slaves were sometimes rotated from plantation to plantation to break up family stability. Planters feared that slaves would become less easy to control if they had the interests of a family to protect. Christian priests and missionaries were usually kept away from the slaves for religion might give them a common bond and unite them against their masters. Slaves were not taught to read and write for this might mean they would pick up and pass on ideas which threatened the system.

Slave society

In Chapter 11 we saw the rich variety of African culture. This was not something which could be crushed altogether by police laws and plantation regulations, especially when contact with West Africa could be renewed each time a slave was brought to the Caribbean. What happened when slaves were given a newly arrived African-born man to 'season'? From the master's point of view they were teaching him the ways of the plantation and, of course, he did learn to use some of the European language and to live and work in the way enforced by European planters. But, at the same time, he was a link with the traditions of Africa; in some cases he could even make slaves better informed about their homeland, for men and women from different African groups were able to discover how much heritage they shared in common.

As in Africa much of the culture of the West Indian slave survived in his dance and song. Many planters believed that when the slaves danced it was a sign of the contentment of a simple people. In fact, they were keeping alive their history and cultural life; sometimes they were enlarging their heritage as people from different West African groups mingled together and developed new dances and stories. The dance for which there are most records in eighteenth-century Jamaica was the John Canoe, and the descriptions of

Fig 14.2 *A picture of slaves dancing in Dominica, painted by an Englishman in 1779. The picture gives a false impression of* *plantation life as the slaves are shown to be healthy, well-dressed and apparently contented.*

the dance leaders' masks remind us of the headdress worn by secret society elders in African village ceremonies and processions. Today, although time and distance have made changes, all the forms of Caribbean song and dance still carry signs of African origins, which appear in the rhythms of jazz, the satire of calypsoes, the vigour of reggae and 'jump ups' and the feeling of soul. Drumming has survived as an important part of religious and social festivals too. Planters feared it and made it illegal, perhaps knowing that it was the main way of drawing African people together. But it was one of the things which no laws could suppress even if it had sometimes to be disguised. The planter, Bryan Edwards, described the Leewards slaves as very fond of beating on a wooden board with a stick. The musical instruments used by slaves in their dances were all of African origin. Many, such as the marimbas and marracas, have changed little in three hundred years.

The planters only succeeded partly in breaking up the family relationships of their slaves' African background. The position of fathers suffered most. Few lived in the huts of their children's mothers, and in a society where men and women, children and the old all toiled, there was no special place for the man as provider of food or the family protector. But the tradition of age-sets continued in slave society. Bryan Edwards commented that 'old age was held in great veneration' and noted that older slaves had considerable authority over the younger ones. Slave children grew up to address the men and women of their mother's generation as 'Daddy' or 'Uncle', 'Mammy' or 'Aunty'. Among newly arrived slaves strong bonds were often created among peoples wrenched from different villages and different societies in Africa. Those who came over on the same boat would know each other as 'ship-mates', an important relationship which lasted a lifetime.

To keep up the relationship with ship-mates or a loved one some slaves risked the dangers of leaving the plantation at night without permission and going 'night walking'. But the most common place for such meetings was the Sunday market, described by David McKinnen, in 1802, as the 'day of market and also the day of mirth and recreation when the whole negro population seemed to be in motion'. The market was of course the place where slaves sold or exchanged provision crops and articles they had made such as bedmats or baskets. But it also gave an opportunity to consult a herbal doctor or Obeah-man, listen to stories or music and take part in dances. Some descriptions of markets show how the slaves would divide up and spend the day in the company of their own age-set.

African customs and beliefs

Slave funerals were carried out with much of the ceremony of Africa, and the belief that the dead person remained part of the community was not abandoned. Corpses were carried in processions which 'stepped up' to the places that the dead person had known in life. Sometimes a bowl of soup was placed at the head and a bottle of rum at the feet to help the dead man to join his spirit relatives.

At first it was common for slaves to believe that they would return over the seas to join spirit relatives. As the years passed and more ancestors were Caribbean born the direct links were broken, but slaves continued to draw many of their ideas and beliefs from the African past. This was true of the beliefs held by followers of *Vodun*, *Shangoism* and *Obeahism*.

Vodun was chiefly found in French St Domingue, modern Haiti. Most of the slaves came from the Dahomey region where Africans recognised a creator male-female god, Maur-Lisa, and a host of lesser gods, or voduns, each caring for some aspect of life. Many slaves were compulsorily baptised into the Roman Catholic Church and it may have been at these services that priests of the Vodun gods noted that a Catholic Church has an altar to a high God and shrines for saints. Out of this arose the mixture of Catholic and African beliefs which has usually been called Voodoo. Shangoism, which became particularly strong in Trinidad, stemmed from the Yoruba stories about Shango, the god of thunder or lightning. Obeahism and Myalism were active cults in the slave

society of the eighteenth century, kept alive by Obeah-men and Myal-men who came on the slave ships. Myal-men were often skilled in herbal medicine and some of them were allowed by planters to practise in plantation hospitals.

The lesser spirits of things like rocks, trees and streams, which were so important in the African explanation of the natural world, often found a place in the Caribbean. Tales of duppies and other spirits were widespread, but so were the fables and stories which were so important a part of the oral, or spoken language, traditions of Africa. Anancy stories were told to plantation children. Originally based on the spider hero Ananse of the Akan people, they became known to Africans of other groups as well, and gradually were given a West Indian setting. In the plantations of the southern American states the tortoise tales of the Yoruba and the hare tales of the Igbo were retold.

African crafts survived in the West Indies. The most common were basket work and straw plaiting used to make bed-mats, wicker-chairs, baskets and occasionally plaited shoes. Traditional pottery skills continued in the making of earthen pots and jars. Some groups kept alive some of the highly decorative fashions of Africa, such as those found in the combs, paddles, stools and doorposts of the free 'Bush Negroes' in Guyana. Women's fashions lasted through the years of slavery to the present day. The practice of wrapping women's heads with distinctive ties can be traced to West Africa. Today, among the Asante, there are at least fifty recognised styles of tying headkerchiefs. The braiding and plaiting of hair into delicate cane rows and pieces is a fashion still shared by women in the Caribbean and West Africa.

One of the great tragedies of the slave societies was that so few records have been left of the cultural and social lives of the African people. Even when Europeans bothered to describe slave life they rarely understood it and, of course, they knew very little indeed about the African society from which they had taken their plantation labour. So their attitudes to African culture in the West Indies show not only fear but also ignorance. Sometimes, therefore, we can best work out how much African tradition survived on the slave plantation by looking at what has lasted to the present day. For instance, it is only recently that careful studies of language have shown that the syntax (or grammar) and idiom (or forms of speech) of the many

West Indian dialects and patois are based on elements found in the speech of peoples such as the Yoruba, the Ewe, the Twi and many others. In most cases the African word has been replaced by an English, Spanish or French equivalent. Sometimes, too, slaves took Amerindian words. But African terms survived too. Many West Indian dialects still retain the word *Tata* for a beloved relative or grandmother. *Nyam*, to eat, is probably the same as the Twi word for meat.

Free coloureds

A threat to the supremacy of the white plantocracy came from the increasing numbers of free coloureds. White men were allowed to free their slaves and this was sometimes done as a reward for long and obedient service. Sometimes assemblies passed legislation freeing certain slaves for help in putting down a revolt or for bravery in fighting a European invader. But the most commonly freed slaves were the coloured children of white men and slave women. As all children took the legal status of their mother such children were born slaves even though their father was a planter, overseer or book-keeper, but many such fathers wanted their children to grow up free.

Limitations on coloureds

Yet freeing slaves was not the same as allowing them to rival the wealth and social position of the plantocracy. There were many local laws to prevent this. Free coloured had to register with a vestry which gave them a ticket of freedom valid for seven years. Failure to show the ticket on demand could lead to fines, imprisonment or enslavement. Free coloureds could not give evidence against a white in court, they could not vote or hold a public office. Other laws limited their chances of becoming wealthy. Most islands forbade them to own plantations and, in Jamaica, they could not inherit more than '2,000 pounds currency or worth of property'. There were less strictly kept laws against coloureds taking up certain crafts such as carpentry and masonry, or working on plantations as book-keepers and overseers.

All these limitations depended on knowing who was or was not a coloured. This was carefully defined in laws which laid down that a coloured person was anyone from a full black to a quintroon, who had one part black ancestry to thirty-two parts white. The child of a quintroon and a white man, defined as an octoroon, crossed the colour line and was legally recognised as white and free.

Added to the laws, the coloureds suffered from social discrimination. Although many had close private relationships with whites they could not appear at white dances, racing meets, banquets and other entertainments. At the end of the eighteenth century the two groups did attend the same Baptist and Methodist churches but, according to the Reverend William Jones, the whites kept away from coloureds, 'searching for seats as distant as possible from them'. Yet, despite this, the coloureds were necessary to Caribbean society. Many of them worked as skilled artisans on the plantations or in the towns. They made up the greatest part of the part-time soldiers in the local militias which were kept chiefly to deal with slave disturbances. They also filled positions in the towns which had been left vacant by poor whites. Coloureds were clerks, traders, tavern keepers, butchers and higglers.

The exceptions

There were just a few who escaped all the restrictions. A coloured who was lucky enough to gain money or education could petition his island assembly for a private Act which granted him the same rights as a free white apart usually from voting and holding public office. As a result of special Acts some free coloureds rose to influential positions as newspaper editors, teachers and lawyers. Planters regularly got permission from the assemblies to allow their coloured sons to work on their plantations as book-keepers and overseers. James Swaby, the illegitimate coloured son of a planter from St Elizabeth, Jamaica, successfully petitioned the assembly for a private Act which allowed him to inherit his father's sugar plantation, 217 slaves and 337 head of cattle. Yet despite these exceptions, most coloureds remained desperately poor.

A creole society?

The plantocracy which ruled the British Caribbean

was white, but this was not the same as being completely English in its life-style or totally loyal to Britain in its politics. But was the plantocracy so different from the upper class in England that we ought to speak of a quite separate creole way of life? This is a difficult question to answer because the people who wrote about the Caribbean in the eighteenth century gave so many different impressions, as we will see from the following examples.

Some travellers' accounts stressed how like Britain the West Indian islands were. Janet Schaw who visited Antigua in the 1770s wrote that the ladies there 'have the fashions every six weeks from London, and London itself cannot boast of more elegant shops than you meet with at St John's'. Going into the countryside she was impressed by the homes of the planters and by the many banquets and balls and by being taken on a 'charming ride through many rich and noble plantations'. The traveller Oldmixon wrote in a similar way about Bridgetown: 'a city of 1,200 houses, built of stone, the windows glazed, many of them sashed; the streets bounding the houses high, and the rents dear'. In the countryside, he declared, 'the Master Merchants and Planters live each like little sovereigns'.

To Oldmixon and Janet Schaw the islands were places where the planters could live the ideal life of leisure of English gentlemen. Yet, occasionally, their writings show signs of the tension and fear which lay below the surface. Janet Schaw spoke of the Christmas holiday when the 'inhuman whip' was not being used as a time when 'every man on the island is in arms and patrols go all around the different plantations as well as keeping guard in the towns'. Fear of the African was obvious and many writings defended the use of the whip to keep them in their place. Matthew Lewis, writing from his knowledge of Jamaica, said, 'I am indeed assured by everyone around me that to manage a West Indian estate without the occasional use of a cart whip, however rarely, is impossible'. Sometimes, too, travellers were shocked by signs of immorality by white men; as Janet Schaw wrote, it 'appears too plainly from the crowds of mullatoes'.

One visitor who stressed ways in which the plantocracy was creole rather than British was Lady Nugent, wife of the Governor of Jamaica from 1801 to 1805. Her diary reports many times when she considered the men and women of the plantocracy to be not up to the best English ways of behaviour. She saw signs

that white creole language was moving away from the English. When she mentioned a breeze blowing through a window a planter's wife replied, 'Yes, Ma-am, him rail-ly too fra-ish'. At a ball she followed the English tradition and danced just once with the oldest servant – but, of course, he was a black slave and this horrified the whites.

Lady Nugent thought that being surrounded by black servants had a bad effect on young creole whites who quickly became little tyrants in their parents' house. This troubled the Reverend John Roland, a campaigner against slavery, whose parents were planters. Of his boyhood he wrote:

> My parents, kind and humane as they generally were to their slaves, yet allowed me to insult, strike and hit them as I pleased. I used to think them on a level with the mules and horses on the estate.

Charles Leslie, speaking of Jamaica, was troubled by the poor education of creole whites:

> Learning here is at the lowest ebb; there is no public school in the whole island . . . to read, write and cast up accounts is the education they desire.

It was far better he thought for young whites to be educated in England, but such young men came to have a dislike for the West Indies as a crude and cruel society and failed to return. By the end of the eighteenth century there were no longer enough wealthy planters to fill all the seats on the councils and assemblies in the Leeward Islands. So the property qualifications were lowered to allow managers and attorneys to stand for elections. This was done rather than have coloured property owners take a share in government and law-making. As John Waller described after a visit in the early 1800s:

> No property, however considerable, can raise a man or women of colour, not even when combined with education, to the proper rank of a human being, in the proper estimation of an English or Dutch creole.

English governors and officials

Lady Nugent's journal was mostly concerned with the ways in which creole social life was different from the English society she knew, but in one place she comments on a political problem. It was the case of a young boy sentenced to death whom her husband wished to save from the gallows, but 'Nugent couldn't do it without giving great offence and alarm to the

Fig 14.3 *Governor Parkes of Antigua.*

white population'.

Like all British governors of the West Indian colonies, Lord Nugent had to be very careful not to offend creole opinion. In the seventeenth century several governors had suffered from trying to have their way against the wishes of the planters. The speaker, or chairman, of the Bahamas Assembly had first fired a shot at the governor and then 'broke the governor's head with the butt of his pistol'. Governor Parkes in Antigua was less lucky. When the planters in the assembly failed to persuade the British Government to remove him, they dragged him from Government House and beat him to death. Not surprisingly, eighteenth-century governors did not usually challenge the local power of the creole planters. Very few of them stayed long enough to understand the ways of creole society as the average term of office was only three and half years.

Another difficulty for governors was that many other officials appointed by the government in Britain did not bother to take up their post in the colonies at all. Englishmen were given posts as island secretary, provost-marshall, surveyor-general, receiver-general and clerk of the supreme court. As was the custom

with many jobs in the civil service in England, they paid a deputy to do the work and kept part of the salary for themselves. Their deputies in the Caribbean were usually planters or attorneys who were more likely to side with the other creoles than with the governor.

French colonial society

As the eighteenth century went on the French islands developed a form of society very similar to that in the British colonies. Yet they never had a plantocracy which was so fully in control. One reason was that, until 1785, there were no French local assemblies for the planters to dominate; all laws and policies were decided in France and carried out by the governor or the intendant and the many officials on the islands. Another reason was that sugar production never had such a central place in the French as in the British colonies. In the mid-eighteenth century the Abbé Raynal visited Martinique and listed four distinct classes of planters.

The first class owned 100 large sugar plantations and 12,000 slaves; the second 150 sugar estates with 9,000 slaves and the third, thirty sugar plantations with 2,000 slaves. The fourth class was much the largest. There were 1,500 planters with over 12,000 slaves who grew provisions, coffee, cocoa and cassava rather than sugar. Even St Domingue, which was by far the largest sugar producer of any European colony, had only 648 sugar plantations compared to 2,587 growing coffee, cacao and indigo.

So the rich white class of landowners – the *grands blancs* – were divided between planters of sugar and other crops. But the French islands also had a large class of small whites or *petits blancs*. These were smallholders, craftsmen, small shopkeepers and the poorer clerks and officials. They were important as suppliers of food and manufactured goods to the plantations, either those produced in their own workshops or small-holdings or those imported from North America and Europe.

These differences in white society affected the position of slaves and free coloureds, especially in the early days when many of the Africans had been brought to the French islands not to work in large field gangs but to serve small farmers, craftsmen and traders. In 1685 the French Government issued the *Code*

Noir, or black code, to regulate the treatment of slaves in the colonies. The Code was divided into three sections. The first dealt with religious questions, the next with the position of slaves and the third with the procedures for granting freedom.

The religious section was drawn up to make sure that the French colonies remained true to the Catholic faith, the official religion of France at the time. Whereas the English planters resisted the idea of religious care and teaching for slaves, the French were compelled to give instruction in the faith and to encourage baptism and legal marriage. Sundays and holy days were to be observed and slaves were to be buried in holy ground. The Code forbade concubinage between slaves and freemen, although this was usually ignored from the start.

The second part of the Code defined the slave as a 'type' of private property. Because they were the property of another man, slaves could not own property themselves, nor could they make contracts, hold public office or take part in trials. Other parts of the Code forbade slaves to carry arms, assemble in crowds, take up trades or use violence against free people. On the other hand, the planter was forced to have some respect for basic human rights. He was obliged to give allowances of food and clothing, to care for the disabled, and punishments were limited to whipping or putting in irons. Owners could not break up families by sale. The Code gave slaves a right unknown in the English colonies; they could go to the legal official known as the *procureur général* (or attorney general) and complain if a master did not carry out obligations.

Easy procedures for freeing slaves were laid down in the final section of the Code Noir, which stated that those freed were to have the same rights as other Frenchmen. The number of free coloured rose more rapidly in the French colonies than the British. Small owners were sometimes more willing to free slaves they knew personally than were large planters to whom slaves were just names in a stock book. Petits blancs often married slave women and thus freed them.

Restrictive laws

The influence of the Code Noir in keeping some respect for human rights weakened as the number of

both slaves and free coloureds rose. In the eighteenth century the French whites showed the same fears of competition from the coloureds and mutiny from the slaves which led to the harsh police laws in the British colonies. They pressed for restrictions on the coloureds and in 1766 the French Government gave in, declaring that it was absolutely wrong for the coloureds, who were still close to slavery, to expect to share in the positions held by white men. It ordered that coloureds were not to serve in the island militia or to carry arms. Coloureds were no longer to have equal rights in law and certain professions were closed to them. To mark their difference from the whites, free coloureds were forced to wear identifying clothing. Ladies were allowed to wear a scarf but not a hat; cotton petticoats were permitted but not silk, which was reserved for white women. Petticoat inspectors stood at church doors where they checked the coloured ladies as they came to mass. To save embarrassment the ladies pinned up their hems a few inches to make viewing easy. This practice is still reflected in the national costume of Martinique and Guadeloupe. In 1779 the freedom of movement of coloureds was restricted by a curfew which kept them indoors at night.

Despite the many controls on the free coloureds their right to own property was never taken away. Many became wealthy and could send their children to France to be educated. Wealth and education made the French free coloureds more influential than those in the English colonies. The time would come when coloured leaders, many of them with friends in France itself, would play an important part in overthrowing the supremacy of the whites who had imposed so many restrictions and humiliations on them.

Restrictions on slaves

As the number of slaves in the French islands grew in the eighteenth century the Code Noir was increasingly ignored by owners. Concubinage became common, marriages were not encouraged; once they were baptised slaves were not allowed to return to church. No-one checked to see that food and clothing allowances were being given. Instead of acting as protectors of the slaves, the procureurs-générals in each colony took the lead in laying down regulations which were very similar to the police laws in the English

Fig 14.4 *A woman in Martinique, photographed in the 1890s, wearing a skirt hitched up so that the petticoat can be seen.*

colonies. Masters were ordered to prevent meetings of slaves and not to send them out as hucksters or day workers without passes. There were efforts to force planters to buy food so that they did not give slaves provision grounds and time to work them. Shopkeepers in the towns were sometimes forbidden to buy from slaves.

These changes in the management of slaves were officially recognised in 1771 by the French Government, which wrote to the governor-general of the French colonies:

> It is only by leaving to the masters a power that is nearly absolute, that it will be possible to keep so large a number of men in that state of submission which is made necessary by their numerical superiority over the whites. If some masters abuse their power, they must be reproved in secret, so that the slaves may always be kept in the belief that the master can do no wrong in his dealing with them.

In the end, it is clear that the slave societies in both the French and English colonies depended on the use of force. This was well understood by the planters. One of them, Bryan Edwards, wrote:

> In countries where slavery is established, the leading principle on which the government is supported is fear: or a sense of that absolute coercive necessity which leaving no choice of action, supercedes all question of right. It is vain to deny that such actually is, and necessarily must be the case in all countries where slavery is allowed.

15 Eighteenth-century wars

Four wars

The last war of the seventeenth century ended with the Treaty of Ryswick in 1697. By the treaty, Spain agreed to French ownership of St Domingue and this was to be the last important change in ownership of the Caribbean colonies for a hundred years. Yet the European powers still fought wars here, seven of them between 1702 and 1814. This chapter deals with the first four: the *War of Spanish Succession 1702–1713* (ended by the Treaty of Utrecht); the *War of Jenkins' Ear 1739–44* and the *War of Austrian Succession 1744–1748* (ended by the Treaty of Aix-La Chappelle); and the *Seven Years War 1756–1763* (ended by the Treaty of Paris). To begin to understand these wars try to look at the map of the Americas in 1700 (p. 113) from the point of view of a prime minister, general or admiral of France, Spain and England.

Spain

Spain still owned the largest territories in the Caribbean, but her four colonies in Santo Domingo, Cuba, Puerto Rico and Trinidad together held only a few thousand Spanish settlers, mostly living as cattle ranchers. Both the Spanish Government and her enemies agreed that the mainland was more important. Far more Europeans, or people of European descent, lived in Spanish America than in any other part of the world outside Europe itself. From the Spanish Government's point of view the main purpose of the American empire was to provide wealth for its treasury. Spain's rulers still insisted that trade had to be undertaken by Spanish ships unless a non-Spaniard had paid for a special licence, or asiento, to trade.

The main effect of this monopoly system was that it made goods scarce and prices high in the Spanish colonies. Because of this everyone apart from the Spanish Government wanted to break the monopoly. Creole Spaniards were willing to disobey the law and trade with foreigners. French and Englishmen were ready to fight for the right to trade with Spanish America. Usually France expected to do best by fighting alongside Spain while Britain was on the other side. The question of trade with the Spanish colonies played a part in all the wars described in this chapter.

France

The richest part of the French Empire was her sugar colonies, especially St Domingue, Martinique and Guadeloupe. Just as the English planters had to send raw sugar to England for refining, so the French planters had to supply French refiners. There was bitter competition between the two countries to supply sugar to the rest of Europe. Success could mean high profits for planters back in the Caribbean, but failure to sell could mean losses and even ruin. Several times in the eighteenth century, English and French planters tried to ruin their rivals with raids which simply aimed to destroy their sugar production by burning the crops and equipment and carrying off the slaves.

France had settlements along the St Lawrence River and in Louisiana. But the number of Frenchmen there was small and most of them lived as hunters and trappers. Because of this the French mainland colonies were of little value as a source of timber, machinery, grain, iron goods and other materials needed as estate supplies on the plantations. Therefore, French planters tried to buy them from the English colonies, especially in New England. In exchange they could offer all their molasses and rum, which they were not allowed to sell in France because they would damage the brandy-making industry there. The New England colonists were willing to trade but the British Government and the English planters saw it as giving aid to the French.

Map 26 *Right. The Americas in 1700.*

Hudson
Bay

Newfoundland

Nova Scotia

New England

Campèche

Sp

Fr   Sp

Sp

Br

Honduras

Fr & Br

Small British Settlements

Porto Bello

Sp

Spanish

French

British

England

England's North American colonies were more valuable than France's. The most important were those in New England where there were no plantations but the settlers grew grain, cut timber, built ships and made some iron goods. Many of these goods were sold as plantation supplies to the British colonies and, despite the French Navigation Acts, to the French islands as well.

Although the mainland colonies were valuable and growing in population, the government in London always favoured the sugar islands. In 1733 Parliament passed the Molasses Act which laid down heavy duties on rum and molasses sold to North America by French planters. This Act had been pressed for by the West Indian planters, although it was easily ignored by the North American traders who simply failed to declare the molasses they imported from the French.

Causes of the wars

There were three conflicts behind the first eighteenth-century wars. One was the struggle between England and France for the right to enter the South American market. The second was the rivalry between French and English planters. The third was the aim of both England and France to gain a firmer control of North America and its trade with the Caribbean islands. All three conflicts played their part in bringing wars, which usually started with some European quarrel, to the Caribbean.

What the Europeans could not usually bring were sufficient ships and men to produce an outstanding victory for either France or England. Losses from disease were so high that it was very expensive to keep regiments in the West Indies. Soldiers feared service here so much that many deserted in France or England before their troop ships set sail. So it rarely made sense to try to capture a rival's island and keep an occupying force there. A quick raid was much less costly in men.

War at sea was generally thought more worthwhile than fighting on land. But here again the difficulties kept the scale fairly small. It was costly to keep fleets in the Caribbean well supplied and repaired, so both England and France had only a few warships here during peacetime. In war they sent larger fleets, but they were more likely to be used to cut off the enemy's trade or supplies than to take part in great battles.

The War of Spanish Succession 1702–13

The war took its name from a European quarrel about who should be ruler of Spain after her king, Charles II, died in 1700. Charles had said that he should be followed by the grandson of Louis XIV, the King of France. This family connection between France and Spain was soon seen to threaten England's position in the Atlantic. In 1701 the new Spanish King granted France the *asiento* to carry slaves to the Spanish colonies. It was also arranged that Spanish fleets crossing the Atlantic would be escorted by French warships. England, however, was not alone in her fears. Both Austria and Holland expected claims to be made by the Spanish on some of their lands. They joined with England in a 'grand alliance' which aimed to replace the French King of Spain by the son of the Emperor of Austria, an ally of England.

In Europe the armies fought a new kind of 'limited' warfare. Regiments dressed in bright uniforms were drilled to move about the battlefield in smart formations. Generals tried to move them into positions which would force the opposing armies to retreat or surrender. But they did not try to seize enemy lands which would be costly to occupy. At sea and in the American empire it was the same story.

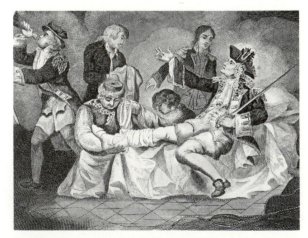

Fig 15.1 *The British Admiral, Benbow, had his leg shattered in the only naval battle in the Caribbean during the Spanish War of Succession. Here he is shown ordering the battle to continue. Benbow later died of his wounds in Jamaica.*

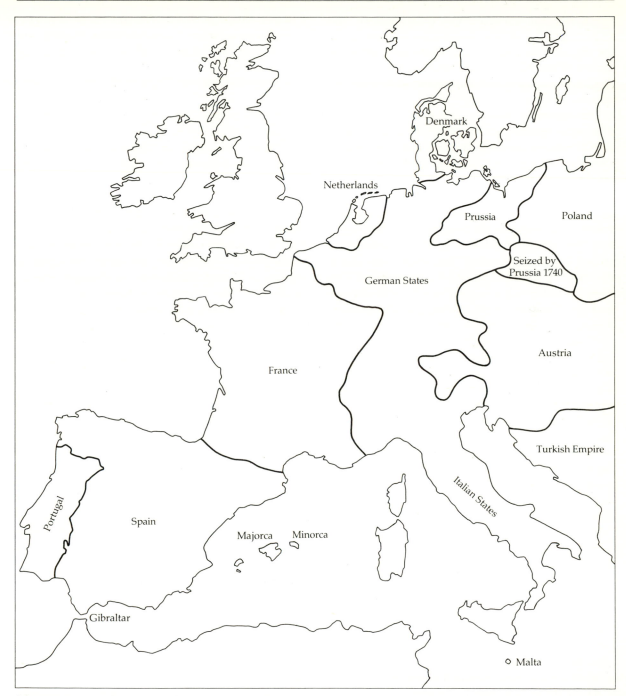

Map 27 *Europe in the first half of the eighteenth century.*

The war in the Caribbean

Each side sent fleets to the Caribbean and soldiers to garrison the main towns. The two main French bases were at Martinique and Guadeloupe, while the

British fleets used Port Royal in Jamaica and English Harbour in Antigua. But there was only one inconclusive naval battle, for the main purpose of these fleets was defensive, to prevent the other side seizing a valuable undefended position. During the hurricane season even the defensive force was withdrawn. The English fleets made for ports in North America and the French sailed home. The most important naval actions in the war were not in the Caribbean but the Mediterranean, where Britain seized Malta and Gibraltar.

This defensive movement of ships and men displeased the planters who hoped for a chance to strike at their rivals' sugar trade. But they had to act on their own without support from their European governments. As soon as news of the outbreak of war reached Barbados, its planters organised a raid against the French settlers in St Kitts, now a British colony. The French were deported to St Domingue and Guadeloupe. Another English expedition then raided Guadeloupe where they burnt cane fields, destroyed mills and carried off many slaves. The French on Martinique replied in 1706 with raids on English plantations in St Kitts, Nevis and Montserrat. A joint attack by the French and Spanish drove the few English settlers from the Bahamas.

The colonists also organised their own naval warfare. Each side gave commissions to captains who would turn privateer and raid the other's merchant ships. These raids led to heavy losses; in the one year of 1703–4 French privateers captured 163 merchant vessels. But none of this private warfare in the Caribbean had any effect on the peace which was signed at Utrecht in Holland in 1713. England and her allies had not been strong enough to alter the Spanish succession, but they had won enough victories to make demands on the French and Spanish.

The Treaty of Utrecht

1 England took away from France her strong trading position in the Spanish Empire. The *asiento* to carry slaves to the Spanish colonies was granted to Britain for thirty years. In addition the British had permission to send one 500 ton (505 tonne) merchant ship with small supply boats known as tenders to the annual trading fair at Porto Bello and the agents of British merchants were to be allowed to live in some Spanish American ports.
2 Britain kept the French part of St Kitts.
3 British naval and trading power was increased in two areas. In the Mediterranean she kept Minorca and Gibraltar which had been seized from Spain. In

North America, France was forced to recognise British ownership of Newfoundland, Nova Scotia and Hudson Bay. All these were a threat to the safety of French Canada.

The uneasy peace 1713–39

The Treaty of Utrecht was followed by twenty-six years of uneasy peace in the Caribbean. English and French planters continued to be bitter rivals for a greater share of the European sugar market. Both sides believed they would never prosper until the other's plantations had been destroyed. But the main trouble came over trade with the Spanish mainland.

The English Government had given the rights of legal trading which it had won at the Treaty of Utrecht to the South Sea Company. Officially only its ships could carry slaves to the Spanish ports and the annual trade ship was also to be sent by the Company. In fact these rights became the cover for widespread smuggling by British merchants. The Company in England was sometimes involved, but more usually it was their agents and captains in the Caribbean who made profits from many forms of smuggling. Ships carrying slaves, allowed under the *asiento*, often unloaded illegal goods as well. While the annual trading ship was anchored off Porto Bello, it was reloaded at night from its tenders. There was an even larger smuggling business carried out by merchants from the British islands, especially Jamaica. They took many goods to the mainland, including poor quality slaves which they sold at cheap rates to Spanish settlers. They also paid visits to Campeche and Honduras where small settlements of Englishmen were cutting logwoods and hardwoods, which fetched good prices from English cloth and furniture makers. The Spanish believed that these foreigners had no right to be on the Central American coast.

The Spanish navy was far too small to deal with the smuggling of the British and the lesser numbers of illegal Dutch and French boats. So the King of Spain ordered Spanish American governors to give commissions to privately-owned ships, known as *guarda-costas*. The crews and captains of guarda-costas were paid from the sale of captured ships and cargo. They were allowed to take any English ship which was carrying a Spanish colonial product such as indigo, cocoa, logwood or Spanish coins. These

Fig 15.2 *The capture of Porto Bello by Admiral Vernon's fleet, 1739.*

goods made poor evidence for smuggling, for the English colonies produced some of them and Spanish coins were in common use throughout the West Indies. Between 1713 and 1727 at least eighty-six English ships were seized and sold with their cargoes in Spanish ports and many of these were undoubtedly not smugglers' vessels.

Despite the loss of so many ships, the English Government tried hard to keep out of the war with Spain. Many supporters would lose the chance of profits from the legal trade if war came. This attitude enraged British merchants both in England and the Caribbean. They wanted war with Spain to force her to open up her American ports to an unlimited number of English traders.

The case for war against Spain was taken up by the opposition party in Parliament. In 1738 they brought Captain Jenkins to the House of Commons where he described how his ear had been cut off by the crew of a guarda-costa which had stopped his ship. He said he had been told to carry the ear, pickled in brandy, back to the English King as a reminder of what would happen to other sailors caught by guarda-costas. As he refused to remove his wig it is very likely that Jenkins' story was made up to swing opinion into support for war. If so it worked, for the government felt it had to give way and declared war on Spain in October 1739.

The War of Jenkins' Ear 1739–44

Most of the fighting was done by the British navy. Early in the war, Admiral Vernon's ships captured Porto Bello and destroyed the fort which guarded it. He then opened the port to all British traders and set his warships to protect English vessels which landed cargoes of slaves and trade goods. For the rest of the time the war was a half-hearted affair. The British sent out forces to attack Cartagena and Santiago de Cuba, but both were too well defended to be taken. The failure did not displease the English colonists, who did not want to lose the good will of Spanish customers by raiding their towns. The French islands were quite another matter; the English planters were impatient for a chance to strike a blow at their rivals. This came when the fighting became part of a new European war in 1744.

The War of Austrian Succession 1739–48

This took its name from a quarrel between the Empress of Austria and the King of Prussia, Frederick the Great. Frederick tried to prevent the Empress keeping control of all the lands left by her father when he died in 1740. In this quarrel about the succession to the throne of Austria, Britain supported Austria and France backed Prussia. As well as fighting England in Europe, France took the Spanish side in the Caribbean war, hoping to win back the trading privileges she had lost in the War of Spanish Succession.

In the Caribbean neither French nor English planters wanted to conquer the other's sugar islands. They feared that new colonies would simply lead to extra sugar production and lower prices on either the French or British markets. It would probably also make estate supplies scarce and push up their prices. On the other hand the planters did want to do as much damage as possible to their rivals. Governor Trelawney wrote to the British Government with the views of Jamaican planters about their French neighbours:

> Unless French Hispaniola (St Domingue) is ruined during the war, they will upon the peace, ruin our sugar colonies by the quantity they make and the low price they can afford to sell it at.

On the French side, Admiral Caylus was ordered to take Barbados, 'not so much . . . in order to keep it as to destroy it and take away the Negroes'.

In fact Caylus did not take Barbados and the British were successful in stopping any raid on their islands. Yet both sides suffered heavy losses to their trade. By the time peace came in 1748 the British navy had captured 1,249 Spanish and 2,185 French ships. The combined Spanish and French navies had taken 3,238 British vessels. But the larger British merchant navy was not hit so hard by the loss of ships as the smaller French and Spanish fleets.

The neutral islands

Most of the Caribbean fighting took place around the 'neutral islands', which had never been claimed by either France or Britain. St Vincent and Dominica were supposed to belong to the Caribs while St Lucia and Tobago were neutral only because they had never been fully settled by Europeans. The islands were more important to the French who used them to collect timber and other estate supplies which the English could buy more easily from the North American colonists. Although there were some English settlers on St Vincent and Dominica there were far more Frenchmen. By 1740 they had bought more than half of Dominica from the Caribs. The English planters did not need the islands but they did not want the French to have them as sugar plantations or naval bases. So the British occupied all four neutral islands during the war but, when the peace came, looked for a way to evacuate them without having them fall into French hands.

The Treaty of Aix-La-Chapelle, 1748

The treaty signed at Aix-La-Chapelle said nothing about the causes of the war. Spain's claim to stop and search British ships and Britain's claim to settle Honduras and Yucatan were both ignored.

1 The British right to the slave *asiento* and to an annual trading ship was recognised, but in fact they sold these privileges back to Spain for £100,000 in a final part of the treaty signed in 1750.
2 Dominica, St Lucia, St Vincent and Tobago were declared neutral islands and the French and English agreed not to colonise them.
3 The only exchange of land in the American territory was Louisburg, which the British handed back to France in return for Madras in India.

Wars for empire

The Treaty of Aix-La-Chapelle did not bring peace to the colonial empires. In the Caribbean things continued as before. The English still smuggled goods into the Spanish Empire and cut logwood in Central America. English planters enjoyed a time of great prosperity; sugar prices were half as high again as

Fig 15.3 *British ships in line of attack firing on Spanish or French vessels off Havana in 1748.*

they were before 1739. But they were still facing great competition from the French islands. The English were angered, too, to find that French settlers did not leave the neutral islands and they objected strongly when, in 1755, the Governor of Martinique claimed St Lucia for France.

Many English were far more concerned about North America, where the French had begun to build a line of forts which threatened from the rear the long thin line of English colonies. While the English population of the islands had not grown much since the beginning of the eighteenth century, numbers on the mainland had risen six or seven times to nearly two million in 1755. So the thirteen English colonies there had become by far Britain's most important overseas market. Their products, especially tobacco and timber, were in great demand in Britain. Englishmen were also eager for war in India, for here again the French had attacked English trading settlements.

The Seven Years War 1756–63

The Seven Years War which broke out in 1756 had its beginnings in this world-wide conflict between the English and French. The French were the first to act by

sending large fleets to their naval stations at Louisburg, Martinique and Guadeloupe; at the same time they captured Minorca in the Mediterranean. Shortly afterwards a general European war broke out, once again because of an invasion by Frederick II of Maria Theresa's lands. This time, however, France supported the Empress of Austria and Britain backed the King of Prussia.

In reply to the French moves, Britain rushed armies to attack the French in Canada. By the end of 1758 they had gained the upper hand and were ready to press on to capture the main French ports and towns in 1759. The British Prime Minister, William Pitt, now turned his attention to the West Indies. This time instructions were given to capture the French sugar islands, not to ruin them but to keep them to bargain with when the time came to make peace. The French were almost powerless. St Bartholomew and Guadeloupe were occupied in 1759. In the same year the British captured the main French slaving station on the African coast at Gorée. In 1761 they seized Dominica. Spain then entered the war in support of France but this did not stop the run of British successes. By May, Martinique, St Lucia, Grenada and St Vincent were taken as well as Havana on Spanish Cuba. Only St Domingue of all the French colonies was unoccupied.

But St Domingue like other French settlements in America, Africa and India was cut off from France by the English navy which had almost complete mastery of the seas. The problem for the English Government was now what kind of peace to make. The planters were keen to hand back Guadeloupe and Martinique. Since their capture their sugar had gone to the English market and caused a serious drop in prices. Other Englishmen were eager to keep at least Martinique as an English naval base. In the end the new Prime Minister, Lord Bute, decided that he wanted peace as quickly as possible and handed back the most valuable islands in return for other French territory. This was done at the Peace of Paris signed in 1763.

Peace of Paris

1 France gave up all claims to colonies in North America except for a few small fishing islands in the St Lawrence River. The vast regions of French Canada passed into British hands.

2 In the Caribbean the British took over French Grenada and the Grenadines and also made themselves masters of three of the neutral islands: Tobago, Dominica and St Vincent. France took over the fourth, St Lucia, and Martinique and Guadeloupe were returned to her.

3 The English handed back Havana to the Spaniards and in return received Florida. The British failed to get the Spaniards to agree to trading rights in Latin America or to hand over Honduras and Yucatan. However, the Spaniards agreed that Englishmen could cut and export wood provided they built no forts in the area.

4 In Africa the English returned Gorée to the French, and in India they allowed France to keep her trading factories provided she kept no troops or built forts there. From this date the British Empire in India grew rapidly.

The later eighteenth century

The first four eighteenth-century wars led to very few changes of ownership of Caribbean colonies, and the fighting had no lasting effect on the French and English plantation societies. In the half century after 1763 three wars were fought which had more profound effects. One result was that Britain became owner of Trinidad, Tobago and the main Dutch Guyanese colonies, but there were also important social consequences. The War of American Independence (1775–1783), which widened into a general war between England and France, weakened the influence and prosperity of the West Indian planter. The two French Wars (1793–1815) marked stages in the development of black freedom. The British abolished their slave trade and the first free Caribbean state, Haiti, was created. So the wars of the later eighteenth century form only part of the story told in the next two chapters.

16 *The West India interest*

In the four wars between 1702 and 1763 Britain had become the ruler of a world-wide empire with lands in India and the Far East as well as the Caribbean and North America. Most people of the time looked on the West Indian planters as the leading figures in the Empire, richer than traders or settlers in any other colony. The basis of their great wealth was the demand for sugar in Europe, which had been growing steadily throughout the eighteenth century. Prices had risen too: from 16s 11¼d in 1733, the price of a hundredweight (fifty kilograms) of sugar had become 38s 6d in 1763.

Plantation profits

What this prosperity meant can be seen from the account books of an Antiguan planter in 1756. His plantation contained 202 hectares and had a labour force of 300 slaves, who produced 200 hogsheads of sugar and 120 puncheons of rum. The land, slaves, building and equipment were valued at £20,000 sterling. For the sugar and rum the planter earned £3,600 and his expenses for the year were £1,900. This left him a profit of £1,700 which equalled 8.5% of the £20,000 invested in the estate. This was the account for a good year. In a bad year when a hurricane struck, or perhaps when French sugar reached Europe at a much lower price, the plantation's sales and profits could fall. At the same time the planter's expenses would be no smaller and so his profit could be cut to a few hundred pounds or nothing at all.

This is why many planters never became wealthy. On the other hand, men who became masters of several plantations could stand a bad year on one of them and still make a profit on the others. In this way a smaller number of planters became very rich. One way of becoming owner of several plantations was to marry the daughter of a planter neighbour who had no sons. But often the most successful planters were those who used their property as security to borrow money which they lent out at higher rates of interest.

Wealthy planters

In the 1740s and 1750s such successful planter-businessmen were among the wealthiest men in the British Empire. They were able to lend money to poorer planters, to newcomers to the Caribbean and to the local governments of the islands. But much of their money was invested in Britain in sugar factories, merchant companies, canals and some of the earliest factories to be built.

Such men turned the flow of wealth to run in the opposite way from the early days of the Caribbean colonies. Then, in the seventeenth century, merchants in Europe put up the money to start sugar plantations. At that time the food, equipment and building supplies coming across the Atlantic from Europe had been worth more than the sugar and other products sent back. Ships had arrived with full cargoes but often returned with only part loads. In the eighteenth century it was the other way round; cargoes to Europe were larger and more valuable than those to the Caribbean. Instead of borrowing money, the wealthiest British planters were lending it to Europe. The sums were vast; it was reckoned in 1775 that nearly £11 million went to the European countries with Caribbean colonies. Another calculation is that in 1773 just over two-thirds of the year's profits for the whole of Jamaica went to Great Britain.

Absentees

Very many of the really wealthy planters used the profits from sugar to become powerful in English society. These were the absentee planters who left their estates in the hands of attorneys and lived in England. Absentees built some of the finest English country houses of the time and were known, from the number

Fig 16.1 *Caribbean trade was so valuable to Britain that a whole section of the London docks was built to receive West Indian goods. This is an eighteenth-century painting.*

of carriages and servants they could afford, to live in grand style. This still left them the wealth to make their way in banking, business or industry and, most important, in politics.

In eighteenth-century England only a few voters and sometimes single landowners could elect a man to the House of Commons. Most Members of Parliament simply bought their seats by bribing the electors or paying the landowner. Here was one use for the profits made in the Caribbean. Between 1730 and 1775, seventy absentee planters became MPs. Antigua alone produced twenty-two MPs, one Lord Mayor of London and nine absentees whose wealth was great enough to buy the title of lord or knight. The Beckford family, whose wealth came from their Jamaican plantations, had three brothers in Parliament at the same time. Two members of the family also became Lord Mayors of London.

The West India interest

These powerful absentees made up the most important part of what was known in Britain as the West India interest. Another part was made up of merchants who traded with the sugar colonies. Finally there were the men appointed by the colonial assemblies to be their agents in England and to press for changes in British law which would benefit the West Indies. The West India interest in Parliament was often successful in seeing that laws were passed to benefit the Caribbean colonies more than other parts of the British Empire or even Britain herself. An example was the Molasses Act of 1733.

Both British and French planters sold molasses to North American colonists in exchange for timber, food and manufactured goods needed on the plantations. The Molasses Act placed higher duties on molasses from the French islands and would have made French molasses more expensive than British. In fact the American importers simply smuggled in French molasses or claimed they had bought them from English plantations, so the Molasses Act made little real difference. The West India interest was soon campaigning for a new law to stop this smuggling.

The West India interest played a part behind the scenes in deciding the terms of the peace treaty with France which followed the British victory in the Seven Years War of 1756–63. An important question was whether England should keep Canada or the sugar islands of Martinique and Guadeloupe. Canada produced little wealth and the islands a great deal. Yet Britain kept Canada and returned the islands. This was a victory for some supporters of the West India interest, led by the Beckford family, who had no wish for sugar from Guadeloupe and Martinique to continue to flow into England. It brought the price down and thus cut the profits that came from their estates on the British islands. This view, in the end, counted for more than the opinion that England would benefit as a sea-power and trading nation from owning all the Caribbean islands.

The same year the West India interest successfully pressed Parliament to pass the Sugar Duties Act, which set up a special force to stop the smuggling of molasses into North America from the French islands. This was bitterly resented by the thirteen colonies who saw that the West India interest had far more power in Britain than supporters of the American case. One American colony objected, saying:

> This Act (concerning Sugar and Molasses) was procured by the interest of the West India planters with no other view than to enrich themselves by obliging the northern Colonies to take their whole supply from them.

At the end of the Seven Years War the West India interest seemed at the height of its power, but this was just the time when planters began to see signs that the golden age of sugar could soon end. The plantation system on most British islands was a hundred years old and many weaknesses were beginning to show up.

Weaknesses in the plantation system

Most planters earned their living from a single crop.

In a year when the profits from sugar were small they could not turn to another product to make up the gap in their income. As the plantations grew older the expenses of running them rose. Buildings had to be repaired and renewed. The first fields were often exhausted from a hundred years' cropping, and planters were faced with the cost of clearing the more difficult, hilly ground.

The slave system, too, no longer seemed so cheap. Every year the number of disabled and old slaves grew. Although they produced very little they had to be fed, clothed and housed. Thousands of pounds had to be spent on buying new slaves to replace them in the fields and mills. Yet few planters thought of switching to cheaper, labour-saving devices such as harrows and ploughs. Most believed that the slaves had to be burdened with heavy work for the sake of order, even if this meant raising the price of sugar to cover the increasing costs.

Planters who became absentees and lived in England added to the costs of the estates. Attorneys and managers had to be paid in the Caribbean. Very little of the profits earned by an absentee's plantations stayed in the colony. Few absentees showed any interest in improving the conditions of life in the islands. During the colonial period hardly any public roads, schools or hospitals were built. Unlike the North American colonies, the West Indian islands became places for Englishmen to come, make money and leave. Those who stayed permanently in the Caribbean and kept few connections with England were generally the less wealthy planters.

French competition

As the English planters were facing these difficulties the French sugar islands were just entering their time of greatest prosperity. The French colonies were larger; St Domingue was greater in area than all six British islands combined. French planters paid only a 1% export duty compared with the 4½% paid by their English rivals. Most of the costs of local government on the French islands were paid by France; the British planters had to pay for them with local taxation.

The French even profited from their losses in the Seven Years War. All the sugar islands, except St Domingue, had been seized by Britain but this did more good than harm to the plantations. They were allowed to sell their sugar on the English market and to import cheap British supplies and slaves. After the war they benefited from the fact that France had lost most of her other overseas territories in Canada, Louisiana and India. This meant that France had the money, ships and men to develop her West Indian colonies. The cost of shipping and insurance fell, bankers were eager to lend money to planters at low rates and merchants sold them estate supplies at lower prices. Unemployed soldiers found work in the Caribbean building roads, irrigation systems, bridges and water mills. Over 40,000 hectares were artificially irrigated in St Domingue.

Fall in prices

After the Seven Years War the French were always able to export more sugar than the English and sell it at a lower price. The result was that refiners in France could sell sugar to almost any European country while the high price of English colonial sugar meant that English refiners could not find markets outside Britain. To meet this French challenge the British planters increased production in the years after the Seven Years War, especially in Grenada and the neutral islands. In Grenada the slave population rose from 12,000 before the war to 30,000 in 1776. Tobago had been almost deserted in 1763; only seven years later the island held 3,093 slaves and 238 whites, who had mostly come from the overcrowded Leewards. Nearly all of them borrowed the money to pay for clearing the fields and buy their first slaves and supplies. Production in Jamaica and the Leewards was also increased by clearing cane fields in areas which earlier had not been thought worth the expense. These planters too had to borrow the money.

It was soon obvious that the extra production would not save the planters. Sugar piled up on the English market and brought prices down, but the fall was not enough to undercut the French. But it was enough to ruin many English planters who found that the average price of 38s 6d per hundredweight (fifty kilograms) in 1763 had fallen to 35s between 1771 and 1775. The 3s fall was a serious blow to planters who had borrowed money. In 1770 they owed between them £16m. (Compare this with total value of a year's sugar from Jamaica, which was about £1m). The bankers and businessmen who had lent the money were quick to see that they might do better lending to planters and traders in the new parts of the British Empire in Canada, Africa and India. The result was that interest rates rose sharply, especially in 1772, when many planters handed over their properties to creditors.

Decline of the West India interest

The planters could see only one way out of their difficulties. That was to change from trying to increase the amount of sugar to actually reducing it. They hoped to create a scarcity in England which would force up the price. At the same time they could cut the costs of running their plantations by buying fewer slaves and supplies from England. Both actions annoyed the men who had been their business partners and supporters in Britain.

Grocers, refiners and distillers in Britain were already alarmed at losing their customers in Europe to the French. Now they found planters trying to make sugar too expensive for the average Englishman. Slave dealers and manufacturers of textiles, hardware and other estate supplies complained of lost trade in the West Indies. Many such businessmen in England began to ask whether the Navigation Acts were still necessary. Only the planters benefited from laws which kept cheap French sugar out of Britain and closed the French islands to British manufacturers and traders.

The West India interest in England tried hard to answer these complaints against the planters. Absentee planters set up a number of societies to put their point of view. The two largest were the Society of West Indian Merchants and the Society of West Indian Planters and Merchants in London. They published pamphlets, arranged speaking tours and sent members to lobby MPs who might support them. But their activities probably did more harm than good. Many of the English landed gentry which had then the most powerful voice in Parliament objected to the West Indian 'upstarts', and the way they used their money to buy a block of seats in the House of Commons.

The Campbell decision

A setback to the planters' efforts to gain support in England came with the Campbell decision in 1774.

Fig 16.2 *A nineteenth-century cartoon showing a wealthy plantation owner of the eighteenth century.*

Alexander Campbell, a planter from Grenada, asked an English court to declare that the government had no right to place a 4½% duty on goods exported from Grenada and the neutral islands. His reason was that the rate of tax had been laid down in the government's order, issued in the name of the king, which gave these islands the right to elect assemblies. Alexander Campbell argued that it was unjust to set up assemblies which had the power to decide on taxes and then tell them what amount they must collect.

The Chief Justice, Lord Mansfield, agreed with Campbell, and he ordered that the collection of the 4½% duty in Grenada and in the neutral islands should be stopped.

The Campbell decision angered many members of the English Parliament. It appeared that the planters were refusing to pay their share of the cost of defending the British Empire; yet they took full advantage of a protected market to get high prices for their sugar. From this time on it was much harder for the West India interest to get support.

17 The decline of sugar

Trade with North America

Between about 1700 and 1775 there was a close link between the British colonies on the mainland of America and the sugar islands in the Caribbean. Both had similar forms of local government with governors, councils and elected assemblies, but their closest connection was through trade. The mainland colonists made their living in a wide variety of ways, as timber cutters, farmers, manufacturers, shipbuilders, merchants and traders. A large part of the goods they produced were sold as estate supplies to the sugar plantations in the Caribbean.

The key to the trade was the huge quantities of molasses which were left after the cane had been milled for export to Europe. In Barbados and Antigua some planters distilled the molasses into rum but on most plantations it was simply stored in large tanks. Merchant ships from the mainland toured the islands, calling in at plantations and filling hogsheads with molasses from the tank. The ships usually carried coopers to make the hogsheads out of staves and to seal them after filling. With the credit they earned by selling the molasses, planters bought the goods they needed for their estates. In 1771, just two of the North American ports exported these goods to the West Indies:

New York		Boston	
Tallow		Whalefat	
Candles:	64,500 lbs (29,200 kg)	Candles:	55,710 lbs (25,230 kg)
Lard:	44,140 lbs (20,900 kg)	Bricks:	341,800
Corn:	63,319 bushels	Shook	
		Hogsheads: 12,539	
Sugar:	4,362 lbs (1,975 kg)	Hoops	
		for hogs-	
		heads:	513,580
Bread and		Dried fish:	57,472 quinals
flour:	3,250 tons	Pickled	
	(3,302,000 kg)	fish:	8,386 barrels
Butter:	35,100 lbs (15,400 kg)		

In the same year New York imported over two million litres of molasses and Boston about a million. Much of this was turned into rum and sold either throughout the American colonies or exported to England. Apart from Boston and New York there were about a dozen other important American ports from which traders set out for the Caribbean. Some of them specialised in goods such as livestock or timber, although all supplied some items of food. No-one knows just how much of the trade was with British islands and how much with those of the French. However, the French planters imported their wine, cooking oil and nearly all their flour from France itself, while the British were much more dependent on the North American colonies. As we saw in Chapter 16, it was common for ships to go to the Caribbean from England only partly loaded.

However, most planters believed that the growing success of the French islands in producing sugar in greater quantities and more cheaply than the British owed much to the fact that they, too, could buy North American supplies in exchange for molasses. This is why the planters, and the West India interest in Britain, supported the Molasses Act, 1733, and the Sugar Duties Act, 1763, which tried to damage the French trade with North America by placing high duties on French molasses. Yet, when the American colonists quarrelled with the British Government over other matters, the Caribbean planters gave them their support.

Support from the Caribbean assemblies

After the Seven Years War the British Government tried to make the Americans pay a share of the costs of defeating the French. The colonists refused to pay, saying that their assemblies alone had the right to demand new taxes. This was a point on which the Caribbean assemblies agreed with the Americans and backed their objections to the taxes.

In 1767 the stamp tax was replaced by the

Fig 17.1 *American colonists burning paper carrying the tax stamp.*

Townshend Duties on all lead, paint, paper and tea imported into the colonies. Again the colonists objected. There were riots against the duties and the British Government withdrew them all except the one on tea. The protests continued and when the British East India Company tried to unload tea at Boston the citizens dumped the cargo into the harbour. These protests were again supported in the West Indies where there were riots against the Stamp Act. In St Kitts and Nevis the rioters destroyed £2,000 worth of stamped paper.

Both Americans and West Indians were alarmed when Parliament passed the Quebec Act in 1774. This made Canada into a separate British colony but without its own elected assembly. Alarmed by the rebelliousness of her other New World colonies, the British Government had decided that Canada would be ruled directly from Britain. In the same year the British Government decided to punish the people of Boston by ruling their colony of Massachusetts directly. Again the Caribbean colonists gave their support to the Americans; the Assemblies of Barbados and Jamaica sent official protests to the English King.

The assemblies change sides

But in 1775 the British Government sent an army to the mainland to force the Americans to obey the regulations. The colonists decided to fight for independence. This move brought about a change of opinion in the Caribbean colonies. Although many West Indians had family or trading connections with the Americans, more had closer connections with England. The planters also feared to lose their special position within the British Empire. Their prosperity, based on sugar, would collapse if rebellion kept them out of the protected market in Britain. Many depended on loans from British banks and merchants for the year by year running of their plantations.

The island colonists also faced the unpleasant fact that their white population was much smaller than the mainland's. They felt they needed British soldiers and warships to protect them from foreign invasions and from their slaves. So, instead of protests, the island assemblies rushed to send petitions to England, stating their loyalty. The Jamaican Assembly's petition made their reasons clear:

> Weak and feeble as this colony is from its very small number of white inhabitants, and its peculiar situation from the encumbrance of more than two hundred thousand slaves, it cannot be supposed that we now intend, or ever could have intended, resistance to Britain.

The petition must have surprised West Indian governors who had struggled to get the Jamaican Assembly to agree to taxes or naval officers who had tried to force planters to obey the Navigation Acts. But the message was clear. The planters and the West India interest were forced to admit that they needed the protection of the British army and navy. Yet the islands paid a heavy price for their loyalty during eight years of war that followed.

The War of American Independence 1775–83

The British navy soon found itself hard-pressed. France and Spain both joined the war on the side of the Americans in 1778, and two years later Holland sent ships to help the rebels. Several other European nations objected to British attempts to stop and search all ships which might be carrying arms to the Americans. They signed an agreement of 'armed neutrality' to fight back when ordered to stop by the British.

In the Caribbean these enemy forces were joined by American privateers who attacked British shipping from bases in the Dutch, Danish and French islands. Their activities caused great hardship to the British islands. In the first year of the war the quantity of sugar shipped to Europe fell by a half. Estate supplies, which had come mostly from North America, quickly became scarce and their prices rose. The cost of grain is said to have risen by 400% by the end of 1777. Insurance rates on British ships in the Caribbean rose from 7% of their cargo's value to over 20%. The cost of shipping rose still further after France joined the war, for it became safe only to travel in convoys which meant costly delays while ships waited in harbours.

Planters tried to grow local provisions to replace those which fell into the hands of the enemy, but most of the crops failed after a series of hurricanes ripped through the islands in 1780 and 1781. In the Leewards there were long droughts in the periods between the hurricanes.

Several islands were captured in the war. Dominica was taken by the French in 1778. The British replied by taking St Lucia in the same year, but in 1779 they could not stop the French capture of St Vincent and Grenada. In 1780 Sir George Rodney was put in charge of British operations in the Caribbean. He had quick successes against the Dutch, capturing their poorly defended island colonies and their Guyana settlements. Then, in 1782, the Americans won their greatest success of the war on the mainland when the British army under General Cornwallis surrendered at Yorktown. Britain was now powerless in North America, and both the Spanish and French fleets left their patrolling of the coast to open full-scale war in the Caribbean.

The French fleet quickly retook St Eustatius and the Guyana colonies, following this with the capture of Tobago in 1781 and St Kitts, Nevis and Montserrat in 1782. Meanwhile the Spanish had taken Florida and some of the Bahamas. The two allies were then ready for a joint expedition to capture Jamaica. The island was saved by Rodney, who caught up with the joint fleet as it passed by the Saintes islands between Dominica and Guadeloupe. Only seven of the Spanish-French ships were taken, but the rest of the invasion fleet was scattered. The Battle of The Saintes saved the West Indies from further attack and while the French were re-organising their fleet, Britain

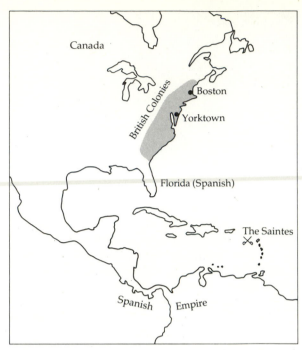

Map 28 *North America and the Caribbean at the time of the War of American Independence.*

signed a truce with the Americans in November 1782. In the following year, a general peace treaty was signed by all who had taken part in the war.

The Treaty of Versailles, 1783

The treaty recognised the independence of the thirteen colonies which became known as the United States of America. In the Caribbean, all the territories were returned to their pre-war owners except that France kept Tobago and gave St Bartholomew to Sweden in return for an agreement that French ships could trade in Swedish ports.

After the war

The end of the war brought no end to the hardship and suffering. Britain refused to allow planters to buy supplies from the Americans even when they were needed to save lives. It was estimated that 15,000 slaves died in Jamaica between 1784 and 1787 'of famine or of disease contracted by scanty and unwholesome diet'. Some planters tried to trade illegally with the Americans and the British navy was sent to prevent this smuggling. Horatio Nelson, then a young naval officer, came to dislike the West Indian smugglers, calling them 'vagabonds' and 'as great rebels as the Americans'. In place of trade with the Americans, British officials encouraged Caribbean planters to buy from English colonists in Canada or from merchants in England. Estate supplies from both places were more expensive because of the greater distances.

In the end the British Government slowly changed the orders against trade with the Americans. They first allowed British ships to stop and load supplies in American ports. Then, in 1794, American vessels were allowed to bring supplies direct to British ports in the Caribbean and elsewhere. But although Americans did return to trading, many of them had already found better markets in the French and Spanish islands where sugar production was growing. The cheap American estate supplies were now helping the competitors of the English sugar planters.

Attempts to reorganise

Before the war had ended the assemblies on all the island colonies set up committees to find solutions to their great difficulties. The committees recommended that costs might be cut if the islands produced their own estate supplies. Planters and small farmers were encouraged to raise cattle to supply beef and working animals for the plantations. In Jamaica and Antigua unused salt pans were opened so that local turtle and fish could be salted. New food crops were planted. Ackee trees were brought from West Africa in 1778; mangoes arrived by accident in 1782 when a French ship carrying trees from Mauritius was captured by a British frigate. Captain Bligh's ship brought the first breadfruit trees from Tahiti in 1793. Funds were set aside to open botanical gardens where the plants could be grown and then passed on to planters.

The committees also suggested ways of setting the colonies free from the risks of depending on one crop. Cinammon, clove, nutmeg and black pepper trees

Fig 17.2 *Botanical gardens at Castleton, Jamaica.*

were planted. New coffee plantations were opened in Jamaica, and in Barbados several planters grew cotton in part of their cane fields. To increase the profits from sugar some owners tried new varieties of canes, such as the Bourbon and Otaheita, which were richer in sucrose. Cash prizes were offered for anyone who could improve the recovery of sugar from the boiling and curing processes.

The attempts at reform had very little success. The eastern islands had little room for large-scale cattle raising. Slaves everywhere did not welcome the new foods, but insisted on their usual rations of wheat or corn flour and salted cod. The breadfruit was thought of as fit only for pigs until after emancipation.

It was found that the spice crops could not compete with cheaper spices which the British and Dutch took to Europe from the Far East. Only nutmeg became an important cash crop for Grenada. Jamaican coffee was successful, but only until large-scale plantations were opened in Brazil and Central America. For a while it seemed that cotton might be a profitable alternative to sugar. By 1790 the islands were supplying about 70 per cent of all cotton imported into Britain, but then the demand for West Indian cotton declined sharply when English manufacturers began to import cheaper cotton from the southern United States. The improvements in sugar production were just as dis-appointing; the yields went up but the extra income was taken up by the cost of dearer estate supplies and the high interest repayments on loans. Besides, the extra sugar continued to push down prices in England.

The decline of sugar

By the end of the eighteenth century the British Caribbean colonies were in a desperate position. The golden age of sugar had come to an end and the West Indies had lost their pride of place as the most favoured part of the British Empire. Yet this very decline made possible the next stage in the development of the English-speaking Caribbean. The West India interest could put up only a weak fight against the growing campaign for emancipation. When emancipation did come in the nineteenth century, it would be necessary to count the cost of a century in which all chances of social and economic improvement had been neglected unless they contributed to the profits of the plantocracy. But, before that stage in the story of the British colonies was reached, there first took place the revolt of the black people of St Domingue against French domination on their island.

18   The Haitian revolution

The French colonies in 1789

The French islands, like the British, were shaped most of all by the sugar plantations. Yet there were some differences. One was that sugar and slavery had developed a little later than in the British islands and in 1789 was still profitable. Slaves were still being shipped to the Caribbean in large numbers; in some years as many as 40,000 were taken to St Domingue. Many of the French plantations were large, and large estates with many new slaves to be 'broken in' meant that conditions for Africans were harsher than on the British islands.

The main wealth of the French islands was in the hands of its plantocracy, which had many absentees like the British. Yet the French planters had less control over the government of their islands. There were no assemblies until 1787, and then they were set up with the power only to advise, not to make laws. On the British islands the few colonial officials were often resisted by the settlers; in the French colonies there were many royal officials to enforce the countless regulations made in France. They were in endless disagreement with the planters who continually pressed for the right to govern themselves. Sometimes the officials had the support of the poor whites, or *petits blancs*, the shopkeepers and craftsmen who made up a much larger group than on the British islands.

Many of the free people of colour on the French islands were far wealthier than those in the British colonies. French laws allowed them to own unlimited amounts of property and a large number actually became masters of plantations and slaves. Yet, however wealthy, the French free coloured resented the fact that they were denied equality with whites. They were not allowed to join the colonial militias, wear European dress, play European games or meet together for feasts or wedding celebrations. Nor could they use the European titles of Monsieur and Madame.

Each group on the French islands felt the others to be its enemy. The planters hated the officials, despised the poor whites, distrusted the growing wealth of coloureds and feared the slaves. The coloureds and poor whites wanted the privileges of the planters. The slaves, especially on St Domingue, had revolted several times and were ready to do so again. This was the uneasy situation when revolution broke out in France in 1789.

The French Revolution

The background to the French Revolution lay in the sharp social divisions of the country. The noble families and the leaders of the Church, which was extremely powerful and wealthy, had many privileges, paid no taxes and yet often gave little service to the state. Their wealth and privileges were resented by the millions of French peasants and by middle-class lawyers, officials and merchants. When the French Government became bankrupt an ancient form of parliament, known as the 'Estates-General', was called in 1789, its first meeting for 175 years. At the meeting, the middle-class leaders demanded changes in the government of the country and the

Fig 18.1 *On 14 July 1789 the people of Paris broke into the Bastille, a tower which was said to be used by the king as a gaol for political prisoners.*

abolition of the privileges of the nobility and Church. The King gave way and the revolutionary members of the Estates-General turned themselves into a National Assembly, the real rulers of France.

By 1791 the King and Queen were prisoners, many noblemen had fled the country, the city of Paris was in revolutionary hands and the Church's lands and other properties had been seized. The National Assembly issued the Declaration of Rights of Man which stated that 'men are born free and equal in rights'. The watchwords of France's new revolutionary leaders were 'Liberty! Equality! and Fraternity (or brotherhood)!'

The French wars

To many people in Europe the idea of Liberty, Equality and Fraternity brought hope of a better and more just life; to blacks and coloureds in America it gave the hope of freedom. But the kings and ruling families of other European countries feared the spread of revolution to their lands. In 1792 war broke out between France and her European neighbours and these 'Revolutionary Wars' lasted until 1802.

For the first period of the wars the most important French revolutionary leaders were the Jacobins. Led by Robespierre, the Jacobins were fanatical in trying to build a new society based on Liberty, Equality and Fraternity. At the same time they had their rivals executed at the guillotine in what their enemies called a 'reign of terror'. Eventually other French leaders sickened of this and overthrew the Jacobins. Power then passed step by step into the hands of the French army, and especially to one of its most successful generals, Napoleon Bonaparte.

In 1799, Napoleon Bonaparte seized control of the government of France and until 1814 he was the sole ruler of France, first as consul then as Emperor. At the beginning of his rule he needed time to strengthen his position at home so, after defeating most of his enemies, he made peace with them in 1801 and 1802. War broke out again in 1803 and the 'Napoleonic Wars' continued until 1814. In that year, and again in 1815, Napoleon was defeated in battle and his Empire came to an end. The events which took place in Europe between 1789 and 1814 had a profound influence upon the Caribbean region in general, and upon the French Caribbean islands in particular.

The planters revolt

In the Caribbean the planters were the first to revolt. The governors of St Domingue and the other French islands ordered them not to send representatives to the Estates-General. But the planters disobeyed and sent six delegates to the meeting in Paris. In the Estates-General they demanded that the colonial assemblies set up in 1787 be granted the power to make laws like those in the British islands. The royal government refused to listen to this request and the planters joined with other members of the Estates-General who took part in the overthrow of the French Government. They became members of the new governing body of France, the National Assembly. On 2 March 1790, the National Assembly granted the West Indian assemblies the right to make their own laws.

The coloured revolt on St Domingue

The planters had scored a victory over the old royal government of France and its officials in the Caribbean. But the free coloureds feared that the planters would use their new powers to pass even more repressive racist laws. They began to organise their own protection. In Paris they were helped by an abolitionist society, *Les Amis des Noirs* – the Friends of Black People. Members of Les Amis des Noirs argued that the revolutionary slogans of Liberty, Equality and Fraternity should apply to black just as much as white men. But, in 1790, the National Assembly was not prepared to listen to this plea. A young coloured living in Paris, Vincent Ogé, petitioned members of the National Assembly asking them to grant free coloureds the right to be represented in the colonial assemblies. This was refused and Ogé left France to lead a coloured revolt against the planters in St Domingue. He stopped first in England where he was given help and money by the abolitionist, Thomas Clarkson. From England he sailed to the USA where he bought guns and ammunition, which he unloaded on the north coast of St Domingue in October 1790. He appointed his two brothers and a friend, Marc Chavannes, as his chief lieutenants. But the free coloureds in St Domingue were not yet ready to fight for their rights and only a few joined the young revolutionaries. A planter militia was hastily called together and succeeded in defeating the small band

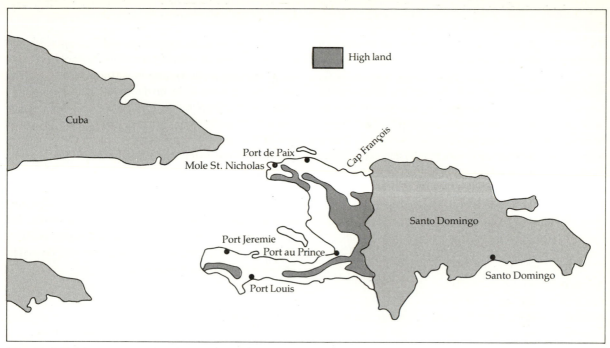

Map 29 *St Domingue.*

with very little difficulty. Ogé and Chavannes were captured and brutally executed.

The slaves are armed

News of the executions weakened support for the planters in the National Assembly. The French members were shocked at the cruel deaths of men who had fought for the cause of Liberty, Equality and Fraternity. Les Amis des Noirs again asked for free coloureds to be given the right to join the island assemblies. On 15 May 1791 the National Assembly agreed to a law allowing 'persons of colour, born of free parents' to have the right to vote for members of the colonial assemblies. Unfortunately they left it up to the planter-controlled assemblies to put the law into effect. The planters refused, even though only the wealthiest coloureds would have qualified, and instead talked about leaving the French Empire and joining the British. In desperation the coloureds on St Domingue began to form their own militias and arm their slaves. The planters did likewise. These were dangerous steps to take as it was unlikely that slaves would fight for planter or coloured masters in a war

which would bring them nothing. The petits blancs supported neither side: they would gain nothing from a planter victory and did not wish to see the coloureds gain equality with whites. Instead, they followed the example of Parisian workers and formed their own separate revolutionary councils.

The slave revolt on St Domingue

The threat of slave revolt had always been greater on St Domingue than most other colonies. Most of the slaves were African-born. They remembered freedom and saw slavery as temporary. The colony was large and mountainous with many deep valleys which were hiding places for escaped slaves who joined together in maroon gangs. The slaves on the plantations were linked by the spread of the Voodoo religion based on mingling the worship of Catholic saints and the Voduns, or gods, recognised by the people of Dahomey in West Africa. Voodoism already had its own priests who met regularly to pass on news from one plantation to another. News of the French revolution and the disputes between planters and coloureds were talked over eagerly at Voodoo meetings.

Mackandal

The St Domingue slaves also shared a number of common myths and heroes. Among the most popular was the story of François Mackandal who, in 1757, devised a plan to destroy the whites by dumping arsenic in their water supplies. At the last minute he was betrayed by the jealous husband of his lover. Mackandal was chained and burned alive, but a legend grew among the slaves that he had escaped the flames by changing into a mosquito and flying away. Many believed he would return to lead them to freedom. (Both the English and French later discovered that the mosquito was indeed their most deadly enemy in St Domingue.)

Boukman

In 1790 and early 1791 Boukman, a creole slave who had been born in Jamaica, was quietly moving from plantation to plantation in the rich northern plain of St Domingue. At each place he explained his simple plan: all slaves should stop work until the planters agreed to pay them wages as free workers. Boukman was supported by other slave leaders such as Gilles, Jean Baptiste and a Maroon leader, Jean François. Eventually the plan was put into operation.

The strike started quietly on 22 August on the Turpin plantation. Boukman led the slaves down the road gathering support from the Flaville, Clement and Termes plantations. The strike then broke into violence. On the Noe plantation the slaves hacked to death an unpopular refiner's apprentice and set the cane fields on fire. Within two weeks the whole plain was a smoking ruin. Only a few whites escaped with their lives. They barricaded themselves in the capital of the area at Cap François and, desperately needing assistance, they waited for help to come from the southern and western provinces.

No help came. The masters were too busy quarrelling. In the west the coloured leader, Rigaud, had fought and defeated a planter army. In the south planters began to arm their slaves who were still loyal for war against the coloureds. The petits blancs had no love for either side; to protect themselves they revolted in the capital, Port au Prince, and set up a revolutionary council. Two-thirds of the city had been burned to the ground.

France supports the slaves

Not one of the warring groups had enough arms or trained troops to defeat the others completely. For more than a year the looting, burning and killing went on. The planters held on to their strongholds and called on the French Government to send an army to restore order. But the National Assembly had come under the control of politicians who had little sympathy for the planters and their slave system. Besides they were facing a war in Europe and could hardly spare troops and arms for St Domingue. When an army was finally sent in September 1792, its commander, Sonthonax, was a supporter of the Jacobins, the group which most strongly believed that 'Liberty, Equality and Fraternity' should apply to all, not just to the more prosperous whites.

Emancipation

Sonthonax refused to help the planters unless they first agreed to allow the coloureds places in their assembly. When they refused he offered his support to the coloureds; but they would not accept his demand that there should be no reprisals against the rebellious slaves. Finally he decided that order would come to the colony only if his forces had the support of the slaves. In August 1793 he granted emancipation to the slaves of St Domingue. It was a year later before the French Government made the emancipation legal, but by then it had had a deep effect on St Domingue. Sonthonax's emancipation decree had united the planters and coloureds against him, but it had won him the support of many slave generals.

The British

In February 1793 England had gone to war with revolutionary France. One of her reasons had been alarm at the execution of the French King and the fear that the revolutionary movement would spread to other European countries. The emancipation of the slaves on St Domingue made them fearful, too, about the spread of black freedom movements across the Caribbean. So it was decided to send troops to the French islands, where they could join forces with the planters. If successful they would both put an end to slave emancipation and destroy the power of revolutionary France's forces in the Caribbean. In 1794 landings were made on St Domingue, Martinique, Guadeloupe and St Lucia. The most successful was on Martinique where the French planters willingly helped the British to take over the island. The same happened on Guadeloupe and St Lucia but then the Jacobin government in France sent a commissioner and an armed fleet. He turned the tables on the British and French planters by announcing emancipation, and he was then able to recapture the islands with black support.

St Domingue

The British hopes for success in St Domingue were high. The French planters had sent messages to Jamaica in which they agreed to surrender the colony to the British for as long as the war lasted. The British also had the support of the Spanish who ruled the eastern half of the island, known as Santo Domingo. They, too, feared the results of slave emancipation.

In September 1793 a force of 900 British soldiers left Jamaica and landed at Port Jeremie on the south-west of St Domingue. At the same time Spanish troops crossed the border from the east. The invasion had one effect which had not been expected. The free coloureds were quick to join the side of Sonthonax and the ex-slaves. They feared that a British victory would lead to the introduction of the laws that restricted the freedom of the coloureds in the British colonies.

Despite this, the British and Spanish troops were very successful for the first few months. The French planters greeted them as allies. By March the whole southern province was in British hands and they were making plans to move north to help the Spaniards. But further successes depended on more troops being sent from Jamaica, and in 1795 no reinforcements came. The reason was a Maroon revolt in Jamaica. The British commander there needed every soldier on the island to put down the rising and hunt for the French agents who were thought to have landed to encourage the Maroons. New recruits for St Domingue were sent from England but they were not seasoned for the Caribbean; they quickly died in thousands from yellow fever. In the same year the British lost their allies when Spain made peace with France and handed over

Fig 18.2 *Toussaint L'Ouverture.*

Santo Domingo to her. The British invasion might yet have succeeded but for the new commander of the black armies, Toussaint L'Ouverture.

Toussaint L'Ouverture

Toussaint was born a slave on the Breda plantation in the northern plain. Before the revolution he had a privileged position as steward of the livestock. When Boukman, Jean Baptiste and the other slave generals had started the revolt in 1791 Toussaint had held back. He was then forty-five and had his wife and two young sons to think about. When he did join, it was not as a soldier but as a physician in Jean Baptiste's regiment. But before long he had proved himself to be a very able army commander because of his excellent horsemanship and ability to lead men. He quarrelled with Jean Baptiste and led part of the regiment away to fight as a paid band with the Spanish army in Santo Domingo. Then came the news of the British and Spanish plan to invade St Domingue and bring back slavery. Toussaint took his regiment back to fight with Sonthonax's forces. His real aim was to make St Domingue safe not for the French but for ex-slaves.

Toussaint defeats the French and British

By 1797 Toussaint had risen to be commander of the united French revolutionary and black army which was made up of 20,000 armed men. He then began to suspect that the government in France was weakening in its support for the cause of freeing the slaves. So Toussaint ordered Sonthanax and his soldiers to leave St Domingue. He was now in sole charge of the fight for black freedom.

In just a year Toussaint's armies completed the defeat of the British. By October 1798 the enemy could hold no more than a tiny stronghold at Mole St Nicholas. The British then withdrew to Jamaica.

The coloured war

Toussaint now turned against the coloureds. The coloured commanders, Rigaud and Alexander Pétion, had no love for the ex-slaves. They wanted to set up their own coloured republic in the south of St Domingue. Toussaint immediately sent two of his generals, Jacques Dessalines and Henri Christophe, to crush this move to divide St Domingue. In a brutal campaign Dessalines' forces massacred over 10,000 coloureds. Rigaud and Pétion fled to France.

Santo Domingo captured

The coloured defeat left Toussaint as master of St Domingue. In 1799 the French Government reluctantly recognised this and made him governor-general. Two years later Toussaint invaded and conquered the once Spanish Santo Domingo.

The independent colony

But France was now ruled by Napoleon Bonaparte who intended to restore slavery in St Domingue and hand the plantations back to their French owners. Toussaint knew that it would not be long before Napoleon sent a strong force to the Caribbean. Before that day he had to make his position as strong as possible. He had a constitution drawn up for the island declaring it to be self-governing. Most of the power was in his own hands and he shortly had himself declared governor for life. Yet he also tried not to offend France too greatly, so the constitution described St Domingue as an 'independent colony of France'.

More important than the constitution were Toussaint's efforts to build up the prosperity of the island. Only if they could grow crops for export could the ex-slaves buy the guns and ammunition they would need when the day came to fight to keep their freedom. So Toussaint ordered his followers back to the plantations and insisted that they worked long hard hours in return for a quarter of all they grew. At the same time he persuaded many of the planters to return, knowing that they had the skill needed to manage sugar production. It was also meant as a sign that the new government of St Domingue wanted the goodwill of her neighbours, especially the United States. President Adams had already helped with arms and supplies needed to defeat the British. He now agreed to a trading treaty with Toussaint's new state.

The French return

The invasion Toussaint feared came in January 1803. It was ordered by Napoleon as a first step in his 'American Scheme' to rebuild a French Empire in the Americas. He sent his brother-in-law, General Leclerc, with secret orders to remove Toussaint and then restore slavery and the old plantation system. France would then have a base for the reconquest of the other sugar islands; she had just taken Louisiana from the Spanish and this was intended as a new source of estate supplies.

Leclerc's force had fifty-four ships and 23,000 troops. He landed at Cap François in January 1803 and quickly occupied most of the larger towns including Santo Domingo and Port au Prince. But he found it impossible to defeat the main ex-slave armies which moved swiftly from one mountain stronghold to the next. When the April rains came to slow down the fighting, Leclerc had already lost 5,000 men killed and another 5,000 in hospital. But he eventually succeeded by deceit. He kept his orders to re-introduce slavery secret and negotiated with Toussaint's generals. Dessalines and Christophe both agreed to accept a pardon, provided that they were given good pensions. Leclerc allowed them to keep command of their troops which were made part of the French army. Disheartened by his generals' actions Toussaint himself negotiated. Leclerc promised that his soldiers would not be disbanded, and Toussaint agreed to give up his leadership and retire to the plantation where he had been born.

Toussaint exiled

Leclerc dare not carry out Napoleon's orders to re-introduce slavery while Toussaint remained on the island for fear that he would once again lead the people against the French. Christophe and Dessalines made it clear they no longer supported Toussaint, so Leclerc felt safe in removing him by trickery. He invited Toussaint to his camp with the greeting, 'You will not find a more sincere friend than myself'. But Toussaint was arrested and shipped off to France where he was imprisoned in the icy Fort de Joux high in the mountains near the Swiss border. He died in solitary confinement late in 1803. His body was buried in the basement of the castle's chapel. In the late nineteenth century the chapel and graves were destroyed to make way for a new wall.

Revolt of the generals

The arrest of Toussaint did not help Leclerc. As the news spread, groups of ex-slaves formed armed bands in the hills. The only thing which stopped them breaking out into general revolt was the fact that Christophe and Dessalines remained loyal to Leclerc. But this lasted only as long as Napoleon's orders to restore slavery remained secret.

Just a few weeks after Toussaint was seized, some slaves escaped from a ship in Le Cap harbour and swam ashore to bring the news that the French had restored slavery in Guadeloupe. Napoleon's plans for the Caribbean were now in the open. Shortly afterwards Christophe, Dessalines and some of the coloured generals deserted Leclerc and took their men into the hills.

Like the British before him, Leclerc found it impossible to defeat armies who knew every trail through the mountains. His men did not know how to live off the land. Threatened by famine, they had to buy food from American traders at extremely high prices. Yellow fever killed the new French troops in thousands. Leclerc himself died in August 1803. He was replaced by General Rochambeau who found the task of defeating the blacks impossible. The British blockaded the coast of France preventing supplies from getting through to the Caribbean. In December the last of the French troops surrendered to the British in Jamaica rather than to the victorious black generals.

Haiti

The French surrender brought independence to the island and its population of ex-slaves. Yet the cost had been terrible. The country was bankrupt and the population had fallen from 500,000 to less than 350,000. Slave-owning nations, including the United States, joined together in an economic blockade which cut the islands' exports down to a mere trickle.

Fig 18.3 *President Pétion.*

The great plantations were broken up, and the new small farms never had a chance to provide more than a bare subsistence for the families which owned them.

The newly freed land was also leaderless. Toussaint was dead. There was no government and no form of assembly to create one. Power lay with the soldiers. In 1804 Dessalines won the support of a number of generals to proclaim himself the first Emperor of Haiti, an Arawak word meaning mountainous. So the first independent state in the Caribbean had an Amerindian rather than a European or African name.

Following the death of Dessalines in 1806 civil war broke out. For a number of years the north was ruled by Christophe, who took the title of King Henri I. His rule did not cover the south which became a coloured republic ruled by President Pétion. In 1821 the two halves of the country were united by another general, Boyer. But until recent times, as Book 2 explains, Haiti continued to suffer from economic problems and a series of civil wars and military dictatorships.

19 *Trinidad and Guyana*

Britain and the French wars

In 1791 Britain went to war in an effort to overthrow the revolutionary government of France. These 'Revolutionary Wars', as they were known, continued until 1802 when Napoleon and Britain signed a truce which lasted only until the following year. There then followed a long period of warfare, known as the Napoleonic Wars, which finally ended with the defeat of Emperor Napoleon in 1814.

For most of the Revolutionary Wars and the Napoleonic Wars the French armies were masters of Europe and occupied many other countries, including Holland and Spain. But Britain was beyond the reach of the French armies and time after time encouraged the European nations to build another alliance against the French. Britain did send an army to Spain, under the Duke of Wellington, but most of her help to her European allies was in the form of money and arms. Her own war against the French was fought at sea, not only in European waters but in the Indian Ocean and the Caribbean. Chapter 18 showed how she used the war as an excuse to interfere in the French West Indian colonies on behalf of the planters and against the rebellious slaves. Although Britain failed to take the two most prosperous sugar islands, St Domingue and Guadeloupe, all the others were in her hands by 1795. In that year came a chance to extend the British Empire still further. The French armies occupied Holland and the Dutch people invited the British to take their colonies rather than see them fall into the hands of France.

The Guyanese colonies

In April 1796 General Abercromby appeared with a fleet off the town of Stabroek and British troops landed to occupy the two Dutch colonies of Berbice and Demerara-Essequibo. There was no resistance, for the Dutch governors of the colonies did not wish them to fall into French revolutionary hands and, in any case, about two-thirds of the white population was British. Most of them had migrated from the sugar islands to join the three tiny settlements on the Berbice, Essequibo and Demerara rivers during the years 1742 to 1772 when L. van Gravesande was the Dutch Governor. Before his day the colonies had developed very slowly from the 1630s when Dutch planters had first settled there. The Dutch had been far more successful as traders than planters. Yet, although much of the wealth to develop the colonies was British, the Dutch had provided the skill in drainage which made it possible to clear the long narrow plantations which ran from the bush through to the low lying land on the estuaries of the three main rivers of the region.

The buildings of Stabroek, too, were built in the Dutch style. Stabroek had been founded in 1783 when the Dutch took their colony back after a brief French occupation in the War of American Independence. It had become the capital of the colony of Essequibo-Demerera when the two colonies were united in 1789. It was to be renamed Georgetown and become the capital of the new colony of British Guiana (as the Guyanese colonies were known for most of their time under British rule).

Trinidad

Spain also joined the war on France's side and Abercromby was ordered to attack Trinidad, the Spanish colony which lay near to the Guyanese coast. He arrived in Port of Spain with eighteen ships and landed 7,650 men. Against him, the Spanish Governor, Chacon, had four ships and only five hundred fit men. He surrendered the island without a shot being fired.

Like the Guyanese colonies, Trinidad had developed only very slowly. Before the arrival of Governor Don José Maria Chacon in 1783 its population,

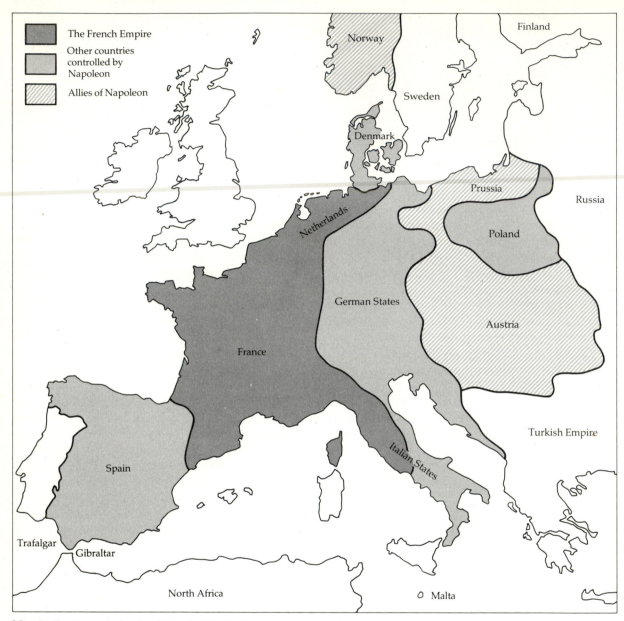

Map 30 *Europe at the height of Napoleon's power.*

not including Amerindians, was never more than a few hundred. In that year the Spanish Government issued a decree which allowed non-Spanish Roman Catholics to immigrate. This had attracted planters from the French sugar islands and also French-speaking free coloureds. In 1797 the island's population was 17,643. Of these 10,000 were slaves. Most of the 2,086 whites were French, but for every free white there were two free coloureds.

The Peace of Amiens

After the capture of the Guyanese colonies and Trinidad, Britain went on to take the Dutch islands of Curaçao, St Eustatius and Saba. When Denmark and Sweden were defeated by France, the British also moved in to occupy their colonies on St Bartholomew, St Thomas and St Croix.

This run of victories was halted for a while. In 1801

Fig 19.1 *A painting of about 1830 showing a plantation on the west coast of the Demerara estuary in British Guiana. Notice the low-lying land and the use of windmills.*

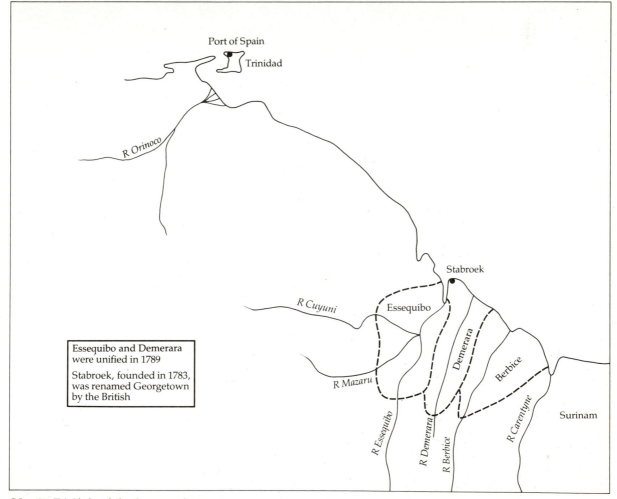

Essequibo and Demerara were unified in 1789

Stabroek, founded in 1783, was renamed Georgetown by the British

Map 31 *Trinidad and the Guyana colonies.*

Fig 19.2 *Warships in action at the battle of Trafalgar.*

Napoleon made peace with France's European enemies. Left alone, Britain had little choice but to agree to a truce which was signed at Amiens in 1802. For the time of the agreement, British forces withdrew from all her new conquests except Trinidad. But as soon as war broke out again in 1803, the Royal Navy immediately began to re-occupy the overseas colonies of France and the countries which lay under her rule.

Nelson and Villeneuve

Napoleon tried to stop the British reconquest of the colonies by sending Admiral Villeneuve to the Caribbean as commander of a strong French and Spanish fleet. For several months in 1805, Villeneuve and Admiral Lord Nelson played a hide and seek game in the southern Atlantic. The two fleets finally met off the Cape of Trafalgar in October 1805. Nelson won the battle that followed and Britain was not challenged again at sea for the rest of the war. By 1810 she had occupied all European colonies in the West Indies except those of Spain. Meanwhile the British navy was blockading all the main European ports so that

France and her conquered Empire were cut off from overseas trade.

By 1812 Napoleon's vast Empire was crumbling and in 1813 he was defeated by a strong alliance of European states. In 1814 the victorious armies entered Paris, forced Napoleon to give up his throne and made the new French Government accept the Treaty of Paris.

The Treaty of Paris

The British had such complete control of the seas that they could dictate which colonies they would keep.
1 In the Caribbean Britain kept St Lucia, Trinidad and Tobago and bought the Dutch colonies of Demerara-Essequibo and Berbice.
2 On the American mainland they claimed the right to settle the Oregon country in the north-western section of North America.
3 In Africa they took the Cape of Good Hope from the Dutch. They paid Holland five million pounds for this and the Guyana colonies.
4 In the Indian Ocean Britain retained Mauritius.

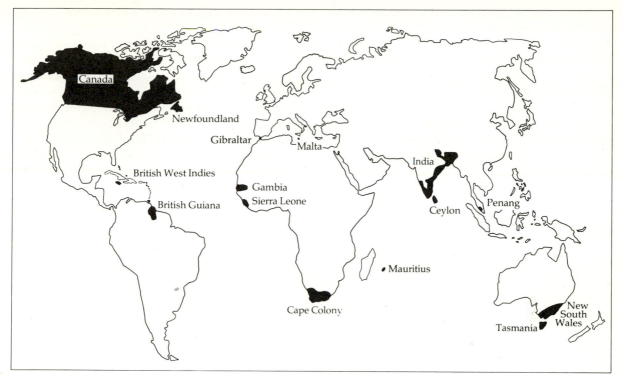

Map 32 *The British Empire in 1815.*

5 In Europe she kept Malta, the Ionian islands and Heligoland.

The new British Empire

These additions to the British Empire were not taken up haphazardly. Each had its part in Britain's aim to make herself the centre of a world-wide trading empire. The possessions in the North Sea and Mediterranean gave the navy stations from which it could protect merchant ships as they set out from Europe for the other continents. The route to India and the Far East was guarded from the Cape of Good Hope and Mauritius. Naval stations in the Caribbean enabled Britain to exercise maritime control over the Atlantic Ocean.

For a time at least, the long struggle for empire was over and Britain would have many years of world domination. But it was the newer parts of the Empire which took most of her attention. The West Indies lessened in importance as fortunes were made from trade with India and the Far East. Those who left Britain to seek their fortune were more likely to go to Australia or South Africa than the Caribbean. Even in the Americas many merchants saw greater possibilities in trade with Latin America than with the sugar islands.

Crown colony government

The British Government was not ready to allow the new colonies in Trinidad and Guyana the same law-making assemblies that ruled the older sugar islands. There were several reasons for this. It was feared that without firm control trouble would break out in the colonies, which would involve the British in heavy costs in men and money. For instance, both colonies had white populations divided between different European peoples: Spanish, French and English in Trinidad; Dutch and English in Guyana. As well as quarrelling between Europeans, there was a fear of revolt from the 60,000 slaves in Guyana. In Trinidad there were so many free coloureds that, even if only a small proportion had been wealthy enough to claim the right to vote, they might have controlled an assembly on the island.

Another reason was that Britain abolished the slave trade in 1807. This particularly annoyed planters who had moved to the new colonies in the hope of starting plantations in the huge areas of unfarmed land. Planter assemblies would have tried hard to find ways of importing slaves illegally. So the power to make laws for Trinidad was kept in the hands of the British Government. It became a crown colony, ruled by a governor who took his orders on all matters of importance from the Colonial Office in London. The colony had no assembly, only a council whose members were all appointed by the governor and which could only advise him.

Crown colony government was then forced on the Guyanese colonies but with some differences. The governor was advised by a Court of Policy which had grown up under Dutch rule. Planters in each district were allowed to elect men to sit on a *Kiezer*, or college of electors. The electors then put forward eight names and the governor chose four of them to sit on the Court of Policy with four of his senior officials.

At the end of the French Wars crown colony government was applied only to Trinidad, Guyana and St Lucia. Later in the nineteenth century the other colonial assemblies had their law-making powers replaced by crown colony government.

No-one opposed slavery more than the slaves themselves. New slaves sometimes refused to work in the fields or to come when called by the new name given them by their masters. Suicide was also a common form of protest, especially among unseasoned men who found the indignity of forced field labour too much to bear. In most West African societies field labour was considered women's work. Seasoned slaves generally protested in other ways: they purposefully worked slowly, damaged tools, pretended to be ill, wounded themselves, or poisoned estate animals. Other slaves acted more directly and tried to poison their overseers instead. Masters feared poisoning by their slaves almost as much as they feared rebellion. Poison was suspected whenever a white overseer died suddenly, although the cause was more likely to be heavy drinking or poor medical care. In his history of Jamaica Edward Long lists over a dozen poisons which he warns masters to be on their guard against. Still, there were many stories like the one Monk Lewis tells of the Jamaican attorney who was:

> . . . brought to the doors of death by a cup of coffee and only escaped a second time by his civility, in giving the beverage, prepared for himself, to two young book-keepers, to whom it proved fatal.

Revolts

Most slave revolts happened where there were uncultivated lands for the rebels to plot and hide in. But no slave colony was completely spared, and the crowded island of Barbados had revolts in 1675, 1686, 1692 and 1702. Some revolts were well organised and aimed at taking over the whole colony. This was the aim of Mackandal who led the slave rebellion on St Domingue. Tackey, leader of the 1760 'Coramantee' rebellion in Jamaica planned a 'total massacre of the whites and to make the island a Negro colony'. In 1763, the slave, Cuffy, led a rebellion on plantations along the Canje River in Berbice. He was successful enough to appoint himself governor of the colony for a while, and it took a year of fighting before Dutch troops overthrew him and forced his followers back to work. The only successful slave revolt was on St Domingue, but the others cost the planters dear. Four hundred slaves and sixty whites were killed in Tackey's uprising and property damage was placed at over £100,000. In the Jamaican 'Christmas Rebellion' of 1831 seven hundred slaves and fourteen whites lost their lives. The assembly spent £161,570 to put down the revolt and property damage was estimated at over one and a third million pounds. The revolts forced all planter assemblies to take defensive measures by passing repressive police laws and setting up local militia forces. But this did not mean they had the situation fully under their control, and the assemblies were sometimes forced to turn to the regular soldiers of the British or French army when slaves got out of hand.

Running away

Many slaves simply ran away. In the small, densely populated colonies most runaways headed for the crowded port towns and tried to get hold of false certificates of freedom which would make it possible to hide among the free coloured people. In the bigger colonies slaves could make their way to the interior where they joined other fugitives in one of the hidden runaway villages. People living in these villages had to be ready to leave their plantings and livestock at a moment's notice if discovered by the militia or troops. But there were always slaves who chose the uncertainties of freedom to the misery of slavery. As early as 1519 slaves in Hispaniola built their first runaway villages. As late as 1819, only twelve years before emancipation, the militia in Trinidad was regularly called out to destroy runaway villages which had grown up since 1802 when English masters had first brought their slaves to the colony.

The Maroons

Runaways stood little chance in the small colonies. In 1684, the Antiguan Assembly posted a reward of £2.10 shillings for a live runaway and £1 for a dead one. Three years later there were fewer than fifty fugitives left to 'excite and stir up the Negroes to forsake their masters . . . and . . . to make themselves masters of the country'. In the larger colonies some runaway villages became too strong to be so easily destroyed. In time they were able to bargain for their freedom from attack in return for agreeing not to interfere with the slave system on the plantations. In 1533 the Maroons in Hispaniola signed a treaty with the Spanish which granted them a large preserve. The Maroons agreed to return all new runaways to their Spanish masters.

Maroons in Jamaica

The first Jamaican Maroons were slaves left behind by the Spanish when they fled from the English invaders. For a few years they joined the Spanish resistance leader, Ysassi, and fought the English. In 1658 one of the Maroon leaders, Juan de Bolas, realised that Ysassi's cause was a hopeless one and came to terms with the English. He was allowed to lead his small band of followers to a preserve in the Cockpit country. Another leader, Juan de Serras, continued to fight the English from mountain strongholds long after Ysassi fled to Hispaniola. No one knows how many slaves ran off to join the Maroons but there were certainly large numbers. In the 1673 rebellion at least 300 slaves from St Anne's parish made their way to Serras's mountain settlement. By 1739, Maroons had built permanent villages at Trelawney Town, Accompong, Crawford Town and Nanny Town.

In that year the English fought several battles with the Maroons. Neither side won but it became clear that the Maroons could not be driven from their strongholds. Instead of fighting on, the English agreed to a treaty similar to the one signed by the Maroons and Spanish in Hispaniola. Captain Cudjoe,

Fig 20.1 *Trelawney Town, in the eighteenth century when it was the largest Maroon village in Jamaica.*

Fig 20.2 *A treaty between British officers and Maroons. Note how many Maroons appear to be wearing distinctive head-ties,* *which suggests they might have come from a Muslim community. They may not have worn as little clothing as shown here.*

leader of the Trelawney Town Maroons, was the first to sign. He and his people were given a 600 hectare preserve in which they could make their own laws and choose their own leaders. The Maroons agreed to stop raiding plantations, to return runaways and to help the militia put down slave revolts. Two white commissioners were also allowed to live in the village 'in order to maintain friendly correspondence'. Soon after, the Maroons in Accompong, Crawford Town and Nanny Town signed similar treaties. Except for a brief revolt by the Trelawney Town Maroons in 1795, the Maroons lived up to the treaties. But this did not stop slaves running away and building new illegal villages like Me-No-Sen-You-No-Come in the Cockpits. There were always slaves willing to take the risks of freeing themselves.

Bush Negroes in Guyana

Maroons were just as successful in the Guyanese colonies of the French, Dutch and English. Nearly all the plantations were either on the coast or the estuaries of rivers just before they reached the sea. The wet marshes and tangled jungle behind made excellent hiding places for the free villages of Bush Negroes. The first of these were slaves who escaped from the colony set up by Willoughby, the Governor of Barbados who fled to Surinam in 1651. This explains why the creole spoken by the Bush Negroes has an English base, although most of the later runaways came from Dutch plantations. In the eighteenth century the death rate among slaves in Surinam was higher than even on the French and British islands. So many replacements were brought to the colony that 90 per cent of the slaves on many plantations had been born in Africa. Such recent memories of freedom led many to risk the torture given to captured runaways and try to make their way to join the free villages.

From their hidden homes the Bush Negroes raided the European plantations and forced the Dutch to send expeditions into the interior to attempt to crush them. These expeditions were costly in soldiers' lives and probably helped future runaways, for the Europeans took slaves with them who thus learned of the pathways through the bush. Rather than continue with the wars the Dutch Governor made treaties in 1761 and 1767 with the two main groups of Bush Negroes. The treaties were modelled on those with the Jamaican Maroons and gave the Bush Negroes freedom in return for an agreement to return any new runaways. The Bush Negroes promised not to approach nearer the European settlements than a two day journey by foot or ten hours by boat. A Dutch official known as 'post-holder' was to live in the village of each Bush Negro chief.

The treaties closed the south of Surinam to further runaways, but this did not stop slaves making their way to the east towards the borders with French Guiana. Others fled from the Dutch colonies of Essequibo-Demerara and Berbice in modern Guyana. Their villages were built on circular pieces of ground cleared of bush. The huts were hidden by planting fruit trees, yams and plantains and the whole area was then defended by a wide ditch filled with water which covered sharpened stakes. False paths were laid to lead enemies away from the underwater firm paths into the village.

21 The churches and slavery

In the early days of the British colonies only one Church, the Church of England, had any importance. This matched the position in Britain where it was the established church, that is the only one recognised by law. In many ways the Church of England, or Anglican Church, played a part in British government. Bishops were members of the House of Lords. The whole land was divided into parishes, each with its church and vicar; each parish had its vestry committee which was responsible for local tasks such as road repairs and the care of the poor. In eighteenth-century England the Anglican vicars were often accused of having little interest in religion and being more concerned with living like landowning gentlemen. Many built themselves large houses, and joined the local landowner in his amusements such as fox-hunting. In many parishes they became magistrates, often dealing out harsh punishments to poor people accused of begging or poaching animals for food.

Most Anglican priests in the Caribbean were very little different from those in Britain. They were connected with the plantocracy, by marriage, by sitting in the assembly or being a magistrate. In most cases the priests accepted slavery and the police laws that went with it. Occasionally a clergyman argued that efforts should be made to convert the slaves to Christianity, but he was usually quickly stopped. In 1680 a Barbadian clergyman, the Reverend Godwyn Morgan, wrote a pamphlet in favour of bringing slaves into the Christian Church. The island assembly immediately protested to the Board of Trade in London that 'converted negroes' would be harder to manage and less valuable for 'labour and sale'. Besides, they went on: 'The Negroes' savage brutishness renders them wholly uncapable of conversion to Christianity'.

A few years later the Anglican Church started the Society for the Propagation of the Gospel with the idea of making Bibles available to 'heathens'. The Society was given three plantations by a Barbadian planter, Christopher Codrington, and built Codring-

Fig 21.1 *The seal of the Society for the Propagation of the Gospel. Note the figure in clergyman's dress and the black people shown rushing to hear him. Was this ever the reality?*

Fig 21.2 *Codrington College, Barbados.*

ton College as a missionary training school. But graduates from the college did little work among the slaves until after emancipation. Until then the college's plantations were worked by slaves, branded with an 'S' for Society.

The Moravians

The first group to make a serious effort to bring slaves to Christianity were the Moravians. They had suffered 300 years of persecution from both Catholic and Protestant Churches in Europe for their faith, which called on Moravian brethren to lead simple lives devoted to spreading the word of God from person to person without the strict rituals of the Churches. In the eighteenth century many moved from their homeland in modern Czechoslovakia to Saxony in modern Germany. From there, they sent missionaries to the Danish islands in 1732. Later missions were opened in Jamaica in 1754, in Antigua in 1756, Barbados 1765 and St Kitts 1775.

Many planters would not accept the Moravians on their estates, believing that it was dangerous to teach Christianity to slaves. Church services would bring them together in large crowds where ideas like love, equality and peace might be discussed. The slaves might learn too much of their masters' language, politics and way of life. But the Moravians were careful to avoid such questions and indeed taught the slaves that Christianity meant accepting suffering on earth in return for rewards in heaven. So a few planters, especially in Antigua and St Kitts, came to believe it was better to have slaves who had been taught that hard work and obedience were Christian duties. The Moravians showed the way of the English non-conformist missionaries who began to arrive in the islands towards the end of the eighteenth century.

The non-conformists

Non-conformists were those Englishmen who refused to conform to the rules and practices of the Church of England. Their numbers swelled in the eighteenth century as a result of the great social changes which were taking place in Britain. The population began to rise rapidly and there grew up new classes of poor people, not only agricultural labourers but workers in the new manufacturing industries. Many Christians became alarmed at the disorder, drunkenness, violence and ignorance in the industrial districts where the Anglican Church seemed able to do very little. Very often there was not even a church, for most of these had been built in the old villages of Britain. So non-conformists, such as the Baptists and Presbyterians, began to send preachers into these areas to persuade people to accept religion as the starting point for a better and more moral life.

The most successful non-conformists actually started within the Anglican Church and then broke away. These were the Methodists. The movement started with John Wesley and a group of students who formed a 'Holy Club' at Oxford University. They were nicknamed Methodists because they methodically set about leading a life given to regular worship, charity and preaching. John Wesley trained himself to rise at four each morning and live on £28 a year. He spent his life travelling in the poorer districts of England and the new American colonies, and preached more than 40,000 sermons. He began as a Church of England clergyman but ended as leader of a separate organisation which was the largest non-conformist church in Britain.

The missionary societies

British non-conformists saw themselves as carrying out missionary work, going to preach in streets, cottages, open spaces, and factories to people who lived immoral lives. Many believed there was similar work to be done in the Caribbean. Here, they were told, there were slaves who had never heard of God and Christ, who were 'immoral' in the way they dressed, by not being properly married, and by breaking the Sabbath by going to market or drinking and dancing on Sundays. So missionaries began to arrive from England in the 1780s and then in large numbers when collections were made in the 1790s to start missionary societies. The Baptist Missionary Society began in 1792, the London Missionary Society in 1795, the Scottish Missionary Society in 1800 and the Methodist Missionary Society in 1813.

The societies took great care to avoid trouble with the planters. Baptist missionaries were told they should 'avoid political and party discussions as beneath your notice'. The London Missionary Society

Fig 21.3 *Buildings of a mission at St Johns, Antigua. Notice the 'respectable' clothing of the black people.*

gave instructions: 'Not a word must escape you, in public or private, which might render the slaves displeased with their masters or dissatisfied with their station'. It chose its missionaries from the 'humblest and most laborious' trades in Britain. This was to encourage them to work humbly among the slaves and not try to challenge the white leaders of colonial society.

By taking such care not to offend the planters the new missionaries were able to get permission to enter some plantations. Soon each island had a small number of Christian slaves. The Methodist Church claimed that it had 6,750 members in the Caribbean colonies in 1793. Occasionally planters, especially on the small islands, welcomed the work of the missionaries in making blacks more loyal. When Antigua was threatened by invasion in the French wars, troops of blacks were raised to defend the islands. One was made up of Methodist slaves and the other had a large number of Moravians.

Opposition from planters

But in most cases the planters tried to hinder the work of the missionaries. Some assemblies passed regulations which required missionaries to hold a licence from the parish magistrates to preach. The fees for the licences were high and some magistrates laid down impossible times and places for services to be held. St Vincent tried to head off the missionaries by passing a law which forbade anyone to preach who had not lived in the colony for a year. Most assemblies made laws forbidding religious services between sunset and sunrise. Some made it illegal for missionaries to use converted slaves to teach others. Occasionally planters threatened slaves attending services or even tore down meeting houses. In 1789 the Methodist chapel in Barbados was stoned, and slaves caught at the services were publicly whipped.

The most successful non-conformists were the Baptists in Jamaica because of the preaching of George

Lisle, a black American, and Moses Baker, a black Bahamian. The island's planters became convinced, wrongly, that the Baptists and Methodists were stirring slaves to rebel. To prevent this they tried to encourage the Anglican Church to undertake missionary work. The fee for a slave's baptism into the Church of England was cut from £3 to a bargain price of two shillings and sixpence. In 1816 the Assembly passed an Act allowing twenty-one curates to work in addition to the parish clergymen, and to hold services in other places than the churches attended by the whites. The scheme failed because no Anglicans volunteered to take any of the twenty-one posts.

The attacks on the non-conformists worked against the planters and their supporters in England. Many slaves became curious to find out more about the missionaries when they saw their masters attacking them. The missionaries often became opposed to slavery on the grounds that it prevented black men from hearing about religion. Their letters home and reports to the missionary societies described the harsh life of the slaves and gave the planters a very bad reputation. For the first time all classes of Englishmen learned about the evils of a slave system, which became a favourite topic of Sunday sermons throughout England. Thanks to the missionaries there was widespread support for the humanitarians when they opened their first attacks against slavery.

22 *Abolition of the slave trade*

Humanitarians

A humanitarian is someone who believes in improving conditions in which men spend their lives. Today we take humanitarianism for granted, but until the eighteenth century it was rare to find men who argued that human life could be improved instead of saying that the state of the world was laid down by fate or the will of God. In the eighteenth century men with humanitarian ideas began to appear in many professions: in politics, writing, economics, industry. They believed that slavery was unnecessary and evil, and some of them made their views sharply clear. Adam Smith, whose ideas helped the development of England as an industrial nation, pointed out that 'the work of freemen comes cheaper in the end than that performed by slaves'. If it were not for the Navigation Acts which forced up the price of sugar, slavery could not exist in the British Caribbean. The poet William Cowper wrote in *The Negroes' Complaint*:

> Why did all-creating Nature
> Make the plant for which we toil?
> Sighs must fan it, tears must water,
> Sweat of ours must dress the soil.
> Think ye masters iron-hearted,
> Lolling at your groaning boards,
> Think, how many backs have smarted
> For the sweets your cane affords.

Samuel Johnson, who wrote the first English dictionary, got a round of applause when he rose and proposed a toast to 'the next insurrection of the Negroes in the West Indies'. People of the time who had a humanitarian outlook began to show an interest in travel books, and descriptions of the cultures of other peoples. Here they could find evidence that Africans were not the ignorant savages that the slavers described but people from well-organised societies. One widely read travel book described one of the African peoples: 'They never suffer any of their own nation to want but support the old, the blind, and the lame equally with the others'. The disabled and old were certainly not as well cared for in Britain at that time, and men began to wonder whether the Africans did not come from societies which were more noble than their own.

Not all humanitarians were religious, but many were, and it was from among their number that the leadership came for a fifty-year campaign against the slave trade and slavery. Perhaps the most important group of religious humanitarians were the Quakers, sometimes known as the Society of Friends. This nonconformist sect had been founded in the seventeenth century by George Fox. Members of the Society of Friends believed in holding religious meetings in ordinary buildings without the rituals of a church service; they were taught to avoid any kind of amusement or elaborate dress, to live lives based on love and never to use violence. Many Quakers went to Pennsylvania and Barbados and were instructed by George Fox to welcome their slaves to religious services, to treat them kindly and to free them after a number of years of faithful service. In 1676 the Quakers in Pennsylvania became the first English colonists to emancipate their slaves. The Quakers in Barbados had to be more cautious because they were few in number. Their meeting houses were torn down by angry planter neighbours; magistrates jailed and fined them for their religious beliefs which forbade them to take oaths or join the militia. The Anglican clergy urged the Assembly to expel 'this base sort of fanatic people commonly termed . . . Quakers'. In 1695 the Barbadian magistrates fined the Quakers over £7,000 for ignoring the colony's laws by allowing slaves to attend religious meetings. At least one Quaker was executed. In face of this opposition the Quakers gave up their open opposition to slavery in Barbados.

But in England they became the first campaigners against the slave trade. In 1727 at their London meeting they passed a proposal against the trade, and in 1761 Quakers who were still engaging in it were expelled. This was just four years before Granville

Sharp had the experience which led to the beginnings of the anti-slavery movement in Britain.

The Somerset case

As a young man, Granville Sharp was apprenticed to a tailor and then became a clerk in the Ordnance (or Supplies) department of the British Government in London. He was a devout Christian and also worked hard to improve his knowledge; he taught himself Greek and Hebrew in his spare time. He was never prepared to give up working for a cause in which he believed. When the American War of Independence broke out, Sharp resigned from his government post because he was in sympathy with the Americans.

In 1765 his interest turned to the abolition movement when he met an African stumbling down a London street. Jonathan Strong had just been beaten and turned out of the house of his master, a Barbadian lawyer living in England. Sharp took the wounded man to his brother's doctor's office where he was looked after until he was fit, and the brothers found him work as a messenger for a nearby pharmacy. Two years later Strong was spied by his master, seized and sold to a Jamaican planter for £30. He was put in prison to wait until a ship was ready to sail. Sharp took the case to court and managed to have Jonathan Strong set free, but the judge refused to give a judgement on whether the English law allowed a man to be bought and sold as a slave.

Granville Sharp, however, would not let this question drop. He was determined to get a clear ruling against slavery in England. First he set to work studying the law and the condition of slaves in the country. In 1765 there were in Britain 14,000 slaves worth over £700,000; most of them had been brought to England from the Caribbean colonies by absentee planters. The absentees had had no worries about taking slaves since in 1749 a judge, Lord Hardwicke, had ruled that a slave running away in England could be legally recovered. They even sold them openly. Advertisements like that in the *Gazette* for April 1769 became common:

> For sale at the Bull and Gate Inn, Holborn, a chestnut gelding, a tin whistle, and a well made, good tempered Black Boy.

Sharp believed that Hardwicke's ruling would be overturned if the question of slavery were taken before another English court. He outlined his opinion in a pamphlet, *A Representation of the Injustice and Dangerous Tendency of Tolerating Slavery in England*. In 1770 he took the case of Thomas Lewis to court. Lewis was a slave who had been seized and put on board a ship bound for the Caribbean. The jury freed Lewis, but this was because his master could not prove ownership, and so the court managed to avoid ruling on the question of whether slavery was illegal. In 1772 Granville Sharp tried again with the case of James Somerset who, like Strong, had been turned out by his master, a Virginian planter, and then seized again. This time the master had clear proof of ownership.

Somerset's case came before the Chief Justice, Lord Mansfield, on 7 February 1772. For four months Sharp tried to force Lord Mansfield to give a ruling. Mansfield was not an abolitionist and wanted to avoid a judgement. He even approached Parliament to pass a special Act declaring slavery legal in England. When Parliament refused, Mansfield proved that he was a great judge who put the law higher than his own feelings. On 22 June 1772 he ruled that his study of the laws of England found that 'the claim of slavery can never be supported'.

Committee for the Abolition of the Slave Trade

Lord Mansfield's judgement that English law did not recognise slavery made it possible for all the slaves in England to claim their freedom. English opponents of slavery then turned to the question of the much larger number of slaves in the colonies, and the Quakers formed an anti-slavery society. Fifteen years later the society decided that the most effective way to end slavery was to begin with the abolition of the slave trade. In 1787 it renamed itself the Committee for the Abolition of the Slave Trade. The Committee's members believed that slavery could be forced to collapse once planters could not acquire new slaves. Ending the trade, rather than slavery itself, would avoid the question of whether the planters should be compensated for the loss of their slave property. Another advantage was that the laws affecting trade were made by the English Parliament, whereas to end slavery itself would mean interfering with laws made by the colonial assemblies.

Fig 22.1 *British humanitarian opponents of slavery.*

Most members of the Committee were Quakers or belonged to the Evangelical movement which was trying to make the Church of England show as much concern about spreading religious ideas as non-conformists. Their enemies mockingly called them 'the Saints'. The leading Saints were also nicknamed the Clapham Sect after the fashionable district of London where some of them lived. The Clapham Sect included Granville Sharp, Thomas Clarkson, who gave his life to investigating slavery, and William Wilberforce, a wealthy politician. Other abolitionists were Henry Thornton, a wealthy banker who spent his fortune setting up a home in Sierra Leone for slaves liberated by the Mansfield judgement, and John Newton, who had been a slave captain until he had been converted to religion and become a clergyman. There was also Zachary Macaulay, a former book-keeper in Jamaica, and James Ramsay, who had served as a surgeon on a warship bound for St Kitts. There he had been called to attend an epidemic on a slave ship and never forgot the horrors he saw in the middle decks. He became an Anglican priest and served in St Kitts for fourteen years, making outspoken attacks on slavery. In 1781 he returned to England and joined the abolitionists.

The campaign

The committee had the support of the Prime Minister, William Pitt the Younger, who suggested that William Wilberforce should be the Committee's spokesman in Parliament. Thomas Clarkson was sent to collect the information Wilberforce would need. He travelled to Liverpool and Bristol where he carefully checked all the information about slaving ships. As evidence about the trade's horrors he collected shackles, thumb screws, teeth chisels and branding irons. The ship's captains kept clear of him 'as if I had been a mad dog' but Clarkson wrote down the names and stories of twenty thousand seamen. He ended with more information on the slave trade than the slavers had themselves. The evidence showed that they were wrong to claim that the trade was necessary to train English seamen for time of war. In fact Clarkson found the seamen's death rate was actually higher than the slaves. Nor did the slave trade bring the greatest profits to Liverpool and Bristol. There were more ships engaged in other trades, and the government earned more revenue from taxes on imported cotton and exports of manufactured goods.

The thousands of stories convinced Wilberforce and many of his fellow MPs that the trade was 'an affront to God and below the dignity of civilised people'. Outside Parliament the movement was widely supported by the missionary societies and humanitarians. They also received backing from many industrialists such as Josiah Wedgewood, who owned large pottery works and produced china decorated with the famous plaque which became the symbol of the anti-slavery movement:

Am I not a man and a brother

Delays and success

Success did not come quickly for Wilberforce and the other abolitionists in the English Parliament. The West India interest still held many seats in the House of Commons, and they were backed by MPs who had their election expenses paid by the slavers in London, Bristol and Liverpool. Twice, in 1789 and 1791, Wilberforce put forward a proposal to abolish the trade only to have it turned down. In 1792, however, he was successful and the House of Commons agreed that the trade should be abolished by stages by 1796.

But in the following year England went to war with France and Prime Minister Pitt withdrew his support for abolition. His argument was that he did not want Parliament to be quarrelling over other questions while England was fighting a war. The abolitionists believed that his real reason was his hope of capturing St Domingue for Britain. If this happened England would control the greatest part of sugar production and would be able to flood Europe with cheap supplies. But to grow sugar on St Domingue required thousands of slaves each year. Certainly Pitt would not support abolition while British troops were fighting on the side of the planters in St Domingue.

Many times in the next fourteen years Wilberforce put forward a proposal to end the trade, but on each occasion it was turned down. The first signs that success might soon come appeared in 1805. After Nelson's victory at the battle of Trafalgar the war was turning in England's favour. It was also clear that the war had changed the shipping and trading interests of England away from slaving towards other goods, and away from the Caribbean towards the much larger empire. In 1782 one in twelve ships sailing from Liverpool had been slavers; in 1807, it was only one in twenty-four. The growth of the British Empire in India had led to the development of a powerful East India interest in British politics. Merchants and industrialists with trading interests in India and other parts of the new Empire objected to the favoured treatment given to the West Indians. The cotton and tea which came from India were not produced by slave labour, so the East India interest in Parliament was willing to back the abolitionists.

At this point, too, some West Indian planters saw that they could benefit from abolition. In 1806 the average planter made no profit at all and this was clearly because they were growing too much sugar and prices were too low; nearly 6,000 tonnes remained unsold in England in that year. One of the reasons was the competition from sugar grown by rivals, especially planters on Cuba, and the British planters believed that their losses would become greater if the new conquests of Trinidad and Guyana were turned over to sugar. This could be prevented if they were not able to import slaves.

Abolition

Finally, the abolitionist movement was helped by the death of Pitt in 1806. The new Prime Minister was Charles James Fox who was a keen supporter of abolition. In the spring of 1807 the English Parliament passed the Abolition Act. The slave trade was to end on 1 January 1808.

British warships were sent to hunt down captains who ignored the law. They also stopped the ships of any nation at war with England and freed their slave cargo. Several nations followed the British example and passed laws against the trade: the United States in 1808, Holland in 1814, France in 1818 and Spain in 1820. However, the Spanish and United States governments took little action against the trade until the middle of the nineteenth century. Each year thousands of Africans were still carried to the southern states of the United States, to Cuba and Puerto Rico, and to Brazil. A small proportion were freed by the British naval patrols sent to stop and search ships suspected of carrying slaves. Up to 1834 most of the Africans they liberated were taken to Sierra Leone to join slaves freed in England after Lord Mansfield's judgement.

23 Emancipation

Slavery after abolition

English abolitionists believed that slavery would soon disappear after the trade was ended. The planters, they thought, would have to protect their remaining slaves and encourage settled family life to increase numbers. As the slaves increased the planters would gradually free them and hire the fittest labourers. The missionaries would be welcomed to teach the ex-slaves how to live as honest, hard-working freemen. Unfortunately, the abolitionists were wrong. Ill-health, overwork and the lack of a proper family life all kept the death rate high, and so many more men than women had been shipped from Africa that the slave population went down for many years after abolition. As numbers fell, those remaining had to work harder.

Plantation profits continued to fall in the face of competition from new areas. Although there was a labour shortage in the new colonies in Guyana and Trinidad, sugar production there was growing. Worse from the West Indian point of view was that England began to import East Indian sugar. This strengthened the East India interest in the British Parliament. At the same time sugar from Cuba and Brazil was passing on to the world market in increasing quantities and British planters found it still more difficult to sell to anywhere but Britain itself. Faced with these difficulties the planters were in no mood to improve the conditions of their slaves or welcome new missionaries.

Reports reached England about Jamaica's Consolidated Slave Act of 1808, which forbade Methodists and other non-conformist missionaries to teach slaves or have them in their chapels. The abolitionists in England complained and the law was disallowed by the British Parliament. However, the abolitionists could not stop planters giving cruel and sadistic punishments to slaves. In 1812 Arthur Hodge, a slave-driver in Tortola, was tried for murdering sixty slaves under his care. He was found guilty but the jury

Fig 23.1 *Arthur Hodge, murderer of slaves.*

recommended mercy. The magistrates, however, decided he should be hanged; the Governor had to declare martial law and call in a British warship to keep order among the planters while the sentence was carried out. About this time the West India Committee in London made an attempt to gain English support by publishing pamphlets in defence of slavery. They paid people like Monk Lewis who wrote: 'Slavery is now so incorporated with the welfare of Great Britain . . . as to make its extirpation (destruction) an absolute impossibility, *without the certainty of producing worse mischief'*.

Fortunately, there were a growing number of people in Britain who were no longer prepared to believe this. One was James Stephen, a lawyer in the Colonial

Office, who read all the reports coming in from the West Indies. In 1812 he asked the Colonial Secretary, Lord Bathhurst, to issue an order to the Governors of Trinidad and Guyana to register all the slaves in their colonies. The British Government had the power to do this because these were crown colony government settlements. Stephen hoped the registration would be the first step towards some protection for the slaves.

The Registration Bill

The planters in Guyana and Trinidad resisted registration so strongly that Stephen tried to strengthen it by making it an Act of Parliament with the help of Wilberforce. In the House of Commons Wilberforce proposed that slaves in all colonies should be registered. The West Indian assemblies all protested, declaring once again that the British Parliament had no right to interfere with their local laws. Wilberforce eventually withdrew the Bill on the understanding that the colonies' governors would persuade the assemblies to pass their own registration acts. Each assembly did so but in most cases the planters simply took no notice.

The Anti-Slavery Society

The failure of registration made it clear to the English opponents of slavery that conditions in the West Indies would not improve gradually as the abolitionists had hoped. New men entered the struggle. In Parliament Wilberforce was replaced as the main spokesman on slavery by Thomas Buxton. He was supported by young anti-slavery campaigners like James Stephen, the Cooper brothers and Joseph Sturge. Unlike the older abolitionists they were not prepared to avoid awkward questions such as compensation or the right of the English Parliament to impose laws on the colonies. They wanted a British Act of Parliament to end slavery once and for all. In 1823 they formed the London Society for the Mitigation and Gradual Abolition of Slavery. Within a year 220 branch societies were opened in cities and towns throughout Britain, and a newspaper *The Anti-Slavery Monthly Reporter* was started. The Society's president was the King's brother, and among its many vice-presidents were five lords and fourteen Members of

Fig 23.2 *The motif of the Anti-Slavery Society.*

Parliament. The most outspoken of them all was the leader of the East India sugar interests in Parliament.

Amelioration

Faced with such a strong anti-slavery movement the West India Committee tried to head off their attacks. They told the Colonial Secretary that they would support some proposals for improving the condition of slaves. The Foreign Minister, George Canning, raised these 'Amelioration Proposals' in Parliament in March 1823, making the promise that his government would, sometime in the future, ask Parliament to agree to emancipation. With this promise the abolitionists supported the amelioration proposals which were agreed in May 1823.

The proposals said that the government should write to each of the colonial governors suggesting that the assemblies should pass local laws to improve the condition of slaves. The laws would state that female slaves should not be whipped and that overseers and drivers should not carry a whip in the fields. Records should be kept of all lashes given to male slaves and all punishments should be put off for at least twenty-four hours. Religious instruction and church marriages were to be encouraged, and slaves should have time off on Saturday to go to market so that they would be free to attend church on Sunday morning. The proposals asked the assemblies to pass laws against selling slaves for debt and breaking up families. The colonies should set up schemes to help slaves save money and buy their own freedom. The most daring proposal was that a slave could testify in court against a free man provided that a minister supplied him with a character reference.

The failure of amelioration

The proposals met with fierce resistance in the colonies. In the crown colonies the governors were ordered to carry them out, but the Governor of Demerara refused to publish them right away for fear of rioting. In Trinidad the planters immediately asked for them to be withdrawn. The assemblies on the older islands greeted the proposals with outbursts of anger. They ignored warnings from the West India Committee that the only way to stop the anti-slavery movement in Britain was 'by doing of ourselves, all that is right to be done – and doing it speedily and effectively'. In Dominica the planters talked about independence; in Jamaica the assembly discussed joining the United States; in Barbados the assembly replied to the proposals by saying that their slave laws were already 'a catalogue of indulgencies to the Blacks'. In the end most of the assemblies passed only a few of the least important amelioration proposals.

The amelioration proposals failed here, but they were an important landmark in the struggle for emancipation. The British Government had promised that emancipation would come one day. The refusal of the planters to accept amelioration meant that the anti-slavery campaign was given a stronger case. It split the West India interest between those in England who had tried to delay emancipation by amelioration, and those in the Caribbean who clung desperately to a passing way of life.

The free coloureds

At first the British West Indian planters turned to the free coloureds for support in their struggle against the abolitionists. It seemed wise to prevent dissatisfied free coloureds joining with the slaves as happened in Haiti. Early in 1795 the Jamaican Assembly had granted pensions to such families of free coloureds 'as shall be killed or disabled in the public service'. In 1813 it passed further acts permitting free coloureds to give evidence in civil and criminal cases, to inherit

unlimited amounts of property, and to engage in trades such as owning and renting boats. The free coloured leaders were aware that the assemblies were trying to buy their support against the slaves. The most active of them wanted to make the most of their opportunity. Throughout the colonies they formed associations to demand that the assemblies remove all their disabilities.

In 1823 the Grenada Assembly gave in and removed all but a few unimportant restrictions on free coloureds. Those in other colonies immediately pressed for the same changes. In Trinidad they sent a petition to the governor demanding 'full enjoyment of civil offices and employments accessible according to capacities and circumstances'. The petition called for the freedom of assembly, the removal of special seats for coloureds at places of amusement, and an end to all 'impediments in the way of marriage between white and free coloured'. Free coloureds in Jamaica threatened to withdraw from service in the militia unless granted full equality with whites. The assemblies had not planned that the free coloureds should take up the improvements they offered in such an outspoken way. In most cases they replied in insulting terms. The Barbadian Assembly gave a definite 'no' to the coloureds and reminded them that keeping the rights they had been granted in the past depended 'entirely on their good conduct'. The Jamaican Assembly was just as insulting, although it did agree to pass more special acts granting full rights to individual coloureds.

Support for emancipation

In the years after 1823 most free coloureds became convinced that their position would be improved only after the entire slave system was brought down. They sided with British officials over the question of amelioration. In return the British officials supported the free coloureds' struggle with the assemblies. In 1823 the Governor of Barbados described the free coloureds as 'by far the most loyal subjects His Majesty has'. In 1828 the Colonial Secretary issued an order removing all disabilities from free coloureds in Trinidad and Guyana. In Jamaica, governors protected the two outspoken coloured leaders, Edward Jordan and Robert Osborn. The two men published a newspaper, *The Watchman*, in which they poked fun at the assembly and published the debates on emancipation which were taking place in England. Jordan was arrested in 1831 for urging in *The Watchman* that the free coloureds 'bring down the system by the run, knock off the fetters, and let the oppressed go free'. Such attacks forced many assemblies to remove the disabilities at last, but by then it was too late. The refusal to help the free coloureds in the 1820s had turned them into strong supporters of the anti-slavery movement.

The emancipation revolts

The slaves knew about the emancipation campaigns. Higglers and jobbers picked up bits of gossip in market places; domestics listened as their masters grumbled about the latest tracts from the Anti-Slavery Society. Slaves who could read followed the reports of debates in parliament in the colonial newspapers. Rumours that the king's 'free paper' had come spread each time a satchel of government letters arrived at the governor's mansion. To many slaves it seemed that the time had come to unite and make their own bid for freedom.

The first emancipation revolt came in Barbados soon after the news spread that the assembly had turned down the registration plan. It began on Easter Sunday 1816 in the parish of St Philip on Bayley's plantation. On one plantation after another first the trash piles and then hated canefields were fired. By Sunday evening cane fields were burning in the neighbouring parishes of St John and St George: '. . . mill after mill on the revolted estates was turned into the wind to fly untended, and bell after bell was rung to announce that the slaves on such plantation had joined the revolt'. News of the disturbances reached Bridgetown early on Monday morning. Martial law was immediately proclaimed and several troops of militia along with regulars marched to the parishes. The slaves scarcely resisted the troops, mainly because many were not yet ready to seek violently what they believed the abolitionists might achieve peacefully. Most had not taken up arms at all, a fact which the Governor, Sir James Leith, honestly admitted. Not a single planter had been hurt and only one militia man killed.

The planters showed no such humanity. Several slaves caught off their estates were murdered on the spot. Others were rounded up and, after passing through a makeshift court of inquiry, were sentenced to death and returned to their owner's plantation where the execution was carried out as an example. Several were deported to British Honduras but, when local officials refused to allow them on shore, they were transhipped to Sierra Leone. Several months later a Select Committee was appointed by the assembly to investigate the cause of the revolt. They tried to use their investigation to discredit the emancipation movement and lay the whole blame on the shoulders of a free coloured man, Washington Franklin, who they reported had read newspaper reports of the anti-slavery debates to the slaves and discussed emancipation with them.

In 1823 the slaves in Demerara revolted after a rumour that the governor would not issue the 'free paper'. Within two days, 13,000 slaves had joined in. Troops suppressed the rebellion, killing over a hundred. Forty-eight were later hanged; others were flogged, deported or put in prison.

The 'Baptist War'

Shortly after Christmas in 1831, a slave Baptist deacon, Samuel Sharpe, led a revolt in the north-west of Jamaica. Sharpe had been kept informed of the latest emancipation movements through a relative who worked in a printery in Kingston. He apparently had not set out to lead a revolt but a general strike, which he hoped would force the planters to adhere to abolitionist demands. The plans were a well-kept secret and for the most part planters and overseers were taken completely by surprise. Missionaries who worked with the slaves like the Baptist, Thomas Burtchell, and the Methodist, the Reverend H Bleby, were equally ignorant of the planned strike. It began quietly enough in St James when the slaves on several plantations peacefully but firmly refused to go back to work after Christmas. The first violence happened when the great house and sugar works at Kensington estate in St James were burnt. The fire at Kensington was the first of many. As in Barbados the cane fields, symbols of bondage and toil, were burned on one estate after another. The militia sent out from Montego Bay were driven back and the revolt spread to Trelawney parish. At the same time minor disturbances broke out in St Elizabeth, Manchester, St

Thomas and Portland. These were quickly put down, but the main trouble areas in the north-west remained in turmoil until after the new year when additional militia troops and a detachment of regulars were sent from Kingston. Over 400 slaves were killed and Sharpe was executed with about 100 followers before the 'Baptist War', as the slaves called it, was put down. Again, as in Barbados and Demerara, the planters and assembly refused to believe that the slaves on their own were capable of joining together in the name of emancipation. Instead the Commission of Inquiry created by the assembly blamed the revolt on: 'the unceasing . . . interference of his Majesty's ministers', '. . . the false and wicked reports of the Anti-Slavery Society', and '. . . the teaching and preaching of religious sects called Baptists, Wesleyan, Methodist and Moravians'.

Attempts by the planters to use the results as propaganda against emancipation failed. Together with the free coloureds' demands, the revolts undermined the planters' determination to delay emancipation; the most far-sighted saw that it was better to end slavery themselves than have the slaves do it. The brutality used in suppressing the revolts, in which over a thousand slaves had been killed but only thirteen whites, led to new efforts by the English abolitionists.

Missionaries become involved

The planters made a great error when they blamed the missionaries for inciting rebellion. In 1823 a mob of 'respectable Barbadian gentlemen' greeted the news of the Demerara revolt by burning the Methodist chapel in Bridgetown and forcing the missionary, William Shrewsbury, to leave the colony. In Demerara itself a Baptist missionary, John Smith, was accused of encouraging the slaves. He was court-martialled and sentenced to hang. It was later proved that he had counselled his converts not to join the revolt, but he died in prison while awaiting the king's pardon.

In Jamaica leading Baptist missionaries like William Knibb, Thomas Burchell and James Alsopp were put on trial, although they had to be aquitted because it was shown that they had pleaded with their congregations not to join the war. The most reactionary planters joined what they called the Colonial Church Union, which was not unlike the Ku Klux Klan which

Fig 23.3 *A handbag carried by an anti-slavery Englishwoman.*

later grew up in the southern United Staes. An Anglican clergyman, the Reverend William Bridges, is believed to have been the main organiser. The Union destroyed sixteen non-conformist churches before it was finally outlawed by Governor Lord Mulgrave in 1833.

The Agency Committee

The planters' failure to carry out amelioration and their brutality during the slave revolts showed clearly that the policy of gradual emancipation would not work. In the Anti-Slavery Society a few young active members such as the Quaker brothers, Joseph and Emmanuel Cooper, called for a policy of immediacy. They started a second organisation, called the Agency Committee, which set out to arouse the British public outside Parliament to the evils of slavery. Five lecturers were paid and each was given a district to organise. Within a year they had set up over a thousand new anti-slavery groups. The flood of support was described by one absentee planter living in south-west England:

In this neighbourhood we have anti-slavery clubs, and

Fig 23.4 *Nineteenth-century English people were often critical of planters. A magazine cartoon mocks at their way of life.*

anti-slavery needle parties and anti-slavery tea parties and anti-slavery in so many shapes and ways that even if your enemies do not in the end destroy you by assault, those that side with you must give up for very weariness.

The Agency Committee received a boost when Knibb and Burchell journeyed to England to report to the Baptist Missionary Society. Their descriptions of attacks on non-conformist churches in Jamaica inflamed English opinion in a way slavery itself never had. It was bad to beat an African but unthinkable to persecute an Englishman. The abolitionist, Zachary Macaulay, was amazed. He wrote:

> The religious persecutions in Jamaica has roused the immense body of Methodists and Dissenters throughout the land to a feeling of the most intense and ardent description . . . I stand astonished myself at the result.

For the first time the missionary societies came completely into the open and joined with the abolitionists in calling for an immediate end to slavery.

Parliamentary reform

The final barrier to emancipation fell down in 1832 when the English Parliament was reformed. For many years there had been growing complaints about the membership of the House of Commons. Most MPs sat for country districts or very small towns and bought their seat in Parliament from a landowner. Among them were many members of the West India interest. Such a parliament had matched social conditions in the eighteenth century when Britain's wealth came mostly from agriculture and overseas plantations. It seemed quite unsuitable now that she had become the world's leading industrial power. Neither the great cotton cloth manufacturing city of Manchester nor Birmingham, where the steam engines invented by James Watt were made, had the right to elect MPs. A widespread campaign for parliamentary reform grew up and, after riots in 1832, a Reform Act was passed. Fifty-six of the privately-owned rotten boroughs were abolished, and these included seats held by the West India interest. Other West Indian supporters lost their parliamentary seats when thirty boroughs had their number of MPs cut from two to one. The vacant seats were then distributed to MPs to be elected by Scotland and Ireland and the new industrial towns. Their MPs were unlikely to back the West India interest.

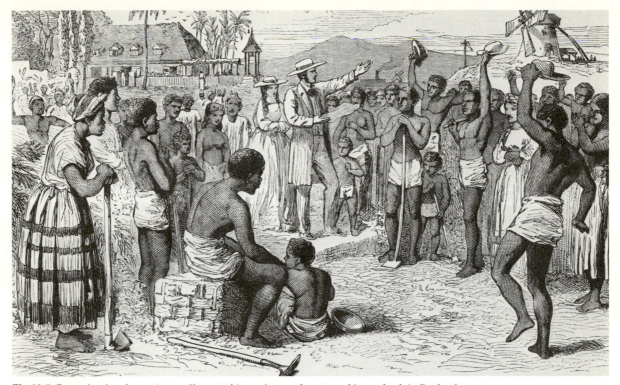

Fig 23.5 *Emancipation day as it was illustrated in a nineteenth-century history book in England.*

The new reformed House of Commons which met in January 1833 had a clear majority of MPs in favour of the immediate end of slavery. MPs from the new manufacturing areas were opposed to the Navigation Acts which gave the colonies protected markets in England. They wanted free trade, without import and export duties, so they could sell their goods cheaply abroad and cheap food could be imported for the new factory workers. They had no sympathy with the planters' struggle to keep their slaves if this meant that Britain had to pay more for her sugar.

The coming of the reformed parliament was a final blow to the planters whose behaviour over amelioration, the slave rebellions and the free coloureds' demands for equality had already united Englishmen against them. With the final collapse of the West India interest the Emancipation Act could not be delayed. It was passed by Parliament in August 1833. A year was allowed to give the planters time to prepare and for the assemblies to pass their own emancipation laws. But it was made clear that no matter what decisions were made in the colonies, slavery throughout the Caribbean, South Africa and Mauritius was to end sharp on midnight 1 August 1834.

The Act

The Act arranged for compensation of £20 million to be paid to slave owners. The West Indian planters received about £16½ million; most of the rest was divided between slave owners in Mauritius and South Africa. Compensation was only to be paid if the colonial assemblies passed their own laws to make certain a smooth changeover to freedom. All children under six years old were to be freed immediately; every one else could be made to serve an apprenticeship if assemblies thought it necessary. Apprentices would have to work 40½ hours a week without pay for their former masters, but beyond that they could demand a wage or hire themselves to another planter. Apprentices could not be sold unless the estate to which they belonged was sold. To settle all disputes between masters and apprentices a number of special magistrates were to be sent out from England. An apprentice could buy his complete freedom at a price agreed between the special magistrate and the master.

The French and Danes continued to use slave labour until 1848, the Dutch until 1865. Slaves laboured on the Spanish islands until 1886 and in Brazil until 1888.

Labour in the nineteenth century

When the British Government abolished the slave trade in 1807 it had the support of some planters on the sugar islands who wanted to check the growth of plantations in Trinidad and British Guiana (Guyana), the new colonies seized from Spain and Holland. At the same time other planters moved to the new territories in the hope of opening canefields on the vast areas of uncleared land. The Governors of Trinidad and British Guiana soon found themselves under heavy pressure to provide them with labourers. As large numbers of slaves could no longer be imported, the governors and planters turned to the idea of using indentured bondservants. They were returning to the system which had been tried in the sugar colonies before slavery, but with one important difference. The bondservants of the seventeenth century had been poor Europeans. In the nineteenth century the search for indentured immigrants was made among the peoples of the many parts of the world which were now dominated by European traders, soldiers and officials.

Chinese from Malaya

The first governor to try to provide indentured labour was Colonel Thomas Picton, the soldier left in charge of Trinidad after it had been taken from the Spanish. In 1802 he wrote to the Colonial Office asking if they would allow him to import Chinese labourers from Malaya. He had been told by friends in Malaya that one Chinese labourer, a plough and a buffalo could do as much work in one day as 'forty stout Negroes'. The Colonial Office agreed to the experiment, saying that it would be a good thing for Trinidad to have a 'race of free cultivators, kept distinct from the Negroes and by their interest attached to the white planters'.

Many Chinese were already emigrating from their homeland to find work in south-east Asia, where European plantations and trading cities were growing fast. It was probably not difficult to persuade some who had moved to Malaya to take up indentures with a promise of small plots of land after five years. 192 made the trip half-way round the world and landed at Trinidad in 1806. They were a disappointment. Only a year later a member of the governor's council asked that they be shipped back since 'their industry was never equal to their maintenance'. Sixty-one returned at their own request in 1807. Seven years later only thirty of the original immigrants lived in Trinidad and not one of them worked on a plantation. For a time Chinese immigration stopped, although it was taken up again half a century later.

Madeirans

As emancipation drew near planters renewed their search for new sources of labour. In the 1830s planters in Trinidad and Guyana turned to Madeira, the Portuguese colony in the Atlantic where sugar was a main crop. Through Mr Seale, an English merchant on the island, they arranged for the first 125 Madeiran caneworkers to come to Trinidad in 1834. A year later 559 landed in Guyana. They were the first of many thousands to come to the Caribbean. Most headed for Guyana because the wages were higher. A few hundred came to Trinidad or found their way to the Windwards and Leewards, but practically none to Jamaica. The numbers of Madeirans declined after 1846, partly because the Portuguese Government objected to so many of their subjects leaving. But it was also because the plantation owners were disappointed in the immigrants. After their indenture was over very few settled as free workers on the plantations. They either returned to Madeira, or became market gardeners, cocoa growers, or entered the retail trade. By 1856 Portuguese Madeirans controlled nearly all the retailing businesses in Guyana and St Vincent.

Indians

In 1838 a Guyanese plantation owner, John Gladstone, decided to try his luck with indentured East Indian labourers. He had read that planters on the island of Mauritius in the Indian Ocean were using indentured labour taken from India. He contacted Gillanders and Company, the firm which supplied Mauritius with the labourers. They assured him that there would be no problem in persuading Indians to sign on for the much longer journey to an unknown land, the 'Natives being perfectly ignorant of the place they agree to go to, and the length of journey they are undertaking'. In May 1836, 396 landed in Guyana. However, the experiment was short-lived. In the same year the British Government forbade recruitment of Indians for overseas labour because of the bad treatment and high death rate they suffered in Mauritius. Sadly, the order had come too late to save the Indians already on Gladstone's estates. Ninety-eight of them died before their time of indenture was over.

Liberated Africans

The abolition of the slave trade brought an undeserved bonus to the planters. The British navy patrolled the seas looking for foreign ships suspected of carrying slaves. Most of the captures they made were of Brazilian or Cuban ships. At first most of the released slaves were taken to Sierra Leone, but after 1838 they were forcibly indentured for up to five years on British West Indian plantations. By 1868, 36,130 liberated Africans had been landed in these colonies:

British Guiana:	13,970
Trinidad	8,390
Jamaica	10,000
Grenada	1,540
St Vincent	1,040
St Lucia	730
St Kitts	460

Free Africans

After emancipation and the end of apprenticeship in 1838, the planters of Trinidad and Guyana hoped for chances to recruit free Africans to work as labourers on their estates. In this search they were in competition with planters from Jamaica, who found that their ex-slaves were leaving the plantations in large numbers to start small holdings in the interior. There were three possible sources of free African labour: from North America, Africa and the other West Indian islands.

The planters were mistaken in believing that slaves who had escaped from the southern American plantations to live in the northern United States or Canada would welcome the chance to work in the warmer Caribbean. Despite their poverty and the harsh climate, less than a thousand escaped American slaves risked increasing their misery by coming to the West Indian cane fields. Attempts to recruit from Sierra Leone and the Kru coast in Africa were hardly more successful. Three hundred years of slavery had given the West Indies a very bad reputation in West Africa. Only a handful of Africans were persuaded to emigrate to Trinidad from the Kru coast and just a few came to Jamaica from Sierra Leone. Some of these were descendants of Jamaican Maroons who had ended up in Sierra Leone after being deported to Nova Scotia in 1796 after the Maroon rebellion.

The Trinidadian, Guyanese and Jamaican planters had more success in attracting freemen from the other West Indian islands. Freemen on the smaller islands sought any chance to go wherever there were better wages and a chance of getting a piece of land, although their former masters made it difficult for them to leave. In Barbados, the Windwards, the Leewards and the Bahamas the assemblies passed acts prohibiting recruitment of emigrants. Ships captains, who were paid a bounty on each immigrant they brought into Trinidad and Guyana, were often not allowed to land in the other colonies. In all of them ministers were asked to help discourage emigration by preaching Sunday sermons on the horrors of the 'Guyanese slave trade'.

Controls on immigration

These attempts to recruit labourers soon caught the attention of the anti-slavery movement in Britain. They did not want unfair indenture schemes to replace slavery. So, as soon as apprenticeship was ended and Africans became free to move in September 1838, the Colonial Office issued a set of regulations to control indenture. They were drawn up by James Stephen, a senior official who was also a leading emancipationist. The regulations stated that no contract could be signed outside the colony where it was to be served, written contracts were limited to one year and verbal agreements to one month. Special magistrates were to be appointed to settle disputes between indentured bondservants and their masters; wage rates had to be reviewed every six months so that they kept level with the average for the district. It was forbidden to pay captains a bounty to bring in Africans, and in 1839 a new regulation made it illegal for the colonies in Guyana to spend public money on assisted passages.

The regulations soon had their effect in cutting the numbers of immigrants. In 1838, 8,000 came into Guyana; a year later only 2,800 arrived. Few planters were willing to pay an immigrant's passage without the power to make him work on the plantation for at least three or four years. The colonies protested to the Colonial Office and asked that the regulations be changed to allow in East Indians. The minister in charge, Lord John Russell, replied saying that, as labour was cheap in India, it was more sensible to grow sugar there: 'the plantation will be found for the labourer and not the labourer for the plantation'.

Bountied European immigrants

James Stephen's regulations aimed at stopping African and Asian immigration. They did not prohibit indenture bonds being signed in Europe or bounties being paid to European immigrants. The assembly in Jamaica was eager to encourage Europeans to settle in the interior so that there would be less room for the ex-slaves who were leaving the plantations in the lowlands. The reasons for the scheme were openly explained in English newspapers:

> I would by my plan, endeavour to supersede the necessity of any black labourers in the mountains, and by having 50 to 60,000 whites there, bring down, say, 100,000 blacks to the lowlands. This would benefit the planters without injury to the negroes: to the former it would give a greater quantity of labourers . . . to the latter it would make the necessity of work greater; consequently less fear of their relapsing into barbarism.

Some planters recruited their own settlers but the assembly also appointed agents to recruit in Europe. New immigrants were paid a bounty, usually of £12, if they stayed for at least six months and promised land after five years. Some were brought to three townships set aside for immigrants by the assembly.

Trinidad and British Guiana attempted similar schemes, although they looked for labourers on the main plantations more than the interior. But planters in all the colonies found that it was difficult to recruit Europeans. During the nineteenth century more than seven million people left Europe for North America, but the West Indies offered much poorer opportunities. The best land was already taken up and stories of the unhealthy climate were widespread. The

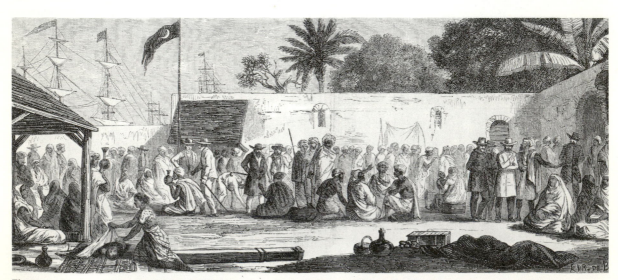

Fig 24.1   *The French brought indentured labourers from North Africa to Guadeloupe. Here they wait to be sent to the plantations.*

few who did come advised others not to follow. They reported that they were not provided with housing or medical care and that they lacked the farming skills to clear the interior lands. Many died within the first months; others wandered off to the port towns and drank themselves to death. A few went home and a few headed west to the mainland.

By 1840 Governor Macleod in Trinidad had had enough of European immigrants. He wrote to the Colonial Office to say how shocked he was by the arrival of 'still another ship, the *Louise*, from Havre, having on board 190 German and French people'. He refused to allow them to stay in Trinidad and begged the Secretary of State to be:

> . . . good enough to take the necessary measures for cal-
> ling on the French Government not to permit any vessels
> to clear from their ports with immigrants to Trinidad at
> least in ignorance of the disadvantages and other evils
> with which they will have to contend here.

By 1843 the colonies had abandoned nearly all schemes for European immigration. A few hundred had settled in the Leewards and Windwards and a few thousand into Trinidad and Guyana. The Jamaican scheme had attracted only 2,685 British and 1,038 Germans. The general opinion of the planters and colonial governors was that paying bounties to Europeans who were unsuitable for plantation labour did nothing to meet the needs of the estate owners. It was, wrote the editor of the Jamaican *Falmouth Post*, a waste of public money to try to substitute 'a European

for an African peasantry in the tropics'.

New immigration schemes

Continual reports from the colonial governors that their territories were still short of labour suitable for plantation work soon led to a complete turn-about by the British Government. In 1843 when European immigration had become an obvious failure, it allowed Trinidad, Guyana and Jamaica to raise loans to pay for the passage of new indentured labourers. In the same year it lifted the restriction on recruiting labour in India. In 1846 the British Parliament passed the Sugar Duties Equalisation Act which removed the protection that West Indian planters had in the English market. To compensate planters for the lower prices they feared now other nations could sell to Britain, the government took away all other restrictions on immigration.

Three years later in 1849 a complete scheme for encouraging immigration under the supervision of the British Government was drawn up. The British Government agreed to guarantee a private loan to West Indian planters to pay for the scheme. But the planters were not trusted to care for their labourers or treat them fairly. So recruitment, shipping and supervision of living conditions on the estates was made the responsibility of the British Government and officials both in the West Indies and the homelands of the immigrants.

Fig 24.2 *Between decks on a ship carrying emigrants from Europe to the Americas in 1851.*

Fig 24.3 *Canton in south China. The buildings along the side of the harbour are the warehouses of British traders.*

Recruiting the Chinese

The British Government's regulations stated that the length of the indenture, wages and arrangements for a return passage were to be clearly explained to each immigrant. Recruiters were not to bribe, threaten or use force. These rules were not obeyed in China where the British Government had little power.

Between 1859 and 1866 about 15,000 Chinese came to Guyana, 2,600 to Trinidad and 4,800 to Jamaica. Most of them came from barracoons at Hong Kong, a small British colony on the south coast of China. They had found themselves in the barracoons after being taken prisoner in the civil war that was being fought across the whole of south China. Their captors handed them over to local indenture brokers who released them for a fee to British immigration agents.

Planters complained that the Chinese did not make good estate workers as few re-indentured themselves; instead they preferred to return to China or open small retail shops in the Caribbean. They were more expensive than East Indian labourers, who usually cost a planter about £15 as against £25 for a Chinese. In 1866 the costs rose greatly when the Chinese Government insisted that indentures had to allow for a full return passage after five years; the planters wanted to pay this only after two five-year indenture periods had been served. The increased cost was enough to bring Chinese immigration to an end. Later Chinese immigrants to the Americas avoided the British-owned Caribbean. By 1890 the Americans and Cubans had signed up 150,000 to work in their canefields. More came to work on the railways in the western United States and the Hawaian sugar fields, where pay was better. Naturally the greatest number of Chinese emigrants did not come to the western world; hundreds of thousands found work in the plantations, ports and warehouses of south east Asia.

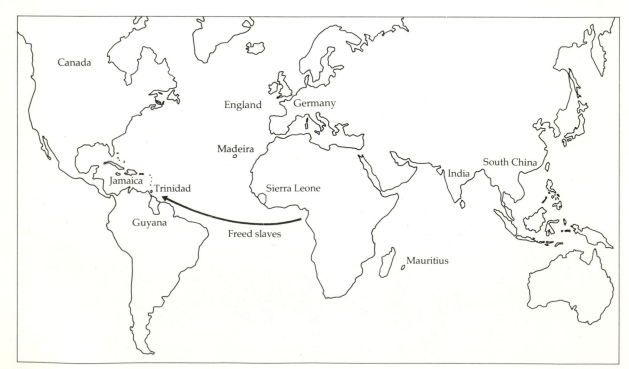

Map 33 *Sources of immigration to the Caribbean.*

25   The Indians

Recruiting the Indians

After 1857 most indentured labourers came from India, the largest territory in the British Empire. It was not difficult to find willing immigrants. Thousands of people had been thrown out of traditional jobs in village craft shops, making cloth and small metal tools and ornaments, because of new competition from the mechanised mills and factories in England. There was simply not enough land to divide among the younger sons, who now had no choice but to remain idle in the country villages. By 1850 the wage for a day's labour had dropped to a ½d. Between 1850 and 1877 a series of famines in the Ganges plain increased food prices beyond the reach of many of the poorest families. For thousands of Indians the offer of a shilling a day and steady work in Trinidad and Guyana seemed the only escape from a life of poverty.

As far as the planters were concerned the Indians made ideal labourers. They were hardworking, used to tropical cultivation, and re-indentured themselves more often than either the Chinese or the Madeirans. They could also be recruited easily. British ships and trading posts provided ready-made collection centres and transportation facilities. The British Government was pleased as well. Because of their great power in India, English officials could supervise recruitment closely. Between 1844 and 1917, 416,000 East Indians were indentured to work in the British West Indies. They were divided among the colonies in this way:

British Guiana	239,000
Trinidad	134,000
Jamaica	33,000
St Lucia	4,000
Grenada	3,000
St Vincent	2,700
St Kitts	300

The Indians

The ancestors of most people living in the modern Indian peninsula belonged to one of three linguistic groups: those speaking the languages of the jungle peoples, the Dravidians and the Aryans. Each language group contained people of several different racial backgrounds. The peninsula's first inhabitants were jungle tribesmen. Today their ancient dialects are spoken in only a few remote villages in the central interior highlands. The jungle peoples were forced to flee there by groups of nomads who moved in from the west more than 5,000 years ago. These newcomers spoke the Dravidian languages; they were dark-skinned and slightly built. Their first settlements were along the broad river plains of the Indus and Ganges but in the following centuries they spread through the whole peninsula.

The Dravidians were driven from the northern coastal and river plains by taller and fairer-skinned people who first arrived about 1500 B.C. These were the men of the Aryan-speaking peoples. Their invasion accounts for the language divisions of modern India. In the south Dravidian dialects are spoken; in the north and along the western coast people tend to speak Hindi, a language derived from the various Aryan dialects.

Western societies owe much to the early Indian civilisations. Arabic numbers, especially the use of '0' which allows for easy counting in multiples of ten, were devised by the first Indian civilisations. Their ancient written language, Sanskrit, has provided clues to the beginning of our own languages and to the way in which early man migrated across the face of the earth. One of the oldest practised religions in the world, Hinduism, was formulated by the first Indians. Hinduism gave rise to other sects like the Jainists and the Sikhs, and at least one other major world religion, Buddhism.

The wealth of India

For thousands of years the people of Africa and

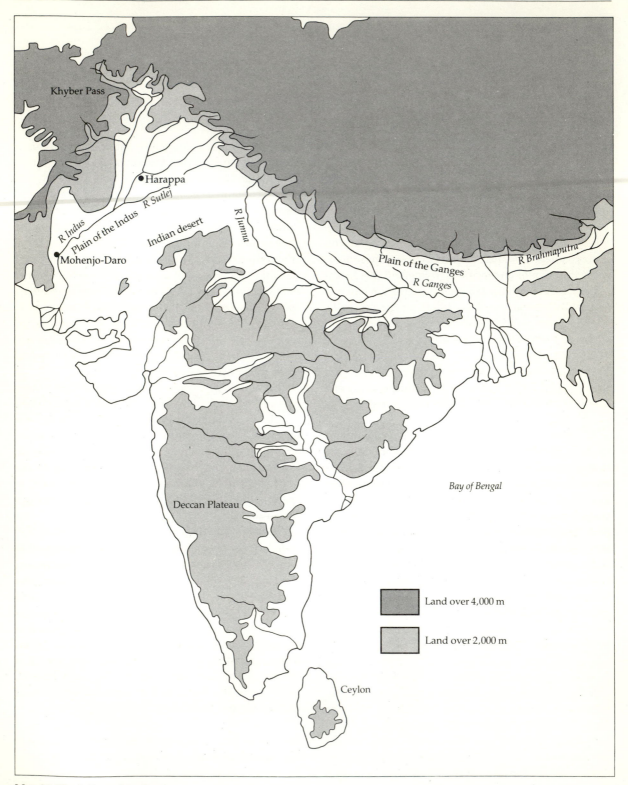

Map 34 *The Indian subcontinent.*

Fig 25.1 *A Hindu temple in India, painted in 1787.*

western Europe spoke in awe of India's fabulous wealth. The fertile plains along the Indus and Ganges Rivers were ideal for growing food crops and cotton, and herding sheep, goats and cattle; the southern forests provided exotic spices, dyes and hardwoods; gems were mined in the central highlands. By 5000 B.C. two cities, Mohenjo-Daro and Harappa, controlled trade along the Indus River. The cities built of kiln-dried bricks contained thousands of dwelling houses and fine palaces, administrative buildings, pillared temples and elaborate public baths. At the centre of each city was a high walled citadel. Enormous granaries and warehouses stored trade goods and tribute which surrounding farmers paid as taxes to their rulers. But the cities were also the homes of craftsmen and artisans. Wheelwrights made carts to be pulled by domesticated water buffalo; potters had learned to use the wheel to turn their clay into thin-walled jugs, pots and jars. Blacksmiths mixed metals and fashioned axes, chisels, knives and razors from copper and bronze. Jewellers carved ivory into needles and combs, and made necklaces, rings and bang-les from gold, silver, jade, agate and lapis lazuli.

About 1500 B.C. the cities were suddenly and violently destroyed, probably by the first Aryan invaders. The newcomers built few cities. Firstly they were farmers, raising crops of rice, barley, wheat, millet, beans and sugar cane. They had come with herds of cattle, sheep, goats and donkeys. But the early city craftsmen did not disappear. Between the Indus and the Ganges thousands of small villages grew up where craftsmen continued to turn out fine leathers, metal items, and woven cotton cloth. While the western Africans and the Europeans were still in the stone age, the Indians were already finding a ready market for their wares throughout Asia and the Middle East.

The invasions

The combination of industry and agriculture encouraged the growth of a large population. By 500 B.C. the whole peninsula was divided into a number of independent kingdoms. Few of the Indian princes were powerful enough to try to join the independent king-doms into a lasting empire. Nor could they stop wave after wave of new invaders from the west. First the Persians and then the Macedonians, under Alexander the Great, led their armies into the peninsula and for a brief while ruled over the Indian kingdoms. They were followed by the Scithians and the Huns and a new round of Muslim conquerors from Persia and Afghanistan. Unlike the others, the Muslims did not leave. By 1400 A.D. a line of Muslim rulers, the Great Moguls, had established their capital at Delhi and united the Indian principalities and kingdoms into a loosely-knit, federated empire.

The Moguls

One of the Mogul rulers, Akbar (1556–1605), tried to make India a more manageable centralised state. Working with the native Hindu princes, he set out to build a network of sound roads to link the peninsula to Delhi. Honest governors and royal officials were appointed; the tax system was overhauled and a standing army was created. Akbar's successors were less capable. Most were content to pass their lives spending the Empire's wealth on such lasting monu-ments as the Taj Mahal and the beautiful alabaster palace of the Moguls in Delhi which held a solid gold, gem-encrusted peacock throne. In 1600 several Hindu princes formed the Mahratta Confederacy and revolted against the Muslim Moguls. The Moguls were unable to suppress the Confederacy and, by 1700, India was once again on the verge of breaking up into several warring states. Neither the Moguls nor the princes were able to put their differences aside long enough to stop a new invasion from Persia in 1739. For the Moguls the consequences of the inva-sion were disastrous. Delhi was sacked, over 30,000 people were killed, and the Moguls' symbol of author-ity, the peacock throne, was carried back to Persia.

By the mid-eighteenth century India was again divided into over twenty-five small principalities and kingdoms ruled by local kings, rajahs, sultans and minor princes who obeyed and disobeyed the Mogul in Delhi as it pleased them. The chief mark of Mogul rule was the conversion of many of the people of northern India to the Muslim religion. Most of their descendents now live in the Muslim states of Pakistan and Bangladesh.

The Europeans in India

Five years after Columbus arrived in the Caribbean, the Portuguese sailor, Vasco Da Gama, was the first European to sail direct to India. Within a hundred years English and French traders had followed and taken over most of the European trade with the Mogul Empire. Both nations set up East India Companies which were given permission by the emperors to open trading stations around the coast. At first these companies kept away from Indian politics but, in the eighteenth century, they took advantage of the civil wars and quarrels to act quite independently of the Moguls in Delhi. East India Company agents built their own forts, garrisoned them with armed soldiers, coined their own money and signed private trade agreements. By the outbreak of the Seven Years War in 1756 Company officials like the Frenchman Joseph Dupleix and the Englishman Robert Clive were hir-ing, drilling and arming their own Indian *sepoy* regi-ments. The sepoys were used against Indian princes, who were slow to grant trading concessions, and also fought in the struggle between the English and French companies for the lion's share of the Indian trade.

The British East India Company had much the greatest success. The French were defeated in the Seven Years War and again in the French Wars. At the same time the East India Company extended its con-trol over many parts of the Mogul Empire, gradually forcing rulers to accept Company officials and tax collectors as the real rulers of their lands. By 1857 the Company had by far the largest army in India, but all its Indian troops were not loyal. British commanders had treated sepoys with little regard for their pride or for their religious customs. Although sepoys out-numbered English soldiers by six to one, few were ever made officers. In late 1857 the sepoy regiments in the Ganges valley mutinied against their British commanders and, for a while, British power in north India seemed to have collapsed. However, the mutiny was soon put down as regiments in the south and west refused to join their countrymen.

The 'Indian Mutiny' convinced the British Gov-ernment that the East India Company could no longer be trusted to manage the affairs of the peninsula. A separate department for India was set up in the Colo-nial Office. At the same time the last of the Moguls, who had supported the mutiny, was deposed and replaced by a British governor sent to rule India in

Fig 25.2 *The Mogul Emperor, Akbar, receiving an ambassador from Queen Elizabeth I of England in 1599.*

much the same way as the crown colonies in Trinidad and Guyana were ruled. One by one the local maharajahs, rajahs, princes and lesser rulers were bribed, threatened and forced to place their territories under British protection. In return most were invited to advise the new British governor in a number of princes' assemblies. The system was completed in 1877 when Queen Victoria was proclaimed Empress of India and a viceroy was sent to rule over the local princes in her name. The real rulers of India at every level from the viceroy down to the district officers in charge of a few villages were officials or soldiers born and educated in Britain. With few changes the Empire of India remained intact until the end of British rule in 1947.

Recruiting in India

It was not the planters but the island governments who recruited Indians. Guyana, Trinidad and Jamaica each appointed immigration agents to work from Calcutta. Most immigrants came from the overcrowded villages on the plain of the River Ganges which flowed, with many lesser rivers, through the United Provinces, Bihar and West Bengal. Throughout the nineteenth century the population of the Ganges plain was rising while traditional village industries such as weaving and iron work were destroyed by competition from English factory-made goods. The result was that hundreds of thousands of villagers left their homes to seek work in other parts of India. To attract these desperate unemployed people to emigrate to the West Indies recruiting stations were set up in the charge of sub-agents. The sub-agents paid recruiters a shilling for every able-bodied person they brought into the station. There was no control over the methods used by the recruiters, but the sub-agents were responsible for explaining the conditions of the indenture and seeing that it was legally witnessed by a magistrate before sending the new recruits on to Calcutta. It is unlikely that many of the recruits

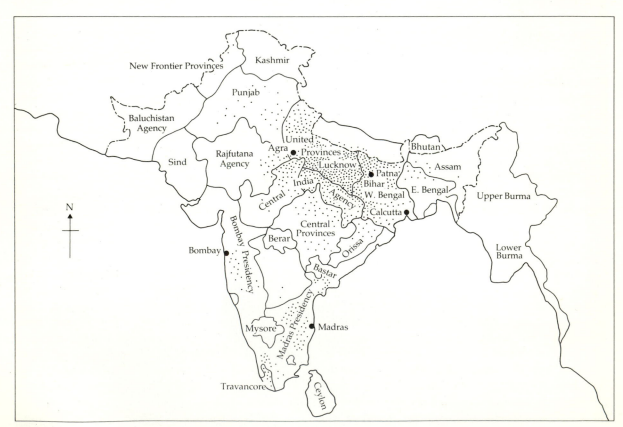

Map 35 *The main homelands of Indian indentured labourers. Each dot represents between 150 and 200 recruits.*

understood clearly what they were told. For each signed contract the sub-agent collected about £3 for a man and £5 for a woman from which he had to pay all his expenses. Higher fees were paid for women in an attempt to correct the greater proportion of men indentured servants on the West Indian plantations.

In Calcutta the emigrants were medically inspected and their contracts were again gone over by an English official. If all was in order, the emigrants were sent to barracks to await passage to the West Indies. For a time immigrants were also recruited by agents at Madras. But the number of indentured servants from the south was tiny compared with those from the Ganges plain. In Trinidad the languages of southern India almost disappeared as the few thousand Madrasi immigrants found it necessary to learn Hindi spoken by the northerners.

The voyage

The first immigrants were allowed less than one and a half square metres deck space, very cramped quarters for a journey that lasted from 93 to 113 days. Death rates were very high at first. In 1858 the *Salsette* from Calcutta to Trinidad landed only 199 passengers; 124 had died of cholera, dysentry and sea-sickness. Such high mortality rates led to new regulations in 1864. Each immigrant was to be allowed at least two cubic metres below decks, with no more than one adult for each bunk. Other regulations checked the deadly outbreaks of cholera and dysentry. Each ship had to carry a medical officer, a dispenser, supplies of drugs, warm clothing and adequate provisions. By 1868 the mortality on immigrant ships had dropped to about 5.45 per cent.

The immigration department

When immigrants landed in a Caribbean colony they came under the control of the local immigration department headed by a protector of immigrants, who was sometimes called agent-general. Each year planters sent in requests for labourers, and the immigration department divided the arrivals among the estates. It was then the protector's task to enforce the many regulations, such as those which forbade the separation of families and those which required the planter to provide sound housing with watertight roofing and adequate drainage. To do this he had a staff of clerks, travelling inspectors and interpreters. There was also a special corps of medical officers, headed by the colony's surgeon-general which had been set up when it was found that many new immigrants died within the first year. Every three months the protector's staff had to prepare a report on each plantation, listing the number of days lost through sickness, all fines on labourers, and the number of births and deaths.

Indenture contracts

The British Government insisted that all indenture contracts had to state clearly the length of service, the number of hours to be worked each day, rates of pay and the conditions for a return passage. Under pressure from planters, the terms of the contracts became harsher as time went on. At first, in the years after 1848, immigrants had to serve at least three years on the plantation of the first indenture and then to remain in the colony for another two years before claiming their return passage. Both the Trinidadian and Guyanese planters thought that a five-year residency was too short, and in 1862 they succeeded in having the contracts lengthened to five years on the first plantation and an additional five years residence. The planters still objected to the free passage home, and in 1895 this was given only to the sick and disabled. The others had to pay a quarter of the fare and in 1898 this was raised to a half. Women paid a sixth in 1895 and a third in 1898.

To encourage labourers to settle near their estates some planters in Trinidad and Guyana sold them small plots of land when their indenture ended. The immigrants were often not allowed to sell the land for years. By 1893 about 32,000 immigrants had bought land in Guyana. Between 1869 and 1881 immigrants in Trinidad were allowed to take up five acres (2.02 hectares) of crown land instead of their passage home. However, many immigrants preferred to buy plots on the land of their choice. By the time the last Indian had finished his indenture only a quarter of all those brought to Trinidad and Guyana had taken a passage home.

Most contracts laid down that indentured labourers should work a five and a half day week with Sundays

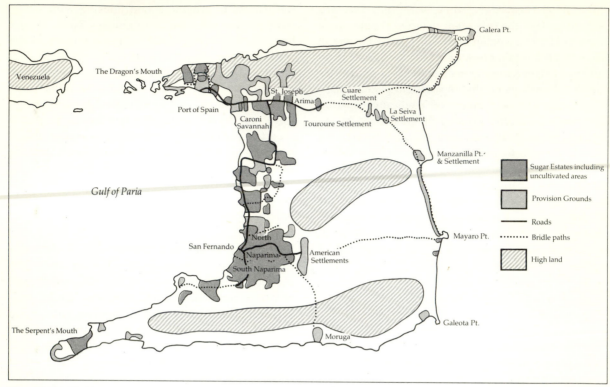

Map 36 *Trinidad in 1850.*

and public holidays off. At first the daily hours of work were ten in the factory and seven in the fields; soon the contracts were changed to a standard nine hours for everyone. Immigrants were to receive weekly wages even if the planter had no work to give them. Most colonies had fairly standard wages of 24 or 25 cents per day for men and 16 cents for women and children over ten. Newly arrived immigrants were supplied with provisions for some months at a rate of 8 cents per day. After this they were responsible for securing their own food. All contracts required the masters to supply housing and medical care.

Immigration ordinances

When the immigrant landed in the West Indies he found that, as well as abiding by the contract he had signed in India, he had to obey a set of special ordinances which applied only to indentured labourers. These special ordinances generally favoured the planters. Indentured servants could not leave the estate without written passes from the owner or the over-

seer; work not done to the owner's satisfaction had to be done again in the servant's own time; servants could not drink liquor in estate housing, use disrespectful language or make insulting gestures to those in authority; it was illegal to congregate outside the plantation to discuss grievances or to refuse 'reasonable' orders. Breaking one of these ordinances could lead to a fine or a fine and a jail sentence. At one time a servant could spend 14 days in jail or be fined $4.50 (two and a half week's wages) for playing sick. In Trinidad leaving an estate without a pass was punishable by a £5 fine and two months in jail. Time spent in jail had to be made up to the planter in the servant's free time.

It was not a criminal offence if the planters broke any of the ordinances. A twenty-four dollar fine was the maximum penalty they could expect if an immigrant managed to sue them in the courts for a breach of contract. This happened rarely since the immigrants were usually unable to speak English and almost always unfamiliar with the workings of English law. The immigration departments' agents were allowed to act on behalf of the indentured servants, but they

Fig 25.3 *African workers in Jamaica in the 1880s. The canefields in Jamaica were mostly worked by African freemen; thousands of* *others emigrated to other islands or Central America.*

had to be careful not to anger the planters or their friends in the assemblies and governors' councils. In Guyana, the Agent-General, James Crosby, a magistrate, William De Voeux, and the Chief Justice, Joseph Beaumont, tried fairly to administer the indenture ordinances. Governor Sir Francis Hinks quickly showed them that they shouldn't interfere with 'planter privileges'. De Voeux was transferred to another colony; Crosby's travel allowances were suspended and his sub-agents had their visits to plantations to hear complaints restricted to twice yearly. The planters certainly never held back on legal prosecutions. Between 1898 and 1905 Trinidadian planters charged 11,149 immigrants for absences, desertions, vagrancy and idleness. In this period of seven years at least one in five of all the indentured servants in Trinidad were brought before the magistrates.

The immigrants were exploited in other ways as the ordinances intended to protect them broke down or were simply ignored. Wages were often withheld, or unfair piece-work was given which made it impossible for those workers involved to earn the minimum

wages stated in their contracts. Housing was seldom adequate. Most estates supplied barrack housing which by law had to contain rooms not less than three metres by three and a half. This was judged space enough for a married couple and their children or three single adults. Few planters bothered to provide their barracks with cooking facilities, sanitary conveniences, or regular water supplies. In 1888 Mr Lechmere Guppy, Mayor of San Fernando, described the barracks in his district as:

> . . . long wooden buildings eleven or twelve feet wide (about two and a half metres), containing perhaps eight or ten small rooms divided from each other by wooden partitions not reaching the roof. The roof is of galvanised iron, without any ceiling; and the heat of the sun by day and the cold by night take full effect upon the occupants. By standing on a box the occupant of one room can look over the partition into the adjoining one, and can easily climb over . . . Comfort, privacy and decency are impossible under such conditions.

The hospitals which each plantation had to supply were little better. Many of the first were holdovers from the days of slavery when they had doubled as lockups. They were so generally detested that the authorities in Trinidad had to pass an ordinance laying down a three month jail sentence for immigrants who ran away from hospital.

The hospitals did nothing to check the poor general health of the immigrant population. In 1911, 24,000 cases of illness were reported for the 10,000 registered immigrants on Trinidadian plantations. There were over 8,400 cases of malaria and 7,100 cases of diseases caused by parasites such as anaemia, hookworm and ground itch. Most of them could be traced to poor diets and unsanitary living conditions around the barracks.

Education

From time to time the immigration department stirred itself to issue ordinances which encouraged the immigrants to send their children to the few schools that were available. In many cases the Hindu and Muslim parents objected to sending their children to the local church schools. But they were almost never encouraged to set up their own schools. The attitude of the Immigration Agent-General for Guyana was all too typical. In 1880 he argued against the need to educate immigrant children on the grounds that:

> . . . large gangs of little children . . . are often employed in light work, such as carrying earth, ashes and manure and this is not only a benefit to their parents but also a source of pleasure to themselves . . . in this country, where their work is as much pastime as labour and is conducive to the promotion of health and vigour, both of body and mind, the necessity of such a restriction as going to school does not appear to me to exist.

Thirty years later his successor was still arguing against 'any steps which may tend to the withdrawal of a single individual from the soil'.

The most important exception to this neglect of Indian education was the Canadian Presbyterian Mission in Trinidad. By 1911 they had opened sixty-one free primary schools for Indians as well as two high schools and a teachers' training college.

Ending indentured immigration

By 1885 nationalist organisations in India were beginning to object to Britain's absolute rule. One of the first abuses they attacked was the indenture sys-

tem. The Indian National Congress, which was mainly Hindu, and the All India Muslim League joined in calling the system unjust, exploitive and an insult to their countrymen's dignity. In 1893 the great Congress leader, Mohandas Gandhi, went to South Africa and was soon leading the Indians there in a campaign to obtain full rights. In 1910 the chance to end indenture came when the British Government first allowed Indians a voice in their government by allowing a few to join a council to advise the Viceroy on future laws. At the first meeting, Gopal Krishna Gokhale asked the Viceroy to consider ending emigration by 1912. The Viceroy refused but agreed to send a Commission of Enquiry to examine the condition of indentured Indians in the West Indies and Fiji. In 1913 the West Indian Commission went back with a report outlining the unhealthy conditions and unfair treatment given to immigrant labourers. After a second Commission reported on Fiji in 1916 the Viceroy first suspended indentured emigration and then, in 1917, it was stopped forever.

Support in the West Indies

Many West Indians welcomed the end of indenture. Cocoa and copra producers had complained for a number of years that the indenture system was unfair to them. Although only about five per cent of the indentured servants were sent to their estates, their cocoa and copra were heavily taxed to provide the public money which paid for indentured immigration. They were supported by some progressive sugar planters, who thought that cheap labour produced backward methods of production and wastefulness.

Some public officials worried that cheap, semi-free labour was holding back the social and moral development of the colonies. In 1897 the Mayor of Port of Spain, Henry Alcazar, complained that the use of indentured servants kept the educated propertied classes 'at the moral level of slave owners'. Spokesmen for the Negro freemen also complained that indentures kept wages artificially low for everybody. In 1904 Prudhomme David, one of the first blacks nominated to Trinidad's Legislative Council, protested at the renewal of government subsidies for immigration. He argued that there was no longer a shortage of labour and that more immigrants would only depress wages further and drive more African freemen to look

Fig 25.4 *One of the small groups of Indian indentured labourers who worked on the cocoa plantations in Trinidad.*

elsewhere for work. David's case was supported by the facts. Between 1901 and 1917 about 84,000 West Indians emigrated in search of better paying jobs on the Panama Canal, Costa Rican banana plantations and Cuban sugar estates. During the same period, West Indian governments had paid subsidies to bring in 24,260 West Indian labourers. Clearly indentured immigration could no longer be justified on the grounds that there was a labour shortage.

The Indians in Caribbean society

Seen from the point of view of planters, Indian immigration succeeded in providing the labour which the earlier attempts to recruit Madeirans,

Europeans, Chinese and free Africans had failed to do. In Trinidad exports of sugar increased five times between 1833 and 1896 and nearly all the field labour was done by East Indians. In Guyana, too, the development of the canefields went hand in hand with immigration as the following table shows.

Period	Hectares under cane	No. of immigrants	Population per hectare
1852	17,927	15,392	0.86
1861	20,738	31,933	1.53
1871	30,681	50,321	1.64
1884	32,118	63,055	1.96
1885–87	30,719	68,977	2.24
1894–96	27,367	72,097	2.63
1903–04	29,488	72,793	2.46

The table makes it clear that, up to 1886, there was a steady increase in the hectares under cane, which would not have taken place without the flow of immigrants. After 1884 the sugar industry was in depression, but the flow of indentured Indians continued at a time when their labour was no longer needed.

The cost to the Indians themselves, the people whose descendants make up well over one-third of Trinidad's population and more than half of Guyana's, was heavy. The indentured population of these colonies in the nineteenth century was constantly sick; the result of disgraceful housing, little sanitation and unnecessarily hard work for masters who made no effort to make cultivation easier or more efficient. Labourers on the plantations were, at best, only half free. For most, there was not even the chance of factory work as an alternative to toiling in the fields. Most plantation artisans were Africans, but very few would work alongside Indians in the field-gangs with their hateful reminders of slavery.

The reputation of being fit only for the poorest labouring jobs followed the East Indian when he left the plantation to join the free society after his indenture. Indians were marked out by their different speech and clothing and despised as 'heathens'. Those who drifted into the towns usually found that there was nothing but 'coolie' work as porters and sweepers. Efforts were made to prevent Indian communities building homes in the towns; one settlement in Port of Spain was burned by the police to force the Indians to trek back into the countryside.

For such reasons most free Indians were reluctant to seek work in the towns after indenture. Besides, for most their only real skill was in agriculture. They preferred to take up small farming on crown lands or on the margins of the plantations. In this way they made a great contribution to the development of Trinidad and Guyana. Free Indians took the lead in showing that the combined field and factory system of the plantation was not the only way to produce sugar. By the end of indenture there were many Indian farmers in Trinidad selling their canes to be milled in large central factories. After 1906 these Indian farmers outnumbered the creole small holders. Indians were

pioneers too. They showed that it was possible to grow rice in paddy fields in the wet low-lying areas. They helped clear the forests of the northern and central ranges in Trinidad where cocoa was grown.

The growth of Indian villages in the interiors helped the immigrants to preserve many features of their traditional societies. About 85 per cent of them were Hindu and 15 per cent Muslim. A few had been converted to Christianity in India but very few changed faith in the West Indies. Indians kept their respect for their religious and social leaders, the Muslim *mulvis* and the Hindu Brahmin priests. Although Hindu and Muslim marriages were not recognised by law until well into the twentieth century, the people themselves respected them and refused to register them with the civil authorities.

The Indians kept their languages alive too, both the various Hindi dialects and the Urdu spoken by Muslims, which is a form of Hindi with a different script. Among other obvious signs of the Indian success in preserving much from their traditional society were the building of mosques and temples, the small coloured triangular flags or *jhandis* which appeared outside houses built in Indian style, and special holidays and celebrations such as Divali, the festival of lights. Less obvious, but important for the future well-being of the Indians, was the firm structure of family life in which all relations supported each other. In the early years of indenture this feature of Indian society had seemed under threat because of the division of families between those who stayed behind and those who came to the West Indies. By the 1870s, however, East Indian life was once again built around close family loyalties.

A fully free society was slow in coming to the West Indies. The slaves were emancipated in 1834 only to find themselves bound to serve apprenticeships for another four years. In 1838 they became fully free but, in the two newest colonies, their place as servile labourers was taken by the indentured immigrants from China and India. Only in 1917 did the end come to the long story of enforced immigration to the Caribbean which had begun with the first shiploads of Africans brought by the Spanish three hundred years before.

Exercises

Chapters 1 and 2

Points to consider

1 How did growing surplus crops make the Aztec, Inca and Maya societies different from those of the hunters, gatherers and subsistence farmers?
2 What evidence can you find to illustrate that the Caribs were more warlike than the Arawaks?
3 What Amerindian inventions and crops are still commonly used in the Caribbean region today?

Checks on understanding

a The three main types of Amerindian societies.
b The Maya city states and temple cities.
c The connections between Maya priests, agriculture and mathematics.
d The similarities between Aztecs, Incas and Mayas.
e The work of archaeologists on Arawak and Carib remains.
f The migration of the Arawaks and Caribs to the Antilles.
g The livelihood of the Arawaks and Caribs.
h The manufacturing skills of the Arawaks and Caribs.
i The social divisions in Arawak and Carib society.
j Religion among the Arawaks and Caribs.

Checks on reading

Names
Aztec, Maya, Inca, Carib, Ciboney, Arawak (Lucayano, Taino, Boriqueno) Nepoyes, Chochos, Cuna, Warraws, Wapisians.

Terms
city state, temple city, slash and burn agriculture, kitchen middens, subsistence farmers, surplus farmers, priest-king, *duhos*, *macana*, *zemis*, *butu*, *obutu*, *ubutu maliarici*, *naharlene*, *tiubutuli canoao*, *piragua*, *nitayono*, *cacique*, *coyiaba*.

Further work

1 Are there any Amerindian sites in your district which you can visit?
2 Which Amerindian group lived in your area? Find out as much as you can about them.

References

European conquest of Arawaks: Chapter 4 and 5.

European conquest of Amerindians on the mainland: Chapter 5.
War between the Caribs and Europeans: Chapter 7.
Caribs in the neutral islands: Chapter 15.

Peter Ashdown, *Caribbean History in Maps*, Longman, 1979, maps 4–8.

Chapters 3 and 4

Points to consider

1 Why did the Europeans want a sea route to Africa and the Far East?
2 Why did the Spaniards begin to search for a *western* sea route to the Far East?
3 What connection can you see between the *reconquista* and the Spanish conquest in America?

Checks on understanding

The Spanish
a The *reconquista* and the formation of the Iberian kingdoms.
b The Spanish *hidalgos*, clergy and merchants prepared for new discoveries.
c The Spanish traders.

A sea route to the Far East
a The Arab trade routes.
b Prince Henry and the African voyages.
c The Renaissance . . . aids for navigation and exploration.
d The Portuguese sea route around Africa.
e The treaty of Alcaçovas and the Canary Islands.

Columbus
a Columbus and his calculations for a voyage westward to India.
b Columbus searches for a patron.
c Columbus' first trans-Atlantic voyage.
d The colonisation of Hispaniola.
e Columbus' second, third and fourth voyages.
f Mapping America.
g Caribbean winds and currents.

Checks on reading

Names
Vikings, Isabella and Ferdinand, Moors, Prince Henry,

Ptolemy, Al-Farghani, Marco Polo, Bartholomew Diaz, Vasco Da Gama, Dona Felipa Menez, Juan Ninas, the Pinzon brothers, Rodrigo de Triana, Bartholomew Columbus, Francisco de Bobadilla, Martin Waldseemuller, Amerigo Vespucci.

Terms
reconquista, *Iberians*, *hidalgos*, *encomienda*, *portolani*, *astrolabe*, cross-staff, quadrant, caravel, Trade Winds, Doldrums, Westerlies, Gulf Stream.

Treaties
Treaty of Alcaçovas 1479.

Further work

1 What Spanish place names can you identify on a map of your section of the Caribbean? What does their distribution tell you about Spanish exploration and settlement? Beware you don't confuse Amerindian and Spanish names.
2 What can you learn about Spanish settlements from pictures or from visiting local sites?

References

Extension of Spanish settlement from the Antilles to the mainland: Chapter 5.
Further European colonisation of the Antilles: Chapters 7 and 8.

Chapter 5

Points to consider

1 What were the consequences of the discovery of America for the Amerindians?
2 Why were the Spanish colonists often dissatisfied with rules and regulations enacted by the Spanish Government?
3 How did the Spanish rulers attempt to keep control of their vast American Empire?

Checks on understanding

Permanent colonies in the Antilles
a Ovando builds a permanent colony in Hispaniola.
b A choice of export crops.
c Forced labour from the Amerindians.
d Extinction of the Arawaks and attempts to find a new source of labour.
e Hispaniola as a base for further conquests in the Antilles.

Spaniards on the mainland
a The Antilles and the mainland conquests.
b The mainland conquests.
c The declining importance of the Antilles.

The Spanish Empire in America
a The new settlers . . . the Antillean creoles.
b Economic life in the Antilles.
c The creoles and local government.
d Royal officials.
e The Church and royal government.
f Attempts to protect the Amerindians.
g Las Casas's social experiments.
h Spain controls the Empire's wealth.
i The Empire's wealth and Spain's economy.

Checks on understanding

Names
Juan de Fonseca, Nicolas de Ovando, Ponce de Leon, Juan d'Esquival, Diego Columbus, Panfilo de Narvaez, Diego Velasquez, Bartolomé de Las Casas, Hernán Cortes, Vasco Nunez de Balboa, Francisco Pizarro, Antonio de Montesinos.

Terms
repartimiento, *cabildo*, *encomondero*, *capiculacion*, *adelantado*, *conquistadores*, 'creole', *peninsulares*, *villa*, *plaza major*, *regidores*, *alcades*, *audiencia*, Council of Castile, Council of the West Indies, presidency, viceroyalty, viceroy, *visitador*, *residencia*, Papal Bull, Holy Office of the Inquisition, friars, mercantilism, *Casa de Contratación, asiento*.

Treaties, laws and special agreements
Laws of Burgos 1512, New Laws of 1542.

Further work

1 What value, if any, was your country to the Spanish Empire?
2 What new crops and animals did the Spaniards bring to your country? How important have these new crops and animals been to your district?
3 What can you find about the conquest or destruction of the Amerindians in your territory?

References

For a full account of the African slave trade to the West Indies: Chapters 10 and 12.
For the overthrow of the Spanish Empire on the mainland: Book 2, Chapter 15.
For attacks on the Spanish Caribbean Empire: Chapter 6.
French and English colonial trade and government: Chapter 9.

Ashdown, *Caribbean History in Maps*, maps 11–13.

Chapters 6 and 7

Points to consider

1 What interests brought the English, French and Dutch to

the Caribbean?

2 What was the chief difference between the first attempts to break into the lands claimed by Spain and those which came later?

3 In what ways was English colonisation different from the Spanish?

4 What was needed to build successful colonies in the Lesser Antilles?

5 What part did the Dutch play in the development of French and British colonies?

Checks on understanding

Foreigners and the Spanish monopoly

a Spain and Portugal claim the Americas.

b Activities of pirates and privateers.

c Defending the Spanish Empire and trade.

d Wars between Spain and France.

e English smugglers and privateers.

f The importance of the Dutch to the Spanish Empire.

g The Dutch revolt and attacks on Spanish shipping.

h Spanish settlers resist the trading regulations.

i Effective occupation.

El Dorado and the Guyanese colonies

a The myth of El Dorado.

b The early history of Trinidad.

c Spanish expeditions to El Dorado.

d English expeditions to El Dorado.

e The tobacco trade.

f Difficulties of planting tobacco in Guyana.

g The first permanent Dutch colony in Guyana.

English colonies in the Lesser Antilles

a The problem of financing colonisation.

b The first successful English colonies in the Lesser Antilles.

c The proprietary system.

d The use of tenants and bondservants.

e The problem of finding a profitable export crop.

f The effect of the English civil war on the colonies.

French colonies in the Lesser Antilles

a The French colony in St Kitts.

b The French joint stock companies.

c Selling the colonies to proprietors.

The Dutch

a The Dutch successes against Spanish shipping.

b The Dutch Empire in Brazil.

c The Dutch end Spain's claim to monopoly.

d Dutch support for French and English colonies.

Checks on reading

Names

Pope Alexander VI, Giovanni da Verrazano, Jacques Cartier, Palmier de Gonnville, Jean D'Ango, François le Clerc, Pedro Menéndez de Aviles, John Hawkins, Sir Walter Raleigh, William of Orange, Don Fernando Melgaréjo, Antonio de Berrio, Domingo de Vera, Robert Harcourt, Captain Charles Leigh, Rene de Montbarrot, Daniel de la Ravardière, Roger North, James I, Captain Painton, Tegramond, Ralph Merrifield, John Smith, Captain Thomas Warner, Earl of Carlisle, John Powell, Sir William Courteen, Sir Anthony Hilton, Pierre Belain, Cardinal Richelieu, Oliver Cromwell, King Charles I, Col. Humphrey and Edward Walround, Lord Willoughby, Amazon Company, Company of St Christopher, Company of the Isles of America, Henry Winthrop, Piet Hein, James Holdip, John Drax.

Terms

Privateering, letters of marque, *corsaires*, *Flota* and *Galleones*, effective occupation, joint stock company, interloping, Lord Proprietor, bondservants, *engagés*, *les trente-six mois*, *trapiche*, *ingenio*.

Treaties

Treaty of Tordesillas 1494, Treaty of London 1604, Treaty of Munster 1648.

Further work

1 Construct a time line for Caribbean colonisation between 1609 and 1648.

2 What export crops are produced in your district? How many of these were grown by the first European colonists?

3 Which sites in your country were first settled by Europeans? Can you account for their choice?

References

For the colonies as part of a new French and English imperial system: Chapter 9.

For extension of the British Empire: Jamaica, Chapter 8; Windwards, Chapter 15; Trinidad and Guyana, Chapter 20.

For the story of the French West Indian Empire: Chapters 8 and 9.

For the Dutch and African Slave Trade: Chapter 10.

Ashdown, *Caribbean History in Maps*, maps 14–17.

Chapters 8 and 9

Points to consider

1 Why did the French and English Governments build empires in the Caribbean?

2 How was mercantilism meant to work? How did it tend to favour the metropolitan country rather than the colonies?

3 What lay behind the wars fought by the French and the English against the Dutch?

4 Do you agree with the authors that the buccaneers deserve little credit for their part in Caribbean history?

Checks on understanding

The English colonies reclaimed
a The demands of English merchants for more colonial trade.
b The capture of Barbados and the type of government granted to the colonists.
c The first Navigation Act.
d The First Dutch War and England's victory.

Further British Caribbean trade and colonisation
a Cromwell's plan to extend trade and colonisation at the expense of Spain.
b The Western Design . . . English naval operations in the Caribbean.
c Jamaica as an English colony.
d The new Navigation Acts and further control over English trade.
e The English slave trade.
f The Second Dutch War.
g Spanish recognition for English colonies.
h The English privateers disbanded.

The French
a The French proprietors.
b Buying back the colonies.
c The French colonial trade . . . the Third Dutch War.
d Spain recognises the French colonies.
e The French privateers disbanded.
f The growth of St Domingue.

The Brandenburgers and Danes
a The Danish and Brandenburger trading colonies.

The English and French colonial systems: economics
a Mercantilism.
b Laws tying the colonial economies to France and England.

The English and French colonial systems: politics
a The British decentralised system of government.
b Colonial government: governors, councils, assemblies and vestries.
c The French centralised system of government.
d Government in the French colonies.

Checks on reading

Names
Sir George Ayscue, General Robert Venables, Admiral Penn, Edward D'Oyley, Christoval de Ysassi, Vice Admiral Goodson, Captain Robert Holmes, Thomas Modyford, Henry Morgan, Jean Baptiste Colbert, Nicolas Fouquet, Sieur de Gabaret, Compte d'Estrées, Sir Charles Wheeler, Company of Royal Adventurers, The Council of Trade and Plantations, Conseil d'Etat.

Terms
Navigation Acts, *flibustiers*, buccaneers, intendant, plantocracy.

Treaties, laws and special agreements
Treaty of Westminster 1654, Treaty of Breda 1667, Treaty of Madrid 1670, 1651 English Navigation Act, 1660 New Navigation Act, 1663 Staples Act, 1673 Plantations' Duty Act, 1676 Consolidating Duties Act, Ordinance of the Marine 1671, Ordinance of Commerce 1673, Treaty of Ryswick 1697.

Further work

1 What British influences can be seen in your local and national government today?
2 Did the Navigation Acts affect the economic development of your country?
3 At what time was your country drawn into the British Empire? What was its history at the time of the story told in these chapters?

References

The British seizure of Trinidad and Guyana: Chapter 19.
The slave revolt on St Domingue: Chapter 18.
Further wars between France and England: Chapter 15.
Further descriptions of the plantocracy: Chapter 14.

Chapters 10, 11 and 12

Points to consider

1 Why were African slaves seen as a suitable 'solution' to the labour problem in the new Caribbean sugar colonies?
2 How did the slave trade to America change the nature of traditional African slavery?
3 Who profited from the slave trade?
4 What is the place of Africa in world history.

Checks on understanding

The new sugar islands
a The growing demand for sugar in Europe.
b The changes brought by sugar cultivation.
c The migration of small land holders.
d The failure of European labourers.

African slavery in the European colonies
a African slavery as a 'solution' to the labour problem.
b The connection between sugar cultivation and the number of African slaves brought to the Caribbean colonies.

The African background
a European ignorance of the African's history and culture.
b The diversity of Africa's history.
c The main African language groups.

West Africa: the savannah
a The division between the savannah and the forest region.
b Trade between the savannah people and North Africa.
c The savannah kingdoms.

West Africa: the forest
a The difficulty of building centralised states in the forest zone.
b The Igbo's independent village system.
c The Asante federal empire.
d The Benin Edo's centralised empire.

West African beliefs
a The similarity of beliefs shared by West Africans.
b The importance of family.
c The spirit world and everyday life.

The slave trade
a The westward movement of sugar cultivation and African slavery.
b Europe's new national slaving companies.
c Private companies and Britain's share of the trade.
d The Atlantic slave trade disrupts traditional African society.
e The West African rulers take part in the slave trade.
f The African kingdoms exploit the weaker village societies.
g Slave routes through Africa to the west coast.
h How the slavers aquired their cargoes.
i Preparations for the middle passage.
j Surviving the middle passage.
k Slave sales in America.

Checks on reading
Names
Ibn Battuta, Igbo, Asante, Uru, Fon, Edo, Ibibio, Mende, Temne, Soninke, Mandingo, Malinki, Shango, Olfert Dapper, John Atkins, C. B. Waldstrom, William Bosman.

Terms
Hamite, Semite, Negro-Bantu, Bushmen, Hottentot, clan society, paramount chief, *Asantehene, Omanhene, Obi,* ancestor worship, the golden stool, coffles, mackrons, slave scramble, middle passage.

Further work
1 What do you think are the most obvious examples of African cultural influences in your society?
2 Can you discover which were the main slaving ports in your country? Have any of them been preserved?
3 Do your national archives, libraries or Public Record Offices have bills of sale, auction notices or other material referring to newly arrived Africans? Would it be possible to examine any of these?
4 At what time did your country become a major sugar producing colony. Where was its labour recruited from?

References
For the life of slaves on the sugar islands: Chapters 13 and 14.
For the ending of the slave trade and emancipation: Chapters 22 and 23.
For the decline of the sugar industry: Chapter 17.

For East Indian and Chinese labourers: Chapters 24 and 25.

Ashdown, *Caribbean History in Maps*, maps 19–28.

Chapters 13 and 14

Points to consider
1 How were so few creoles able to control so many slaves?
2 What were the main differences between plantation societies in the British West Indies and plantation societies in the French West Indies?
3 Which important features of African culture were transferred to the Caribbean?
4 In what ways were the creole whites different from their European relatives?

Checks on understanding
Eighteenth-century sugar plantations
a Capital investment in a sugar plantation.
b The layout of sugar plantations in Jamaica, Barbados and Guyana.
c Different types of plantation factories.
d Sugar making.

Plantation society: the free whites
a The plantocracy . . . life-styles and occupations.
b The great house and plantation life.
c The hired whites.

Plantation society: the slaves
a Slaves as part of the planter's property.
b Slave gangs.
c Skilled and semi-skilled slaves.
d The uncertain position of the domestic and hired slaves.
e Plantation routine.

Maintaining order
a The Deficiency Acts.
b Police Acts.
c Controlling slaves on a plantation.

African Society in the Caribbean
a Keeping alive African culture on the plantation.
b New and old family and age-set relationships.
c African beliefs and customs in the Caribbean.

The free coloureds
a Origins of the free coloureds.
b Free coloureds' inferior position.
c Free coloureds in 'white' society.

Creole society
a The creoles and English society.
b English officials and the plantocracy.

French colonial society
a Differences between the English and French plantocracy.

b Small landowners and professionals.
c The *Code Noir*.
d Restrictions on the free coloureds and slaves.
e Physical force in slave societies.

Checks on reading

Names
Rev. William Jones, James Swaby, Janet Schaw, Matthew Lewis, Lady Nugent, Rev. John Rolland, The Abbé Raynal, Bryan Edwards, Maur-Lisa.

Terms
great gang, driver, Johnny Jumper, grass gang, quintroon, octoroon, Voodoo, *Vodun*, night-walking, *Shangoism, Obeahism, grands blancs, petits blancs*.

Laws and special Acts
Deficiency Acts, Police Acts, *Code Noir*.

Further work

1 Do any sugar plantations in your district conform with the general description of a plantation given in this chapter?
2 Is it possible for your class to inspect any eighteenth century plantation account books? What could you learn from them?
3 What conclusions can be drawn from the charts on page 94?
4 Discover more about an aspect of African culture which may be linked to an aspect of modern Caribbean life.

References

For further information on the plantocracy see Chapter 16.
For slave resistance: Chapter 20.
For changes in the plantation structure: Chapters 16 and 17; Book 2, Chapter 3.
For further information on plantation labour: Chapter 25; Book 2, Chapters 1–3.

Chapters 15, 16 and 17

Points to consider

1 Were the British West Indian planters responsible for their own troubles?
2 How were the British West Indian absentees able to gain political power in England?
3 What effect did the wars described in these chapters have on the British West Indies?
4 Had the slaves anything to gain from the decline of sugar?

Checks on understanding

War objectives in the Caribbean
a Further attacks on the Spanish monopoly.
b Trade rivalry between France and England.
c The French and English colonies attempt to ruin each other's sugar.

Wars between 1702 and 1763
a War of the Spanish Succession.
b The Treaty of Utrecht.
c English smuggling and trading in the Spanish Empire.
d The War of Jenkins' Ear in the Caribbean.
e The War of Austrian Succession.
f The question of the neutral islands.
g The Treaty of Aix-la-Chapelle.
h Rivalry between England and France for the neutral islands and North America.
i The Seven Years War to 1759.
j The Seven Years War in the Caribbean.
k The Peace of Paris.

British West Indian planters
a The expansion of sugar cultivation to Tobago and the neutral islands.
b Investing sugar profits abroad.
c Influential absentees.
d The West Indian interest in Britain.

Decline: cost and competition
a Slave labour and absenteeism.
b French competition.
c Expensive credit and declining prices.
d Decline of the West India interest.
e The Campbell Decision.

Decline: the American revolt
a Trade between the Americans and the West Indians.
b The British West Indies and the War of American Independence.
c The effects of the outbreak of war on the British West Indies.
d The War of American Independence.
e Loss of the mainland trade.
f The British West Indies attempts to regain prosperity.

Checks on reading

Names
The South Sea Company, Captain Jenkins, Admiral Vernon, Governor Trelawney, Admiral Caylus, Lord Bute, The Beckford family, Governor Leybourne, The Society of West Indian Merchants, the Society of West Indian Planters and Merchants.

Terms
Limited warfare, *asiento*, *guarda-costas*, the West India interest, absentees.

Treaties, laws and special Acts
Treaty of Utrecht 1713, Treaty of Aix-la-Chapelle 1748, Treaty of Paris 1763, Molasses Act 1733, Sugar Duties Act 1763, Stamp Act 1767, Townshend duties, The Campbell Decision, the Quebec Act, Treaty of Versailles 1783.

Further work

1 Are there any monuments or place names that commemorate the eighteenth century wars in your country?
2 How many fruits growing in your area are native to the Caribbean?
3 Can you find anything about absentee management of the plantations in your area?

References

For the beginning of the English/French conflict: Chapter 8.
For the French revolutionary and Napoleonic Wars: Chapters 18 and 19.
For the end of the Spanish monopoly: Book 2, Chapter 15.
For the final failure of the West India interest: Chapter 23.
For changes in agriculture, farm ownership and management: Book 2, Chapters 3 and 4.

Ashdown, *Caribbean History in Maps*, maps 31, 32, 39.

Chapters 18, 19 and 20

Points to consider

1 What were the differences in the effects of the French Wars on the French and British Empires in the Caribbean?
2 What legacy for today's Caribbean was created by the events in these chapters?

Checks on understanding

The French colonies and the French Revolution
a The French colonies in 1789.
b Revolution in France.
c The French Wars.

The Haitian Revolt
a The planters' revolt.
b The free coloured revolt.
c Background to the slave revolt.
d Boukman's revolt.
e Emancipation.
f British support for the planters.

Toussaint
a Early life of Toussaint.
b Toussaint's victory.
c Toussaint's rule.
d French defeat of Toussaint.
e The French defeated.
f Independent Haiti.

Trinidad and Guyana
a The French Wars and Britain's gain of Trinidad and Guyana.
b The Guyanese colonies in 1796.
c Trinidad in 1707.
d The new British Empire.

e Crown colony government.

Checks on reading

Names
Boukman, Jean Baptiste, Dessalines, Sonthonax, Robespierre, Leclerc, Christophe, Nelson, Mackandal, Vincent Oge, Toussaint L'Ouverture, Pétion, *Les Amis des Noirs*, General Abercromby, L. van Gravesande, Don Jose Chacon.

Terms
General, National Assembly, crown colony government, *Kiezers*.

Treaties, laws and special Acts
Declaration of the Rights of Man, Truce of Amiens, Peace of Paris.

Further work

1 Make a time line for 1789–1823 divided into three columns: Europe, The Caribbean and Haiti.

References

The French plantocracy: Chapter 14.
Eighteenth century wars: Chapters 15, 16 and 17.
For the last stages of the Spanish American Empire: Book 2, Chapter 15.

Ashdown, *Caribbean History in Maps*, maps 30, 33–5.

Chapters 21, 22 and 23

Points to consider

1 How did the slaves and the free coloureds help to end slavery in the British West Indies?
2 In what ways did the slaves show themselves to be the most militant opponents of slavery?
3 Why were the British West Indian planters either unable or unwilling to block the Abolition and Emancipation Bills?

Checks on understanding

The slaves oppose slavery
a Opposition on the plantation.
b Slave revolts.
c Runaways.
d Maroon villages in Guyana and Jamaica.

The Christian church and slavery
a The established church's attitude.
b The Moravians.
c Non-conformist churches in England . . . the Methodists.
d Missionary societies and the plantations.

e White missionaries and black Baptists.

f Missionaries and anti-slavery movements.

The anti-slavery campaign in Britain

a Humanitarians.

b The Quakers.

c Granville Sharp.

d Lord Mansfield and the Somerset case.

Abolishing the slave trade

a Reasons for abolishing the slave trade before the abolition of slavery.

b The leadership of the campaign that was mounted against the slave trade.

c Activities of the abolitionists.

d The French wars delay abolition.

e Abolition.

f British campaign against foreign slave traders.

Abolition to emancipation

a The planters continue as before.

b Registration.

c Amelioration.

d Planters and the free coloureds.

e Free coloured support for emancipation.

f Slaves fight for their own freedom.

g Support from the missionaries.

h Agency committee.

i The 1832 Parliamentary reform.

j New industrialists in Parliament.

k Provisions of the Emancipation Act.

Checks on reading

Names

Tackey, Cuffy, Ysassi, Juan de Bolas, Juan de Serras, Cudjoe, Moravians, Christopher Codrington, Society for the Propagation of the Gospel, John Wesley, Baptist Missionary Society, George Lisle, Moses Baker, George Fox, The Society of Friends, Granville Sharp, Jonathan Strong, James Somerset, Lord Mansfield, Committee for the Abolition of the Slave Trade, Thomas Clarkson, William Wilberforce, Henry Thornton, John Newton, Zachary Macaulay, William Pitt, Charles James Fox, Arthur Hodge, James Stephen, Lord Bathurst, Lison George, Cooper Brothers, Joseph Sturge, 1823 London Society for the Mitigation and Gradual Abolition of Slavery, *The Anti-Slavery Monthly Reporter*, *The Watchman*, Edward Jordan, Robert Osborn, Samuel Sharp, John Smith, William Knibb, John Burtchell, Colonial Church Union, Rev. William Bridges, Agency Committee, Thomas Buxton.

Terms

Non-conformism, humanitarians, East India interest, new industrialists.

Treaties, laws and special Acts

Abolition Act 1807, Emancipation Act 1833.

Further work

1 What can you find about runaway villages and slave revolts in your district?

2 Can you find records or other evidence of non-conformist missionary activity in your country?

3 Can you trace your family history to emancipation? What evidence have you used to answer this question?

References

For the weaknesses of plantation slavery: Chapter 17.

For the end of slavery in Haiti: Chapter 18.

For apprentices and freemen after emancipation: Book 2, Chapter 1.

For plantation labour in the nineteenth century: Chapter 24 and 25.

For the end of slavery in the other West Indian colonies: Book 2, Chapters 14 and 15.

Ashdown, *Caribbean History in Maps*, maps 37, 38.

Chapters 24 and 25

Points to consider

1 In what ways might Trinidad and Guyana have developed differently without immigration?

2 Why was it possible for the British Government to stop slavery but encourage the indentured system?

3 Why have these chapters been placed in Book 1 which otherwise ends in 1834?

Checks on understanding

The first nineteenth-century immigrants

a The pressure to provide plantation labour.

b Chinese from Malaya.

c Madeirans.

d Indians from Mauritius.

e Liberated Africans.

f Free Africans.

g Controls on immigration.

h Bountied European immigrants.

i New immigration regulations.

j Chinese immigration 1859–66.

The East Indians

a The Indian people and their historical background.

b The Mogul Empire.

c The British in India.

d Recruiting Indians.

e Immigration departments.

f Indenture contracts.

g Indenture ordinances.

h Plantation life and conditions.

i Education.

j The campaign to end indenture.

k The contribution of the Indians.

Checks on reading

Names

Thomas Picton, John Gladstone, Gillanders and Co., Sierra Leone, Kru coast, James Stephen, Lord Russell, Governor MacLeod, Hong Kong, Dravidians, Aryans, Indus, Ganges, Mohenjo-Daro, Harappa, Akbar, Robert Clive, Joseph Dupleix, East India Company, Calcutta, *Salsette*, James Crosby, de Voeux, Lechmere Guppy, Mohandas Gandhi, Gopal Gokhale, Canadian Presbyterian Mission, Prudhomme David.

Terms

Barracoon, Sanskrit, Mahratta Confederacy, *sepoy*, Protector of Immigrants, *mulvi*, Brahmin, *jhandi*.

Treaties, Acts and special agreements

Sugar Duties Equalisation Act 1846, Immigration regulations, 1838 and 1849, West Indies Commission 1913.

Further work

1 Can your family history be traced to any part of the story told in these chapters?
2 Are there any plantations, businesses or townships in your area which owe their beginnings to one of the immigrant groups in the nineteenth century?

Further reading

General

Student sources

P. Ashdown, *Caribbean History in Maps*, Longman, 1979.

F. R. Augier *et al*, *The Making of the West Indies*, Longman, 1960.

F. R. Augier and S. C. Gordon, *Sources of West Indian History*, Longman 1962.

J. H. Elliott, *The Old World and the New*, Cambridge University Press, 1970.

A. Garcia, *A History of the West Indies*, Harrap, 1965.

D. G. Waddell, *The West Indies and the Guianas*, Prentice-Hall, 1967.

Easier books

T. Mills, *Great West Indians*, Longman, 1973.

R. N. Murray, *Nelson's West Indian History*, Nelson, 1971.

A. Norman, P. Patterson and J. Carnegie, *The People Who Came*, Books 1 and 2, Longman, 1968, 1970.

P. Sherlock, *West Indian Nations*, Jamaica Publishing House, 1973.

For teachers

C. Hampshere, *The British in the Caribbean*, Weidenfeld and Nicolson, 1972.

J. Parry and P. Sherlock, *Short History of the West Indies*, Macmillan, 1971.

W. A. Roberts, *The French in the West Indies*, Cooper Square Publishers (New York), 1971.

E. Williams, *From Columbus to Castro*, Deutsch, 1970.

Student sources on particular states

M. Anthony, *A Profile of Trinidad*, Macmillan, 1975.

C. V. Black, *The Story of Jamaica*, Collins, 1965.

V. T. Daly, *The Making of Guyana*, Macmillan, 1974.

W. Dobson, *A History of Belize*, Longman, 1973.

F. A. Hyosos, *History of Barbados*, Macmillan, 1976.

E. Williams, *History of the People of Trinidad and Tobago*, PNM Publishing, 1962.

Early history and European settlement

Student sources

E. Jones, *Protector of the Indians: the life of de las Casas*, Longman 1973.

J. Langdon-Davis, *Columbus and the Discovery of America*, (Jackdaw No.4), Cape, 1967.

E. Newarth, *They Lived Like This in Ancient Maya*, Man Parrish, 1966.

P. Richardson, *The Expansion of Europe 1400–1600*, Longman, 1966.

For teachers

C. A. Burland, *The Maya*, Weidenfeld and Nicolson, 1967.

A. P. Newton, *The European Nations in the West Indies*, Black, 1966.

R. Pares, *Planters and Merchants*, Cambridge University Press, 1963.

J. H. Parry, *The Age of Reconnaissance*, Weidenfeld and Nicolson, 1963.

R. B. Sheridan, *The Development of the Plantations to 1750*, Caribbean University Press, 1970.

African background and slavery

Student sources

M. Crowder, *West Africa: an introduction to its history*, Longman, 1978.

B. Davidson, *Discovering Africa's Past*, Longman, 1978.

B. Davidson, *A History of West Africa 1000–1800*, Longman, 1977.

P. Edwards, *Equiano's Travels*, Heinemann, 1967.

J. Langdon-Davies, *The Slave Trade and Its Abolition*, (Jackdaw No.12), Cape, 1965.

J. R. Milsome, *Olaudah Equiano*, Makers of African History Series, Longman, 1969.

E. Montejo, *The Autobiography of a Runaway Slave*, Bodley Head, 1968.

G. T. Stride and C. Ifeka, *Peoples and Empires of West Africa*, Nelson, 1969.

For teachers

B. Davidson, *Black Mother*, Gollancz, 1968.

R. S. Dunn, *Sugar and Slaves*, Norton (New York), 1972.

P. D. Curtin, *The African Slave Trade: A Census*, University of Wisconsin Press, 1969.

J. G. Fage, *A History of West Africa*, Cambridge University Press, 1969.

Slave societies; resistance and revolt

Student sources

J. D. Bentley, *Toussaint L'Ouverture*, Hulton, 1969.

E. Brathwaite, *Folk Culture of the Slaves of Jamaica*, New Beacon Books, 1970.

L. Mathurin, *The Rebel Woman in the British West Indies During Slavery*, African-Caribbean Publications (Kingston), 1975.

G. F. Tyson, *Toussaint L'Ouverture*, Prentice-Hall, 1973.

For teachers

E. Brathwaite, *The Development of Creole Society in Jamaica 1770–1820*, Clarendon Press, 1971.

M. Craton and J. Walvin, *A Jamaican Plantation*, University of Toronto Press, 1970.

E. Goveia, *Slave Society in the British Leeward Islands at the End of the 18th Century*, Caribbean University Press, 1970.

C. L. R. James, *Black Jacobins*, Random House (New York), 1963.

O. Patterson, *The Sociolgy of Slavery*, Farleigh Dickinson, 1967.

R. B. Sheridan, *An Era of West Indian Prosperity 1750–1775*, Caribbean University Press, 1970.

Abolition and Emancipation

R. Coupland, *The British Anti-Slavery Movement*, Cass, 1974.

M. Craton, *Slavery, Abolition and Emancipation*, Longman, 1974.

E. Williams, *Capitalism and Slavery*, Deutsch, 1972.

P. Wright, *Knibb the Notorious*, Sidgwick and Jackson, 1973.

Nineteenth-century immigration

J. G. La Guerre, *Calcutta to Caroni*, Longman, 1974.

K. O. Laurence, *Immigration into the West Indies in the Nineteenth Century*, Caribbean University Press, 1971.

H. Tinker, *A New System of Slavery*, Oxford Univeristy Press, 1974.

Index